# ISP Liability Survival Guide
## Strategies for Managing Copyright, Spam, Cache, and Privacy Regulations

Timothy D. Casey

**Wiley Computer Publishing**

**John Wiley & Sons, Inc.**

NEW YORK • CHICHESTER • WEINHEIM • BRISBANE • SINGAPORE • TORONTO

Publisher: Robert Ipsen

Editor: Carol A. Long

Managing Editor: Micheline Frederick

Text Design & Composition: North Market Street Graphics

Designations used by companies to distinguish their products are often claimed as trademarks. In all instances where John Wiley & Sons, Inc., is aware of a claim, the product names appear in initial capital or ALL CAPITAL LETTERS. Readers, however, should contact the appropriate companies for more complete information regarding trademarks and registration.

This book is printed on acid-free paper. ∞

This publication is designed to provide accurate and authoritative information in regard to the subject matter covered. It is sold with the understanding that the publisher is not engaged in professional services. If professional advice or other expert assistance is required, the services of a competent professional person should be sought.

Library of Congress Cataloging-in-Publication Data:

Casey, Timothy, 1961–
    ISP Liability survival guide : strategies for managing copyright, spam, cache, and privacy regulations / Timothy Casey.
        p. cm.
    Includes index.
    ISBN 0-471-37748-1 (pbk. : alk. paper)
    1. Internet industry—Law and legislation—United States.   2. Copyright and electronic data processing—United States.   3. Internet service providers.   I. Title.

KF390.5.C6 C37 2000
343.7309'944—dc21                                                    00-022256

Printed in the United States of America.

10 9 8 7 6 5 4 3 2 1

# Wiley Networking Council Series

Scott Bradner
*Senior Technical Consultant*, Harvard University

Vinton Cerf
*Senior Vice President*, MCI WorldCom

Lyman Chapin
*Chief Scientist*, BBN/GTE

## Books in the Series

Geoff Huston, *Internet Performance Survival Guide: QoS Strategies for Multiservice Networks.* 0-471-37808-9

Geoff Huston, *ISP Survival Guide: Strategies for Running a Competitive ISP* 0-471-31499-4

Elizabeth Kaufman & Andrew Newman, *Implementing IPsec: Making Security Work on VPNs, Intranets, and Extranets* 0-471-34467-2

*For more information, please visit the Networking Council Web site at www.wiley.com/networkingcouncil.*

# CONTENTS

The Networking Council Series was created in 1998 within Wiley's Computer Publishing group to fill an important gap in networking literature. Many current technical books are long on details but short on understanding. They do not give the reader a sense of where, in the universe of practical and theoretical knowledge, the technology might be useful in a particular organization. The Networking Council Series is concerned more with how to think clearly about networking issues than with promoting the virtues of a particular technology; that is, how to relate new information to what the reader knows and needs, so that he or she can develop a customized strategy for vendor and product selection, outsourcing, and design.

In *ISP Liability Survival Guide* by Timothy Casey, you'll see the hallmarks of Networking Council books: examination of the advantages and disadvantages, strengths and weaknesses of market-ready technology; useful ways to think about options pragmatically; and direct links to business practices and needs. Disclosure of pertinent background issues necessary to understand who supports a technology and how it was developed is another goal of all Networking Council books.

The Networking Council Series is aimed at satisfying the need for perspective in an evolving data and telecommunications world that is filled with hyperbole, speculation, and unearned optimism.

In *ISP Liability Survival Guide: Strategies for Managing Copyright, Spam, Cache, and Privacy Regulations* you'll get clear information from experienced practitioners.

We hope you enjoy the book. Let us know what you think. Feel free to visit the Networking Council Web site at www.wiley.com/networkingcouncil.

*Scott Bradner*
Senior Technical Consultant, *Harvard University*

*Vinton Cerf*
Senior Vice President, *MCI WorldCom*

*Lyman Chapin*
Chief Scientist, *BBN/GTE*

# ACKNOWLEDGMENTS

I am most grateful to Jacquelyn Fuzell-Casey (my wonderful wife and partner), who had been telling me that I should write a book for many years. She filled me with the strength, desire, and conviction necessary to get through the arduous process of writing this one. My son Skyler Fuzell-Casey is also to be thanked for his enthusiasm and encouragement, even when that meant I couldn't spend precious time with him, and his clever suggestions. They are both very smart and I love them dearly.

I would like to thank Vint Cerf for talking me into being the author when I wasn't so sure I wanted to do it. His thorough review of the text (he caught things the copy editors missed) and technical and historical advice were greatly needed. Yes, Vint, you are indeed a better speller than I. Theresa Swinehart performed invaluable research on international subjects and helped me understand nuances about the European Union that I will not soon forget. Jeff Magenau performed virtually all of the domestic research and provided critical reviews of early drafts. Lastly, my editor Carol Long fought the good fights in the background and for the most part let me do my own thing, which I greatly appreciated.

—Timothy D. Casey

*Be brave enough to live life creatively. The creative is the place where no one else has ever been. You have to leave the city of your comfort and go into the wilderness of your intuition. You can't get there by bus, only by hard work, risk and by not quite knowing what you're doing. What you'll discover will be wonderful. What you'll discover will be yourself.*

**ALAN ALDA**

Each new communication medium forces us from our city of comfort into a wilderness of new experiences. Along the way we confront old thoughts and new risks and hopefully emerge wiser and richer. While some people still haven't heard of the Internet, or if they have, haven't used it and have no desire to try, many younger people, such as my son, have never known it to not exist, so it forms an integral part of their lives. In between those two perspectives lie so many others that it is difficult to describe them all, and even if you tried there might be twice as many before you could finish. This diversity of views is fueled by the rapid changes experienced by the Internet itself, not so much in structure as in function, and the uncertainty regarding the direction it should or will take next.

While people argue over uncertainties (Should content be pushed or pulled? Should electronic commerce transactions be taxed? Should users or advertisers pay for web sites?), one certainty has emerged: No matter what the Internet may mean to people, as long as they continue to use it they will need someone to provide them with at least access services. Hence, Internet service providers (ISPs), the entities that provide such access, as well as many other products and services, have become a critical component of the commercial Internet. Because most traffic flows through ISPs and most users get services from one, ISPs have become the ideal target for any form of content or user activity control. Even though it is the user who initiates the content and the user who performs the forbidden acts, users are so hard to find and track down that the ISP has become the scapegoat for most liability initiatives. This is a frustrating and ignorance-based approach to dealing with content and activity issues on the Internet, a mixture of old thought and new risks, but it doesn't appear likely to change—which is why I have written this book.

Although I've described ISPs within the context of access providers, the term *ISP* presently encompasses a wide array of different types of service providers. An ISP may provide Internet access services on a retail basis to residential and/or business customers. An ISP may operate only a *backbone network* and provide Internet dial and/or dedicated access services to other ISPs on a wholesale basis. Some ISPs provide *hosting* services, whereby customers store information on computer servers operated by the ISP with dedicated Internet access and 24-hour-a-day, 7-day-a-week maintenance and security. Some ISPs provide server *caching,* the local storage of frequently requested third-party web site content. Other ISPs do not provide any of the aforementioned services and operate only *portals.* A portal is a web site that aggregates and organizes information about the content of other web sites so users can readily find desired information. An ISP may provide only a *search engine* or some other e-commerce tool that I haven't described or that is yet to be developed.

If you are an ISP, although this book isn't just for ISPs, you need to know about the laws and regulations that have been or are likely to be created in the near future that will impact you in some way. You need to know how and why these laws were or will be created. You need to know what you must do to comply with these laws and how best to structure your operations to avoid problems and otherwise stay out of trouble in the future, but without spending so much money that you compromise your profitability. This is where I come in and why I may be just the right person to walk you through what would otherwise be a confusing maze of unknown or misunderstood laws and regulations. I will provide you with basic, practical advice to deal with all of these matters to avoid liability, and to survive and provide your services another day. Although the subject matter of this book involves serious stuff, being responsible and serious are two very different things. I want you to be responsible and stay out of unnecessary trouble, but I don't take myself too seriously, so I assume that you will not mind my tasteful play on words and irreverent, opinionated behavior throughout.

So, who am I and why am I the right person to be writing this book? Permit me to explain my background first. Right now, I am a senior vice president and the chief technology counsel for MCI WorldCom, where I manage the Technology Law Group, which has responsibility for the strategic development, management, licensing, and transfer of all intellectual property rights (IPR) and technology-related transactions involving MCI WorldCom. Before that, I did very similar things for Silicon Graphics and Apple Computer in their earlier days, and I worked as an associate at a California law firm. Along the way I obtained a J.D. from Santa Clara University School of Law, where I was editor in chief of the *Computer and High Technology Law Journal.* While attending law school, I worked nights as a test engineer for a disk drive company and as a patent agent for a law firm. I also have a B.S.E.E. from the University of Nevada, Reno, and worked as a digital design engineer for a telecommunications company and as a blackjack dealer for a major casino. As you might imagine, I have an excellent poker face, although in the context of this book that won't do much good unless we happen to meet face-to-face or by videoconference some day.

As a result of this background, I have spent a considerable amount of time working with computer and Internet-related technologies and the laws associated with them, but so what? Well, back in 1995, when I landed in Washington, D.C., the bureaucrats (no offense intended to all you hardworking government employees, but this is a nice, short descriptor for the general function you perform) had just figured out that the Internet was a threat to certain standards of decency as well as to the content industry, so a full-blown effort was under way to rein it in. One such effort was the Communications Decency Act, which became law in 1996 and was almost immediately found, in part, to be unconstitutional. The other effort was the NII Copyright Protection Act of 1995, which sought to hold ISPs *strictly liable* (i.e., without fault) for any copyright infringement that occurred on their networks. In the body of this book, I will explain in greater detail why the Internet was considered a threat and what ended up happening with this and other similar legislation in the United States and Europe. Suffice it to say, however, that ISPs almost experienced a radical, and very negative, transformation of their business, and most didn't know it was happening.

For better or for worse, I did know. I was also one of the few people in town with an understanding of the technology and the law—and with the ability to explain both. I therefore quickly found myself up on Capitol Hill and in the bowels of Congress, with a handful of other people, trying to explain what was reasonable and practical to do legislatively with regard to the Internet.

Luckily, one of the people I was introduced to was Congressman Rick Boucher from Virginia. Mr. Boucher was concerned that the Internet, and therefore his constituents, including many potential users of distance learning tools, would be adversely impacted by some recently introduced copyright legislation. After I acknowledged the legitimacy of his concerns, he asked for some ideas on how to modify the legislation to help correct the situation. This request, coupled with suggestions from others and news about a settlement that had just been reached between the Church of Scientology and Netcom (now part of Mindspring Enterprises), led me to suggest two solutions in the form of proposed amendments. The first solution, which Mr. Boucher rejected as impractical, would have completely exempted ISPs, under certain conditions, from any liability for most forms of copyright infringement on the Internet. The second solution was a combination of an exemption and a form of private injunctive relief, now called *notice and take down* (NTD). In retrospect, even this solution was pretty crude in comparison to what became law. It basically exempted an ISP from liability when it was not in control of the content, such as when providing access or operating a backbone network. When the ISP was in control of the content, such as on a host site, it would have liability only if it actually knew of the infringement, such as through a notice letter, and failed to act. Thus, by preserving the ISP's ability to operate and necessary defenses to infringement, such as fair use, Mr. Boucher would be able to preserve necessary distance learning tools.

Mr. Boucher and his staff were very interested in the latter and passed my proposed solution to an attorney working for the Computer and Communications Industry Association (CCIA), Gregory Gorman. Gorman had been the only other person who had earlier expressed an interest in this matter to Boucher's office, so they figured he would be interested. Shortly thereafter, I was contacted by Gorman and Sarah Deutsch, an attorney for Bell Atlantic, a regional local telephone operating company (at least at that time). Although long-distance and local phone companies did not typically work well together, especially back in 1995 and 1996 when the Telecommunications Act of 1996 was being negotiated, we nevertheless decided that we had aligned interests on this issue. Since we did not share a common industry association, we formed a new coalition, called the Ad Hoc Copyright Coalition (AHCC), to work on what we thought would be a fairly short-lived project. Many other companies, including AT&T, AOL, Prodigy, Netscape, PSINet, BellSouth, and Ameritech, and many additional associations, including the Information Technology Association of America (ITAA), the United States Telephone Association (USTA), and the Commercial Internet Exchange (CIX), joined the AHCC over time. After multiple congressional hearings, hundreds of hours of private and congressionally sponsored negotiations (for which I was an industry representative), numerous trips around the world to talk to copyright experts and government representatives, and a three-week-long diplomatic conference in Geneva, Switzerland, resulting in two new copyright treaties, the exemption and notice-and-take-down architecture was finally implemented in the Digital Millennium Copyright Act of 1998 (DMCA).

The DMCA, and how to qualify for it and comply with its provisions, is covered in great detail in this book. As you will note, the basic architecture, provisions, definitions, and conditions of the DMCA have set the stage for the development of most future laws addressing various aspects of the Internet, and it will continue to largely influence the direction of such laws and how they will impact ISPs far into the foreseeable future. The same basic architecture was also adopted in a *Proposal for a European Parliament and Council Directive on Certain Legal Aspects of Electronic Commerce in the Internal Market,* also known as the *E-Commerce Directive,* and it, too, will be discussed.

Although not everyone likes the DMCA or regards it as a good law, if it hadn't been for the effort that ultimately resulted in the DMCA as compromise legislation, ISPs would have been subject to one of the worst legislative disasters of all time. In the United States, at least, this disaster was avoided, but similar progress has been hard to come by in other countries. Governments around the world are rapidly establishing laws and regulations relating to the Internet that will shift significant burdens onto ISPs. Of even greater concern, these laws threaten to outlaw very basic and necessary operations of the Internet. These laws tend to be directed at attacking the transmission of certain types of content and certain types of activities that are being carried out using the Internet. ISPs have in turn sought some of their own laws to deal with issues such as authentication and certification and to help control certain users' activities like spamming and denial-of-service attacks.

As a result of these and many other activities over the years, I have frequently been interviewed and quoted in local, national, and international newspapers and radio, television, and Internet news programs, including the *Wall Street Journal,* the *Financial Times,* CNN, and even PBS. I am also on the Board of Advisors for the Engineering College at the University of Nevada, Reno, and I am chairman of the Intellectual Property Committee of the Information Technology Association of America. Through all of this, I have emerged as one of the few people who knows a significant amount about ISP liability issues. As an added bonus, I have had the great fortune of working closely with Vint Cerf, who has provided me with access to technical expertise and historical perspective. I have also lived with this stuff in the context of my own company's operations, so I know how it applies to the real world. All this said, I'm not trying to blow my own horn but to provide you with some assurance that you have someone here with appropriate credentials dispensing advice and solutions for running a liability-free ISP.

# Overview

This book is a simple, practical guide for understanding, complying, or otherwise dealing with existing and ongoing efforts to control or regulate the Internet. In particular, this book will do the following:

- Explain who is making the laws and regulations (collectively, the laws), how those laws are being made, and how ISPs can effectively get involved in the process.
- Provide background material and a general explanation of the laws (and goals to be achieved via those laws) that exist or have been proposed that will have an impact on different aspects of Internet-related businesses.
- Explain what ISPs need to do in order to comply with the various laws on content and activity controls that have been developed, particularly with respect to obscenity, privacy, and copyright.
- Identify important issues to consider when contracting with users, vendors, and sales channels to accommodate the laws and avoid breach-of-contract issues when an ISP is forced to take action to comply with or avoid a content/activity law.
- Conclude with suggested policies and procedures that could be adopted by ISPs to more readily comply with a legal requirement or to avoid certain problems that are bound to arise. Some time will also be devoted to dealing with outside and in-house legal counsel.

# How This Book Is Organized

This book starts off with an explanation of how laws and regulations relating to the Internet are being developed. I then go into the gory details about the existing laws and legal environment so you can better understand what you have to deal with and what is likely to come up next. But don't worry, I do try to keep it basic and interesting. I then explain what you need to know to comply with these laws and regulations within the context of your business. The book finishes with a discussion of some related areas and suggests ways to develop policies and procedures to help cope with this aspect of your business.

## Chapter 1  WWW: The Wild, Wild West?

Chapter 1 starts with a discussion of the political aspects of the Internet as a wild thing that desperately requires taming. While I do explain why this approach is wrong, I also explain why the diametric view that the Internet is a wonderful anarchy that shouldn't be regulated at all (or self-regulated, if anything) is also dangerous. In the context of taming the Internet, it is important to understand who (not the people, just the agencies) makes these laws and regulations and the process followed in the United States, Europe, and other parts of the world.

## Chapter 2  Intellectual Property and Other Laws Made Simple

As a network of networks, the Internet itself is actually a physical structure (although widely dispersed). The Internet operates by ubiquitously transporting digital data representing text, software, images, music, and many other forms of intangible objects. Intellectual property laws are used around the world to protect intangible objects from being used without the owner's permission. Intellectual property laws therefore have almost more relevance to the Internet industry than any other industry that has previously existed. Intellectual property laws primarily include copyrights, patents, trademarks, and trade secrets, but also implicate free speech, unfair competition, and antitrust laws, among other legal areas. Virtually all countries have some form of intellectual property law, as well as many related laws on a wide variety of subjects that have had and will continue to have a large impact on ISPs. Chapter 2 describes each relevant form of intellectual property or related law, the history and development of that law, and how that law has been particularly applied to Internet-related activities.

## Chapter 3  A Special Law for ISPs: The DMCA

Intellectual property laws also spurred the creation of the Digital Millennium Copyright Act (DMCA), which is the rather obvious (i.e., eponymous) subject of this chapter. The development of copyright law has always been in response to challenges raised by new technologies that enable the reproduction and distribution of works, such as the original printing press and cable television. A packet network such as the Internet produces automatic copies of every packet transmitted through the network many times over. For example, routers make temporary copies of packets for forwarding purposes. Other devices operating in cooperation with the Internet may make many additional copies. Internet users also make copies, lots of them, and these copies are perfect (i.e., not degraded like an analog copy of an analog recording). These copies can then be distributed around the world in a matter of moments at almost no cost, potentially creating exponential losses for copyright owners. Copyright owners reacted to this potential loss by demanding that ISPs take the responsibility for preventing copyright infringement on the Internet—and if they failed to do so, that they take the liability as well. The DMCA was the first law specifically written to address ISP liability issues.

## Chapter 4  Other Internet-Specific Laws

Whether you like it or not, many other Internet-related laws now exist and many new ones are being created all the time. These laws directly impact the Internet and must be understood to profitably survive in this business. Chapter 4 explains (as simply as possible—I promise) many of the laws that have been developed or are likely to be developed that impact ISPs in some meaningful way. Although many of these laws are interrelated, I have formed a number of the most common groupings, such as spamming, spoofing, and trespassing, under one heading. I end this chapter with a discussion about emerging areas of regulation, such as gambling, guns, alcohol, and money. Taken together, this sounds like an interesting group, but the relationship between each area may not be obvious. Nevertheless, each of these areas is heavily regulated in the physical world, so we can certainly expect that them to be likewise regulated in the cyberworld.

## Chapter 5  What Is an ISP to Do (or Not)? Content and Activity Regulations to Live By

This is where I get into more of the nitty-gritty details about the laws discussed in the prior chapters, some additional laws that were not previously discussed, and what you as an ISP must do in order to comply. The primary focus will be on U.S. laws, but I will include some detail about what is going on in other countries. In particular, just so you don't start feeling too sorry for yourselves, I will describe some of the really ugly regulatory approaches that are being adopted elsewhere. Such Draconian restraints could surface in the United States if ISPs don't get involved in the legislative process (something I will encourage you to do throughout this book). It is also important to understand that to the extent you operate internationally, different rules may have to be applied for each type of content and for each type of activity in each different country. If you think this sounds crazy, you are right, which is why I will describe an idea for trying to deal with all controlled content and activity matters in a uniform manner.

Finally, I will spend some time on consumer issues. If all you do is provide access and no other services, then the consumer issues may not matter to you. Chances are good, however, that you at least run your own web site for your customers, that you provide other services, and that you are a consumer yourself, so you might be interested after all. But wait, there is more. I will finish Chapter 5 with a very important discussion about hate speech and similar laws in different countries and about pornography and its various manifestations.

## Chapter 6  Incorporating ISP Liability Concepts in Contracts

If only we could live without customers, we wouldn't have these problems! Since that is obviously a nonviable solution, this chapter addresses issues associated with customer contracts. How you structure your relationship and responsibilities with your customers will be critical to your successful avoidance of some of the worst potential problems. You also need to incorporate liability concepts into the contracts you have in place with everyone else with whom you do business, so I spend time discussing some of the issues involving your sales channels and your vendors.

## Chapter 7 Policies and Procedures: What to Ask/Tell Your Lawyer

Now that you know all about the laws affecting your business and what you need to do or not do, it's time to implement what you have learned. The problem is that everyone's business is different, so a policy or procedure that works for one business may not work for another. Rather than provide you with a one-size-fits-all policy and procedure for everything, Chapter 7 delves into the concepts and principles that need to be incorporated into those documents, as well as describing what some other companies have done. I assume a lawyer somewhere will be given the task of writing most of these policies and procedures at your direction (unless you like to write everything yourself), so I add a few tidbits of advice that might be useful when it comes time to talk to your lawyer. Finally, this chapter includes a quick discussion about some important developing areas to keep an eye on, such as tax laws.

## Chapter 8 Technical and Legal Glossary

Hopefully, I will explain all the terms you need to know as we go along. Obviously, you will want to read this book from front to back, so you won't need a glossary. But just in case you slip into that nasty habit of reading only what you think you need, I've slipped a little something extra in back.

## Who Should Read This Book?

As the title conveys, this book is a guide for Internet service providers and anyone associated with the ISP business, such as a web hosting provider, a portal operator, an Internet broadcaster, or for that matter, anyone operating a web site, a bulletin board, a news service, or even a mail server. Despite the appearance of the word *liability* in the title, this is not a legal book for lawyers. While I am sure there are many lawyers out there who could benefit from reading it, this is a business book for just about everyone else who could use a better understanding of the law. I am a lawyer, but I am not your lawyer and I do not represent you, nor am I providing you with legal advice. If you need a lawyer, and you might, I suggest you get one, but we will talk about that in Chapter 7, "Policies and Procedures: What to Ask/Tell Your Lawyer."

If you are looking for a legal book that will go into great detail about the law, analyze the meaning of years of various judicial decisions, and include copies of all of the relevant statutes in an appendix, such books exist, but this is not one. Such books assume you have a certain elevated understanding of the basic laws involved, and they start from there. I do not make such an assumption. Interestingly enough, out of all of the Internet law–related books that I have seen, I have recognized few of the authors. Obviously, someone doesn't have to be recognized by me to know a good deal about this area of law. I just find it odd that in all these years, I have not run into them in some significant way. Instead, I am going to tell you what the laws are in plain and simple terms as they relate to the aforementioned businesses. This book is for anyone who needs to understand how laws are applied in practical terms to the technologies and users that such laws are intended to control. This means that politicians, government representatives, trade associations, and lobbyists should also read this book because no one can possibly know what to do about the Internet without knowing what has already been done—and how it works.

## Assumptions

I assume you know something about how the Internet works and some of the business models that have developed around it, such as web sites. I will attempt to explain technology only where I feel it is necessary to create a proper environment for the application of the laws. As previously mentioned, I assume you know relatively little about the laws affecting the Internet, other than what you might have read in newspapers, the trade press, and seen on the Internet.

# CHAPTER 1

# WWW: The Wild, Wild West?

While you may understand the acronym WWW to stand for *World Wide Web*, a significant number of people seem to believe that WWW stands for "Wild, Wild West." Not only have I seen this cliché used in many different articles discussing the lawlessness of the web, I have even seen the slogan on T-shirts and bumper stickers. I generally detest clichés. Nevertheless, I am going to be a hypocrite and use the analogy in this chapter because it works. And besides, as Mozelle Thompson, a Federal Trade Commission (FTC) commissioner, noted, "[T]here are a lot of people who think cyberspace is the Wild West, but it isn't."

Without question, as viewed today, the Internet can be a wild place. Before it turned wild, however, the Internet existed undisturbed and in peace for many years within the relatively quiet confines of government research and academia. It was not until the Internet was allowed to enter the commercial market that its true power was unleashed—and such power! Alas, there are those who will seek to do evil with any powerful object, and the Internet is no exception. Thus, the Internet has quickly attracted many unscrupulous users around the world who have sought to take advantage of its powerful, unregulated nature to practice their illegal acts. But now good intention has arrived, riding into town to tame the Internet by bringing legal order and justice and thereby ridding the Internet of its evildoers. Be careful of what you ask for—you might just get it.

# Whatever Happened to Self-Regulation?

Good question. In between complete lawlessness and a heavily regulated environment, there has been much talk about and a number of attempts at self-regulation of the Internet. From a theoretical perspective, self-regulation is a great thing, but the problem with self-regulation is that it always seems to come too late. By the time an industry realizes that it needs to take action to police itself, the matter demanding an industry's attention has usually attracted too much other attention as well. To make matters worse, rather than immediately condemn the offending matter, the industry usually first tries to deny the existence of the problem. When this doesn't work, the industry establishes a number of working groups to study the problem. As a result, by the time the industry finally gets around to talking about regulating itself on some matter, the matter is often already out of hand.

## The Problem with Content

For example, the online solicitation of private information from children, child pornography, and the online availability of sexual material to children had really gotten out of control before the Internet industry realized that it needed to do something. After several years of study, some of the biggest names in the online industry, including America Online Incorporated, Microsoft Corporation, Walt Disney Company, Excite Incorporated, Lycos Incorporated, and Yahoo! Incorporated, introduced GetNetWise, an elaborate self-regulatory effort aimed at helping parents guard their children from objectionable material on the Internet by using filtering software. While encouraging parents to take responsibility for what their children access online is a good idea, it falls short as a solution. Parents will not exercise any greater control in the online environment than they do in any other area, such as television. As a result, lawmakers have already acted to regulate the collection of information from children, the distribution of child pornography, and the availability of sexual material to children online.

Likewise, despite the fact that any ISP carrying newsgroup feeds has known of the vast amount of objectionable content available on the Internet for many years, ISPs have done relatively little to self-regulate the availability of that content by anyone. After a two-year working group effort, a number of international Internet companies announced the formation of the Internet Content Rating Association (ICRA). ICRA promotes a system based on the RSAC content rating system previously developed by the Recreational Software Advisory Council (RSAC), which will be folded into ICRA. The new system, RSACi, enables web publishers to review and rate their online material, thereby enabling parents and Internet users to screen out undesired content. The original RSAC rating system for recreational software was, of course, developed only in response to legislative threats to regulate software content. (See Side Law: Content Rating Systems.) An ICRA spokesman stated that it was trying to send a message to governments around the world "that the best way to regulate content is through self-regulation, not through Draconian [methods]" (Courtney Macavinta, *Global Groups Seeks Movie-Like Net Ratings*, CNET News.com, 11 May 1999). It's already too late—the dracos (an old French word for dragons) have come.

# The Problem with Privacy

Like a loose pile of feathers, as soon as the Internet industry pounced on one issue, many other issues flew up and began to swirl around. Accordingly, while the industry was focused on one type of content problem, a different type of content problem, this time involving the privacy of user data, become an equally controversial issue. Not only were some well-known web site operators collecting personal information from children and selling that information to companies hoping to market goods to those kids online, a number of other companies received negative publicity for redistributing user data to thousands of other users. Also, in 1998, the FTC released the results of a privacy survey that revealed that just 14 percent of web sites informed visitors of their data collection practices.

While prompt passage of legislation designed to protect children's privacy (which will be discussed in Chapter 4, *Other Internet-Specific Laws*) dealt with one issue, the Internet industry has been slow to deal with other privacy concerns. In response to the FTC study, a number of Internet companies have formed associations to advocate industry solutions, such as the Online Privacy Alliance, which went so far as to hire Christine Varney, a highly respected former FTC commissioner, to lend credibility to the effort. As a result, a number of privacy initiatives have been announced.

The Better Business Bureau, a company called TRUSTe (www.truste.org), and others initiated a program to create a seal that designates web sites that comply with certain privacy protection principles. Microsoft and the Electronic Frontiers Foundation (EFF) alternatively introduced software (P3P) that creates machine-readable privacy policies for web site operators. Users running this software on their computers would not load web sites that had nonexistent or unacceptable privacy policies. Other companies have undertaken similar efforts. IBM and Microsoft have even gone so far as to pull advertising from web sites that fail to post privacy policies (few companies have the leverage of these two companies to carry out similar campaigns).

## Side Law: Content Rating Systems

To address the issue of violence in computer games, Senators Joseph Lieberman and Herbert Kohl held a number of U.S. Senate hearings in 1994. In response to these hearings, and to deflect possible government regulation of this media, two different content rating systems were developed. "RSAC's very existence is a direct result of the legislative initiative taken by Senators Lieberman and Kohl . . . that raise the issue of excessive violence in computer games" (statement of Senator Orrin G. Hatch, Hearings on S. 892, "Protection of Children from Computer Pornography Act of 1995," before the Senate Judiciary Committee [1995]). The Entertainment Software Rating Board (ESRB) proposed a different age-based advisory system that depended upon the decisions of a rating board (similar to motion picture ratings). While video game manufacturers and their developers have adopted ESRB, computer software developers disliked the age-based system.

Nevertheless, organizations like the Center for Democracy and Technology (CDT) note that there is a big difference between companies' policies and how those policies are implemented. As a result, the CDT and others have called for legislation that would establish a baseline standard for privacy protection. To further complicate matters, the United States and the European Union (EU) have been battling one another over whose data privacy standards should control. A number of years ago the EU passed a directive on how private data should be handled within the EU that will eventually require all citizens of the EU to comply with certain data privacy protection rules. I say eventually because an EU directive merely establishes a base upon which each of the member countries must place their own national laws. Europeans tend to be highly protective of their private information and more inclined to let government tell them what to do, whereas Americans tend to be less protective and less enthusiastic about governmental intervention. Hence, each member state of the EU is establishing a privacy office for investigating and enforcing data privacy violations. However, the United States has no national privacy law and is unlikely to establish a new privacy agency, although President Clinton did appoint a privacy advocate to partially placate critics.

## Cats on Drugs

Other self-regulatory efforts are popping up in many other areas. In testimony before the U.S. House Commerce Committee in the summer of 1999, a couple of reporters explained how a seven-year-old child, a man dead for 24 years, and a cat managed to order prescription drugs over the Internet. In one example, an investigative journalist logged onto an online pharmacy and answered a number of questions on behalf of Tom the cat. The answers indicated that Tom had been neutered for 10 years, weighed 15 pounds, and was 6 inches tall. Nevertheless, Tom's Viagra (an anti-impotence drug) prescription was promptly filled and charged to the female reporter's credit card. Online pharmacies have responded to such criticisms by endorsing an industry self-regulation effort—the Verified Internet Pharmacy Practice Sites certification program, sponsored by the National Association of Boards of Pharmacy. Despite the existence of extensive regulations that affect pharmacies, new regulations are being developed to deal with online pharmacies.

## Why Self-Regulation Will Fail to Prevent Regulation

Ideally, people should inherently know how to behave and shouldn't need laws to provide them with instructions and penalties for failure to comply, but most people are incapable of behaving themselves. Because self-regulation depends on the exercise of self-control (something that many people lack), few self-regulatory plans will be completely effective. So perhaps self-regulation won't fail as much as it will fail to live up to everyone's expectations, but either way, the failure of significant self-regulation will lead to regulation.

Speaking of self-control, former U.S. House of Representatives member Robert Walker recently noted that the desire to control something is one of the most important motivations to members of Congress—or to any other bureaucrat for that matter. "People go to Congress to be in control—it's why they go raise money, go through tough campaigns," Walker said. "They go to be at the center of [the] universe and be involved in public policymaking. . . . When something gets high on their radar screen they are going to seek ways to take control of it—and that's what is happening now [with the Internet]" (Chris Oakes, "Cluing Congress into Net ABCs," *Wired News*, 24 August 1999). The political desire to control will override the reasonable desire to wait for self-regulatory solutions.

In addition to the desire to control, bureaucratic self-preservation will also play a significant role in determining the regulatory environment of the Internet. In 1999, the Federal Communications Commission (FCC) released a paper entitled *The FCC and the Unregulation of the Internet*. While the title of this paper sounds very promising, the paper primarily focused on how the FCC's 30-year history of not regulating data services led to the Internet's development and growth. At about the same time, however, the U.S. Department of Commerce reported that although information technology industries accounted for just 8 percent of gross domestic product between 1995 and 1998, they contributed more than one-third of the United States' economic growth. By 2003 to 2004, it is predicted that data services traffic, which is presently considered an enhanced service and is therefore not regulated by the FCC, will represent 99 percent of all communication traffic, with only the remaining 1 percent representing traditional, regulated voice traffic. It was very easy for the FCC to ignore data services when they represented a small portion of the communication services business, but what will they be doing by 2003? What do you think will happen to all of the regulatory people at the FCC, as well to many people at the Commerce Department and the FTC, when regulated voice traffic is reduced to a meaningless percentage of all communication traffic? Will the U.S. government decide to just shut down the operations of these groups, send all the people working there home, and cut our taxes accordingly? Because the Internet will clearly be regulated, maybe it would be a good idea to figure out who is going to do it—and how.

## Who's the Sheriff?

My impression of the Old West leads me to believe that few people wanted to be sheriff. Then again, impressions born from highly authoritative Western films starring the likes of Ronald Reagan are not to be trusted. Today, I am inclined to believe that the ratio of lawmakers and enforcers to ordinary citizens has increased significantly, but this impression is largely based on being a lawyer, so who really knows if that impression is accurate, either. However, without question, there are many people around the world attempting to exert influence over the shaping of the regulatory environment of the Internet. Deciphering who is responsible for or attempting to do what is no easy task, and largely depends on your country of origin.

## Making Laws and Regulations in the United States

Local regulations (e.g., those relating to the local operation of your business and health and safety ordinances) may be some of the most important to many smaller ISPs. The good news is that these rules tend to be pretty simple to understand and easy to follow. If you don't pile up garbage outside of your building, serve food without a catering license, or set up a roller rink in the break room, then you probably won't run afoul of any of these regulations. More important, these rules apply to all businesses and people living in that area, not just ISPs. If you don't know what they are, however, contact city hall, your local town counsel, or even the Chamber of Commerce or Better Business Bureau in your area for help.

If you are building a network or providing physical access lines to customers, your situation will be different because you will need to get right-of-way permits and construction permits to tear up public streets and sidewalks. I would advise getting an attorney who has experience helping cable, phone, gas, or other utility-type companies obtain similar access and licenses. Any rules established by a local community to deal with such matters, however, should also apply to any company with similar needs, not just to ISPs. If a local community has adopted special rules that apply only to ISPs and that make it harder for ISPs to compete against established (dare I say monopolistic?) providers, that community has probably exceeded the limits of its authority. In such cases, I would advise at least going to the state Public Utilities Commission (PUC) or the FCC for guidance.

Because ISPs provide communication services primarily across state lines, even the states have a limited amount of authority to establish ISP-specific laws. A state's authority is limited to *intrastate* activities. And a state cannot establish laws that conflict with the Constitution or with any federal law intended to supersede state law. As you will see in Chapter 2, the federal government is not wasting any time establishing ISP-specific laws.

## Legislative Structure

Most states and the federal government are similarly structured and develop laws and regulations in pretty much the same way. Publicly elected officials develop laws. Regulations implement these laws and tend to be created by appointed officials or employees of the government. Each state has a publicly elected legislature, usually consisting of a house of delegates or representatives and a senate. The federal government has a House of Representatives and a Senate. Each state elects two senators to the federal Senate. Allotting senators to counties serves to populate state senates in a similar fashion. Representatives are allotted on a population-density basis. More-populated areas get more representatives. Some states have only a senate. Some states are large enough to justify a full-time legislature with full-time politicians, but most states meet for only part of the year or every two years, and the legislators have other jobs when they are not in session. When I was in college in Nevada, I worked as an intern at the Nevada Legislature for a senator from Las Vegas. This experience convinced me that at the state level, who you knew meant far more than the justification behind any bill. My experiences at the federal level haven't led me to believe that federal politics is much different. As you can imagine, long-established state communication companies have employees who know everyone at the state level. As a result, if one of these companies wants legislation enacted that will help them and hurt ISPs, it is highly likely that they will get it.

## Making Sausage

Legislation gets enacted by being written and introduced by a legislator. Legislation typically needs to be introduced in both the House and the Senate. Sometimes, a bill is passed from one body to the other, but at other times, two different bills are introduced. Rarely are the two bills the same, so even after the legislation is passed, the two bills must be referred to a conference committee that has the responsibility for reconciling the differences between the two bills. The legislators who introduce the bills do not typically come up with the ideas for the legislation themselves, nor do they even write the legislation. In large states and at the federal level, the legislature has a staff that often helps write the legislation, frequently after the idea for such legislation has been suggested to them by a constituent. In smaller states and sometimes even at the federal level, the constituents write the legislation. These constituents generally aren't who you think they are. Most of us, although we may be constituents of any of a number of different publicly elected officials, cannot simply write up a bill, walk into an official's office, and expect that official to introduce our bill. You have to have power of some kind to get a bill introduced. In most cases, money and political support develop power. A company or political organization that donates money to a politician, that gets the politician good press, or that helps the politician win support on another issue can often get that politician to introduce or sponsor all sorts of bills.

Constituents rarely draft legislation at the federal level because the parliamentary rules and internal congressional politics that have to be followed are too complicated. For example, certain words must be used in a bill in order for that bill to get introduced and referred to the proper committee for consideration. If nonstandard words are used, the bill will get introduced elsewhere, which can be a significant problem, because the bill may be assigned to a committee that knows nothing about your issue and may include no legislators with whom you are friendly. Bills are almost impossible to get moved once a committee has jurisdiction (even if by mistake). In the U.S. Senate, for example, intellectual property–related bills are typically assigned to the Senate Judiciary Committee. Intellectual property often involves commerce, and more frequently now, the Internet, so if an intellectual property–related bill is not drafted in the right fashion, it might be assigned to the Senate Commerce Committee. Given that the chairman of the Commerce Committee and the chairman of the Judiciary Committee are both either thinking of running or are running for higher office, it is unlikely that either would be inclined to give up any authority to the other. This is especially true in relation to an intellectual property– or communication-related bill, which might not get much press but will generate lots of contributions.

Once a bill has been introduced and referred to a committee, the committee will usually then refer the bill to a subcommittee with responsibility for the particular subject matter of the bill. This subcommittee will probably hold a hearing on the bill to solicit public comment. If the person who introduced the bill belongs to the same political party as the chairman of the committee or subcommittee, the bill will get a hearing faster (if it has one at all) and will usually be moved through faster than any bill introduced by an opposing party member. The scheduling, construction, and witness selection for a hearing is highly orchestrated. The supporters of a bill usually outnumber those who oppose the bill, but both are almost always represented, although the opposition can sometimes be token. Although a big deal is made out of hearings, and I have testified numerous times in both the U.S. House and Senate, I have never seen a hearing have any real impact on the course of a bill.

When there is strong support and opposition to a bill, an opposing bill will often be introduced to compete with the first bill. This sometimes results in a forced negotiation between the two sides, but more often than not simply results in neither bill moving forward. If a negotiation is possible, the opposing sides may initiate it themselves, or they may be forced to talk by a legislator who gets sick of hearing both sides and just wants to get rid of the matter. While I have absolutely (and I mean absolutely) nothing in common with Senator Orrin Hatch (a Utah Republican), I still respect the fact that he had enough guts to tell the opposing sides in the Digital Millennium Copyright Act (DMCA) controversy to sit down and truly negotiate or he would modify the bill and push it forward himself. That prospect was horrifying enough to both sides that it forced them to work out their differences. I have since tried to get other legislators to take a similar stand without much success.

Once a bill gets passed out of a subcommittee, it will go to the full committee. The full committee may hold another hearing or two and will sometimes make changes and add explanatory language if it decides to pass the bill. If the bill impacts more than one committee's jurisdiction, it will also be referred to the other affected committees for similar treatment, although the subsequent referrals tend to defer to the original committee's work. Once a bill has cleared all of the committees, it will get sent to the legislative body for a vote. As a whole, the legislature's leadership does not like to vote on legislation that will not be passed (unless they want to take political advantage of its defeat), so bills will often get hung up in the committees until the end of the term. If the term ends before a bill has made it through a legislature, the bill has to start all over the next term, including reintroduction.

In the event that identical legislation makes it through the House of Representatives and the Senate, it will be sent to the president (or governor in a state) for signature. If the two legislatures pass different bills, the bills are sent to a conference committee, which is made up of members from both legislatures. If the conference committee agrees to a compromise bill, it gets sent to the president for signature. If members of the committee can't agree, one or both bills will get sent back to the legislatures. A bill sent to the president may be vetoed. The president will typically veto only legislation that cannot be overridden by the Senate because the president generally doesn't want to give the Senate a chance to flaunt a victory over the president. It takes a two-thirds majority vote of the Senate to override a veto. Unless legislation is strongly supported by the Senate, the number of votes required to override a veto forces the Senate to take the administration's point of view into account when it considers legislation.

What I have described here is a highly simplified explanation of how the legislative process works in the United States. The reality is much more complicated. Due to the complexity and ugliness of this entire process, the creation of legislation is often compared to the creation of sausage—something most people do not want to see.

You can avoid participating in sausage production, but you better not avoid participation in the production of legislation, because the greatest influences on legislation are those that most people do not see. In between the public introduction, the hearings, and the votes comes private meeting after meeting between the lobbyist in support of or opposed to the bill and those who control its destiny. Meetings are required with the legislators and their staffs who introduce and cosponsor the bill. Meetings are required with the subcommittee members and their staffs to influence their support of the bill and to try to get them to make needed changes. Meetings are required with the committee members and their staffs to garner more support and to fix anything left over from the subcommittee. Meetings are required with the leadership and its staff to influence referrals, to gather more support, and to impact the time of voting in the legislature. Meetings are required with the administration and its staff to get them to take or change a position. If the bill is controversial, or if someone wants to make it so, meetings are required with the press to stir up publicity. Sometimes the meetings are useless. Sometimes the meetings result in changes to the bill. Sometimes the meetings result in more hearings. Sometimes the meetings serve no purpose other than to get in someone's face so that they know someone cares about the bill in one way or another. If you don't participate in this process, you simply don't matter.

Legislation before any publicly elected body has everything to do with participation and very little to do with principles. No one really cares whether a bill impacts your business if you never read the bill and voiced an opinion, if you never attended or participated in a hearing, or if you never went to a meeting. Riding on the coattails of the other companies involved can be a very dangerous gamble. During the course of the negotiations on one bill, I contacted a couple of Internet companies in order to get them involved because particular aspects of the bill would have been crippling to their businesses. While they expressed interest, they also assumed the other parties would take care of them. In the end, however, the other companies were forced to give up protection for these Internet companies in order to get something else they wanted. When the Internet companies found out, they screamed bloody murder, and although they did end up getting some (not all) changes made, most of the legislative people involved said, "Where were you before this?" I would therefore encourage you, even if you cannot comfortably afford it, to have some representation in Washington, D.C. Some attorneys at different firms will represent your interests, together with a number of other clients, and will involve your company (and charge you for doing so) only when absolutely necessary. Others will rip you off blindly, so be selective. If nothing else, you should join an association that can represent your interests. While I am sure there are associations operating at the state level, at the federal level the Information Technology Association of American (ITAA), the Commercial Internet eXchange (CIX), and the Computer and Communications Industry Association (CCIA) each have capable representatives working on ISP-related matters—although I like ITAA the best. They all have web sites; I've provided their URLs in the reference section at the end of this book.

## *Making Regulations*

Once the president signs legislation into law, it gets assigned to some agency of the government for implementation and enforcement. The agency then creates the regulations that are needed to see the legislation carried out. Different agencies operate differently. The FCC has a number of commissioners who are appointed by the president, the commissioner's political appointees, and its permanent staff. The FTC operates in the same fashion. The Patent and Trademark Office only has one presidentially appointed commissioner. Presidents, commissioners, and their staffs come and go every four to eight years, but the permanent staffs remain unchanged. The politically appointed people can be more readily influenced than the permanent staff—and that probably is a good thing. Sometimes while proposed regulations are being drafted, it is possible to meet with the officials and employees of the agency in an effort to influence their interpretation of the legislation. Other times, you must wait until the proposed regulations are published. Each agency is required to publish its regulations for public comment before the regulations can go into effect. Once the final regulations have been adopted, the commissioner either signs them into effect, or if there is more than one commissioner, the commissioners will vote. If you participate in a regulated industry, and as an ISP I suggest you already do, then you should also be paying attention to the adoption of the various regulations that will impact your operations, primarily at the FCC and FTC. "What?" you say, "I'm not in a regulated industry." "Ha!" I say. Read on.

## Law and Regulation Enforcement

Some laws create private remedies, such as the right to sue and collect damages, whereas other laws rely on public enforcement. The public enforcement agencies relevant to ISPs at the federal level include the Department of Justice, the FCC, the FTC, and the FBI. For the most part, the enforcement of most laws that apply to ISPs on their face are not that interesting, unless you happen to be the defendant. Where things get interesting is when the Justice Department or the FBI starts talking about enforcement efforts in other areas that will have a significant impact on ISPs. For example, in July 1999, the FBI revealed an antiterrorism plan that involved the monitoring of crucial industries such as banking, telecommunications, and transportation. The FBI is particularly concerned about cyberspace attacks and hopes that detailed monitoring of all communications traffic will help prevent such intrusions. Congress was rather outraged by this suggestion and immediately threatened to cut off any funding that would be used for it, so hopefully it won't go anywhere. The British prime minister recently introduced a similar proposal in the United Kingdom that goes even further and requires each ISP to maintain permanent records of the source and/or destination of every packet transmitted over its network. This proposal has also met immediate criticism.

In August 1999, shortly after the administration's rebuke for its FBI proposal, President Clinton signed an executive order establishing a working group to examine unlawful conduct on the Internet. The working group involved the attorney general and the departments of the Treasury, Commerce, and Education, as well as the FBI, the Bureau of Alcohol, Tobacco and Firearms (ATF), the Drug Enforcement Agency (DEA), the FTC, and the Food and Drug Administration (FDA). In particular, the working group was intended to investigate the effectiveness of existing federal laws to control illegal conduct involving the Internet and the degree to which new or existing technology tools could be used to investigate and prosecute crimes and educate and empower those attempting to prevent them.

## Making Laws and Regulations in the European Union

The European legislative process makes the American process look fairly simple—and so it is, in comparison. The EU presently consists of 15 member states: Austria, Belgium, Denmark, Finland, France, Germany, Greece, Italy, Ireland, Luxembourg, the Netherlands, Portugal, Spain, Sweden, and the United Kingdom. Originally, according to the Rome Treaty, the European Commission (EC) was to propose European legislation, and the Council of Ministers (Council), appointed by each member state, was to decide on whether to adopt such legislation after consultation with the European Parliament (EP).

The EC is composed of 20 commissioners, representing a number of different general areas of responsibility. For example, the Commissioner of Directorate General (DG) XIII is responsible for telecommunications, information market, and exploitation research. France, Germany, Italy, Spain, and the United Kingdom each have two commissioners, and each of the other member states has one. Each commissioner also has a staff, called a *cabinet*, which typically consists of nationals from the same member state as the commissioner, although each commissioner is obliged to act independently of national governments and only in the interests of the EU. Since it was the EC's duty to draft proposals for submission to the council, the EP was initially just a consultative body, made up of representatives appointed by the parliaments of member states (each country belonging to the European Community), having little power or responsibility.

The power and responsibility of the EP all began to change in the 1980s when the direct election of members of the EP (MEPs) gave the EP its own mandate to draft and adopt EU legislation on behalf of the people of Europe. The Treaty on European Union, signed in Maastricht on February 7, 1992, firmly established the EU and granted the EP the right to initiate legislative proposals. The EP now has 626 MEPs, democratically elected to five-year terms, each of which belongs to one of nine recognized political groups. The EP has four official tasks:

1. To take part in the EU's legislative process.
2. To adopt the budget for the EU in conjunction with the council.
3. To exercise general supervision over the activities of the EC and the council, which means that the EP can force the commission to resign (which happened in the summer of 1999).
4. To act as the political driving force for the EU.

Although the EP can initiate legislative proposals, the commission is not explicitly required to respond to an EP request. It is therefore the commission's duty to adopt draft proposals for submission to the council or to the council and the EP. Failure to respond to EP requests can doom commission proposals. Since the commission initiates new legislation, and there are relatively few commissioners in comparison to the MEPs, the commission is the most heavily lobbied body.

## The European Process

The EP participates in the legislative process of the EU through four legislative procedures, depending on the nature of the proposal:

1. The consultation.
2. The cooperation.
3. The assent.
4. The codecision procedure.

A consultation is just the EP's opinion on a legislative proposal from the commission that is intended to influence the council's adoption of the proposal. If the EP's opinion is not incorporated into the council's common position on the proposal, the EP has the right to reject the proposal. Any such rejection by the EP can be overturned only by a unanimous decision of the council. Because unanimity is difficult to achieve, the council usually seeks to cooperate with the EP to come up with a joint resolution. If this cooperative procedure fails, the EP can definitely reject the council's common position through what is called the *codecision procedure*. The EP first used this procedure in 1994 to reject a council's adoption of a law having to do with the enforcement of open network provisioning for voice telephony. If it were not for the EP's action in this regard, there would probably be little voice telephony competition within Europe. Finally, the assent procedure involves the EP's approval for any decision having to do with the accession of new member states (such as former Eastern Bloc countries), the right of residence and freedom of movement, certain budgetary issues, and other matters.

Once the council has adopted legislation, that law prevails over any conflicting national law of a member state, just as federal law supersedes conflicting state laws in the United States. The commission therefore works with each member state to draft national legislation that will conform to the EU laws. Simply put, the EU establishes the EU laws, and the commission works with the member states to adopt the regulations implementing the EU laws. If a national of a member state violates an EU law or if a government of a member state fails to implement national legislation in conformity with the EU law, the Court of Justice can hear the matter and enforce the EU law. As the EU gains more legislative power from the member states and adopts more laws, a common body of law is gradually being developed throughout all of the member states of the EU. Eventually, the legislative authority of the European member states will be very similar to the authority of various states within the United States of America, with limited authority to create nonconflicting laws within their territorial boundaries.

## The European Process Applied

To understand how all of this works within the context of legislation that is relevant to an ISP, consider the WIPO Copyright Treaties that were the subject of the DMCA legislation in the United States. First, Directorate General (DG) XV, which is responsible for internal markets, was assigned the job of drafting a proposal for turning the treaties into EU law. DG XV is divided into different sections, including one that handles intellectual property. Unfortunately, the person responsible for intellectual property matters was an avid and traditional believer in very strong copyright laws who had no clue how the Internet worked. Hence, the Copyright Directive (*directive* is another name for *proposal*) did not incorporate any of the limiting language that was adopted in the treaties to mitigate the liability of ISPs for transmitting copyright-infringing material. Also, because a different DG had already undertaken the task of working on a proposal to handle electronic commerce liability issues in the context of the so-called E-Commerce Directive, the Copyright Directive did not address those issues at all.

Offhand, assuming the E-Commerce Directive did a decent job of dealing with the issue, this sounded like a reasonable way to deal with the issue of ISP liability, except for the fact that the two directives were not tied to one another. It was important for these two directives to be tied together to prevent the directive that would create liability for ISPs (the Copyright Directive) from taking effect before the directive that limited the liability of ISPs (the E-Commerce Directive). While the other members of the EC were considering the Copyright Directive (a process called *inner service consultation*), the ISPs tried unsuccessfully to get the two directives linked.

The Copyright Directive was adopted by the EC and put forward to the EP. The EP, which also has a number of different substantive groups, assigned the Copyright Directive to a main committee, in this case to the Legal Affairs Committee, for consideration. The Legal Affairs Committee assigns a *rapporteur* (an MEP with an interest in the matter) to each directive to coordinate hearings and voting on amendments to the directive. Unfortunately, with respect to the Copyright Directive, a rapporteur was selected who had no understanding of the Internet and very close ties to the content community. Other committees, however, were permitted to review the directive and to offer their own amendments to the main committee. The main committee decides whether to incorporate any such amendments into the committee's report. With respect to the Copyright Directive, the rapporteur actually got into some trouble for refusing to consider certain ISP-friendly amendments offered by other committees. The amended Copyright Directive was then sent to the EP for a vote by the plenary. Unfortunately, at about the same time the Copyright Directive was sent to the plenary, the voting procedures within the EP were changed, which resulted in great confusion regarding which amendments were being voted on and a pretty embarrassing situation for the EP. This was eventually straightened out, although not in the ISPs' favor, and the amended Copyright Directive was sent back to the EC.

Things looked promising for ISPs when the EC decided that it did not like the EP's amendments to the Copyright Directive. The amendments significantly increased copyright protections and would have required ISPs to get a copyright owner's authorization before the ISP could transmit a copyrighted work without liability. Regrettably, while the EC was drafting a response to the EP, an audit highly critical of the EC's management and spending activities was released. This resulted in all of the commissioners resigning. Although a new commission has since been appointed and accepted by the EP, the will to take on the EP over something like a copyright law has ebbed. Nevertheless, the EC continues to work on its response. This delay has at least enabled the E-Commerce Directive to catch up with the Copyright Directive, but it remains to be seen whether the problems with both directives can be fixed.

## Pointed Fingers

As much as I would like to, it isn't fair to blame the EC or the EP for the status of ISP liability issues in Europe—the ISPs themselves are at fault. When the Copyright Treaties were being negotiated at the World Intellectual Property Organization (WIPO), U.S. ISPs tried to get the Europeans involved. While these efforts resulted in the enthusiastic support of Sonera of Finland and British Telecommunications, many companies lacked the vision to realize how significant this could become for their businesses. Even after the disastrous plenary vote on the Copyright Directive, most European ISPs remained inactive. American ISPs, of course, carry only so much weight in discussions with the EC and various MEPs, so the Americans were in no position to help much until the Europeans got it together. While some European ISPs, mainly the large, incumbent telecommunications companies in each country, are finally beginning to get involved, due to years of monopolistic largess they lack the political weight and experience of the content community when lobbying their positions before the EC, EP, and council. For now, all most of us can do is to help where we can and hope the Europeans do not manage to kill the growth of electronic commerce in Europe for the limited benefit of a few music companies and publishers.

# What about the Rest of the World?

As you might expect, each country has its own legislative system, together with different methods of lobbying and allowing or even encouraging industry input. Each system is largely influenced by the cultural and historical baggage that happens to be associated with that country. For instance, former European colonies tend to have legislative systems that are modeled after the system of the former colonist. Many countries, especially developing countries, tend to be less interested in the merits of proposed legislation and more interested in the political impact. For example, some countries simply ratified and adopted the WIPO Copyright Treaties without the benefit of implementing legislation so they could get credit from certain developed countries, who care about such things, for having promptly done so. In particular, a number of copyright infringement havens were under heavy international pressure to clean up their acts and quickly adopted the treaties. Whether these countries will actually enforce them remains to be seen.

Other countries took a more pragmatic approach and quickly adopted ISP-favorable laws, largely based on DMCA principles, in order to encourage electronic commerce within their countries. Singapore, for example, while not a signatory to the treaties, has already adopted liability laws that are favorable to ISPs. Other countries such as Malaysia, Finland, Ireland, Mauritius, and Japan view national policies as a means of establishing new and valuable sources of national competitive advantage. Australia was one of the first countries to understand the importance of coordinating its legislative and government policy approaches, as evidenced by its August 1997 report to the Minister for Communications and the Arts from the Information Policy Advisory Council (IPAC) entitled *A National Policy Framework Structural Adjustment within the New Commonwealth of Information*. Unfortunately, due to the structure of the Australian government, which enables certain individual politicians from conservative, low-populated areas to dominate the adoption of legislation, Australia has largely ignored the IPAC report and gone on to adopt some questionable Internet-related legislation.

In 1999, for example, the Australian Minister for Communications, Information Technology and the Arts (who represents a sparsely populated and highly conservative portion of the country) proposed and obtained the approval of a very egregious regulatory plan that applies to the Internet. This plan is discussed in detail under ISP Liability Gone Amok in Chapter 5, *What Is an ISP to Do (or Not)? Content and Activity Regulations to Live By*. One aspect of the Australian regulatory plan requires all Internet content to be rated and all ISPs (who do not otherwise run a filtered network) to take down (within 24 hours) any X-rated and R-rated content that can be accessed without adult verification. ISPs would also be required to attempt to block access to prohibited material obtained from overseas sources.

As the Internet continues its global and interstellar expansion, and as more service provision competition evolves, so, too, will the laws and regulations that impact each and every aspect of the Internet and your operations. With respect to interstellar expansion, the Interplanetary Internet project is working on extending an Internet network into outer space. (See www.wcom.com/about_the_company/cerfs_up/interplanetary_internet/index.phtml for more information.) You can stand by and observe the process and hope someone else will look after your interests, but hopefully you have learned that you are better off taking your liability issues into your own hands, no matter where in the world, or universe, you happen to be.

# CHAPTER 2

# Intellectual Property
# and Other Laws Made Simple

Virtually all countries have some form of intellectual property law, as well as many related laws on a wide variety of subjects that have had and will continue to have a large impact on ISPs. Intellectual property laws primarily include copyrights, patents, trademarks, and trade secrets, but also implicate free speech, unfair competition, and antitrust laws, among other legal areas. I am starting with a discussion of intellectual property laws in this chapter before moving on to other Internet-specific laws because intellectual property is a legal area most people have heard of but few understand well. Intellectual property laws also spurred the creation of the Digital Millennium Copyright Act (DMCA), which is the subject of Chapter 3. The DMCA was the first law specifically written to address ISP liability issues, and it has formed the basis for many of the laws that have followed and will unquestionably influence the world's legal direction long into the future. Before I go on too much about that law, however, lets start with IP in general. Oh! I almost forgot to tell you, in the legal world, *IP* means intellectual property, not Internet protocol.

## Copyrights, Freedom of Speech,
## and Related Rights

Copyright has always been a law of exclusion. When the printing press was introduced into England in 1476, it scared the hell out of the Crown, which feared it would be used to promote religious heresy and political upheaval. So, by 1534, anyone who wished to publish something was required to get a license and the approval of official censors. This was simplified in 1557 by conferring a monopoly on publishing to a group of London printers and booksellers who could be relied upon to publish only what the Crown approved. This monopoly prevailed until 1694. Competition in the market, however, drove the former monopolist to seek protection, and through its lobbying efforts Parliament passed the first copyright act, the Statute of Anne, in 1710. While the Statute of Anne maintained the monopolist's rights (until 1731) in works that were already in print, it granted copyrights to the authors themselves for new works under the theory that this would encourage learning, and the disclosure of such learning, through reward.

The United States incorporated a similar philosophy into its Constitution in 1787, through Article I, Section 8, Clause 8, the Patent and Copyright Clause, which states in part that: "The Congress shall have power . . . [t]o promote the progress of science and useful arts, by securing for limited times to authors and inventors the exclusive right to their respective writings and discoveries." This statement, of course, is not read today as it was intended. At that time, the term *science*, which was then known as natural philosophy, was defined to include all knowledge, not just what we think is included in the study of science today. As a result, people have assumed that *useful arts* applied to copyrights and *science* to patents, but it was really the other way around. Copyright is now a form of legal protection recognized in almost all countries and is even guaranteed by the constitutions of many countries. In this sense, copyright is a fundamental precept of democracy—the freedom and encouragement (through economic reward) to express your views for the betterment of public welfare.

Copyright is not a tangible right, such as the right to possess an object or real property. It is an intangible right. This is an important distinction, because the Internet by its very nature deals in intangibles and is more likely to be impacted by intangible rights. A copyright is also a negative right in that the government grants the owner of the copyright the exclusive right to do, or to authorize others to do, things with the copyrighted work for a limited period of time. It does not necessarily grant the owner the right to do anything he or she chooses with the copyrighted work (i.e., duplicate it), because the work might be based on or include the works of others who also have exclusive rights.

## Copyright Ownership

You might have noticed that I referred to the *owner* of the copyright, not the author. I drew this distinction because few people actually understand how copyrights are created and, once created, how they are used. You do not need to do a darn thing to obtain copyright protection other than to create a copyrightable work and reduce it to a fixed medium (i.e., a piece of paper, a word-processed document stored in a computer's memory—something tangible). Thus, from the moment you create it and store it in some fashion, it is copyrighted.

Technically, because the copyright is created along with the work, the copyright immediately becomes the property of the author. This general-ownership rule worked fine when most authors worked for themselves. Over time, many authors started working for other people and for companies, or they were specifically commissioned (i.e., by a publishing company) to produce a work. Allowing such authors to own their works while employed by someone else created problems, because the

## Side Law: Work Made for Hire

A *work made for hire* is defined as follows:

> . . . a work prepared by an employee within the scope of his or her employment; or a work specially ordered or commissioned for use as a contribution to a collective work, as a part of a motion picture or other audiovisual work, as a translation, as a supplementary work, as a compilation, as an instructional text, as a test, as answer material for a test, or as an atlas, if the parties expressly agree in a written instrument signed by them that the work shall be considered a work made for hire.
>
> **The U.S. Copyright Act**

*Translation:* A contribution to a collective work could include source code written by a contract programmer as part of a larger software program. Web sites and software programs that operate in conjunction with a graphical user interface, such that they can be displayed on and interacted with on a monitor, would be included in the definition of *audiovisual works.* As for the rest of the copyright statute, based on the specific inclusion of motion pictures, tests and atlases, it is at least clear that no special-interest groups helped fine-tune this legislation.

employers expected to own the works for which they paid. After many ownership battles between employers and authors, a solution to this problem was finally created, which is generally called the *work-made-for-hire* doctrine.

In countries where this rule is applied, when one person under the hire of another creates a work, the employer and not the employee is considered to be the author, irrespective of the real author. There are limits to this doctrine. While you do not have to be at work for the rule to apply, the work you create does have to be within the scope of your employment in order for that work to belong to your employer. This rule can also apply to contractors when there is a contract between the contractor and the employer. As one would expect, jointly created works are jointly owned, absent an agreement to the contrary. Also, the copyright in each separate contribution (a newspaper column) to a collective work (the newspaper) is distinct from the copyright that exists in the collective work as a whole.

All of these rules regarding the initial author or owner of a copyrighted work point to the special care that needs to be taken when you hire someone to do work for you. Many former employees have successfully wrested ownership of valuable works from employers as a result of being able to show that the work was outside the scope of their employment. The situation involving contractors is even worse. Contractors are either self-employed or are the employees of a contracting agency. In such cases, the work-made-for-hire doctrine is limited and specifically requires a written contract. Suggestions for what to include in contracts with employees and contractors will be covered in Chapter 6, *Incorporating ISP Liability Concepts in Contracts.* Disputes can also arise when companies codevelop documents or software and fail to agree in advance on who will own the resulting work. For example, if you operate a retail ISP operation and you codevelop software with your wholesale provider to monitor a

## Side Law: First Sale

Under the first-sale doctrine, you may sell or otherwise transfer your copy of a copyrighted work without asking permission of or paying a royalty to the copyright owner.

*Translation:* Application of this rule of law depends on whether you actually purchased the good or licensed it. Most people would be surprised to learn that when they go to the store and "buy" a copy of Microsoft Windows, even though they may be buying the box, the manuals, the plastic in the CD, and so forth, they are only *licensing* the actual software. Software licenses often bar the copyrighted software from being transferred to another person or allow for such a transfer only subject to the terms of the same license. Nonetheless, there is disagreement among the courts regarding the proper application of licensing law in this case. As a result, some courts have held that even though software was "licensed" by agreement, the copy of the software was purchased and consequently, the first-sale doctrine applied to permit any resale of the software. Other courts have found that a resale in violation of the terms of the license is not permitted. In my humble opinion, the first-sale doctrine is much more likely to be applied to consumer software purchases than it is to business-to-business transactions.

certain type of traffic flow, the absence of a written contract would dictate that both parties equally own that software. Contracts with vendors and suppliers will also be covered in Chapter 6.

As long as I am explaining ownership, I might as well explain the difference between owning a tangible good and owning the underlying copyright that applies to that good. When you buy a copy of a book or a compact disc or a software program, you do not also purchase the underlying copyright. Likewise, just because the copyright owner owns the copyright to your software program does not mean that the copyright owner can prevent you from selling your copy of the program.

## What Can Be Copyrighted?

Computer software, video games, motion pictures, and compact disk players did not exist when the U.S. Constitution was being drafted—on paper with a quill pen. Copyright law has therefore had to adapt over time to new technologies and continually expand the definitions of *authors* and *writings*. The term *authors* has been expanded to include photographers, artists, architects, publishers, programmers, singers, musicians, writers, and composers. Likewise, the types of *writings* eligible for copyright protection have been expanded to include the following:

- Literary works (computer programs, cartoons, books and articles, stories, and similar text from newspapers, magazines, web sites, trade journals, newsletters)
- Music and lyrics (music as written, recorded, or performed)

- Pictures, graphics, sculptures, and architectural works (photographs, cartoon characters, paintings, blueprints, dolls, jewelry, models)

- Dramatic works (plays and screenplays as written and performed, including accompanying music)

- Pantomimes and choreographic works (stage plays, dance routines)

- Audiovisual works (motion pictures, videotapes, video games, and computer software that have audio and video effects)

- Sound recordings (compact discs, cassette tapes, phonographic records, digital music files such as MP3)

## Pseudo Copyright Protection for Databases

As broad and inclusive as the preceding categories may be, the push is always on to extend them further (see Side Law: Performance Rights versus Mechanical Rights). In 1991, the U.S. Supreme Court ruled in *Feist Publications, Inc. v. Rural Tel. Serv. Co.* that copyright protection did not extend to facts and information, or even to obvious, noncreative arrangements of facts and information. Currently, an effort is under way to legislatively extend copyright-like protection to databases. The creators of large commercial databases, the proponents for such legislation, want this protection because they spend a lot of money to compile data and put it together in a useful form (often called "sweat of the brow"). Proponents don't like the idea that someone else could come along and simply take the data. On the other hand, the opponents question why database owners should get copyright protection when they have done absolutely nothing original and have done even less to keep the data from being easily taken. For example, why couldn't database companies restrict access to and use of their databases under the terms of a license agreement, or use technical measures to prevent the data from being readily downloaded, printed, or copied and pasted?

Nevertheless, I expect to see some form of database protection become law some day. Database protection proponents already have a directive in Europe that is slowly being implemented within member states. The term *member states* in European parlance means the individual countries that make up the EC. Broad and narrow forms of legislation have also been introduced in the United States. I have testified before Congress against the broad legislation and in favor of the narrow legislation, and I expect that a compromise will be reached in 2000. If a compromise is not reached in the United States in 2000, it may be many years before this dispute is ultimately resolved. Any legislation will hopefully include exclusions for databases that are necessary for the efficient operation of the Internet. The Internet, which is among other things a combination of network computers and their databases, is particularly dependent upon the open sharing of information. Internet Protocol addressing, data packet routing, conversion (lookup) tables, protocol priority listings, file format information, and domain name registries are just a few examples of the types of critical functions performed within the Internet every minute of every day through reliance on what are presently publicly available databases.

# Side Law: Performance Rights versus Mechanical Rights

In 1908, the U.S. Supreme Court ruled that phono records and player piano rolls were not copies for purposes of copyright. The Copyright Act of 1909 changed this law by awarding composers a royalty each time a song is carried on something that can be replayed mechanically, such as a compact disc or an MP3 file. The mechanical right to a sound recording (music) is quite different from the right to perform such music in public, such as through a radio broadcast, and the two are often owned by different copyright owners. The mechanical rights tend to be owned by the record labels, and the performance rights tend to be owned by the songwriters and composers.

In the United States, copyright agencies such as the American Society of Composers, Authors and Publishers (ASCAP) and Broadcast Music, Inc. (BMI) represent songwriters and composers. ASCAP's catalog includes more than 4 million songs. These agents collect royalties for public performances of their clients' songs (e.g., on radio stations, in elevators, and, increasingly, on the Internet). Digital versions of songs that are *streamed* from a public server to a user's computer where it can be played but not stored will probably be considered a public performance akin to a broadcast. The fact that only one person sitting at home hears the song doesn't change the public nature of the performance, because the song itself was publicly available and could have been broadcast to a larger audience. In contrast, the Harry Fox Agency collects royalties from the sale of recordings, typically on behalf of the recording labels. ASCAP and BMI also represent their clients politically, whereas the record labels tend to be represented by the Recording Industry Association of America (RIAA) rather than the Harry Fox Agency. Under the terms of the Digital Performance Right in Sound Recordings Act of 1995, RIAA finally succeeded in getting the definition of *mechanical rights* slightly broadened to include public performances, but only for sound recordings that are publicly performed by means of a digital audio transmission. Now the Harry Fox Agency can collect royalties for sales of digital versions of songs transmitted over the Internet.

The Audio Home Recording Act (AHRA) of 1992 was intended to extend the record labels' mechanical rights to cover digital recording devices and their respective recording mediums, such as digital audiotape (DAT) drives and DAT tapes. Nevertheless, in 1999, RIAA lost a suit against Diamond Multimedia in which RIAA claimed that Diamond's Rio PMP300 player, which allows users to download music in MP3 format onto the Rio device and replay the music at a later time, violated the AHRA. RIAA lost because the court held that the AHRA outlawed only commercial recordings and did not extend to copying from a computer server to another device such as the Rio. As a result, the Rio was determined not to be "a digital audio recording device subject to the Act's restrictions."

Similar battles are being waged by the same kinds of organizations in many other countries. The Korea Music Copyright Association (KOMCA) recently prevailed on Korean ISPs to remove free MP3 files from their servers. Other organizations around the world have mounted similar attacks on ISPs storing Real Audio (RA) and Real Media (RM) media files. The Society of Composers, Authors and Music Publishers of Canada (SOCAN) has been fighting to get compulsory music licensing extended to the Internet. A compulsory music license would effectively result in a very small, but collectively large, tax (often called a *levy*) being charged for every bit of information transmitted (often called a *bit tax*) in a particular country. The International Federation of the Phonographic Industries (IFPI) and the Confederation of Societies of Authors and Composers (CISAC) have been up to similar no good throughout Europe. Even Australia introduced legislation in 1999 that would not permit *caching* for the purpose of listening to music on a computer.

# Where Copyright Protection Stops

Now that you know where copyright protection starts, it is equally important to know where it stops. Even if a work is eligible for copyright protection, meaning that it falls within one of the categories set forth earlier, it must still be an original work that has been reduced to a tangible medium of expression. Thus, improvisational speeches and music performances, no matter how original, are not protected unless written down or recorded by or for the creator. Likewise, just because something has been written down or recorded doesn't mean it is original. Examples of unoriginal works that are routinely excluded from protection include titles ("chief evangelist"), short phrases and slogans ("This end up"), familiar symbols and designs (smiley faces), and mere listings of ingredients or contents (nutritional data on food products). As basic as these rules may sound, their application to new content-related technologies can be complicated.

## *Original Works*

In 1983, Apple Computer, Inc., won a copyright lawsuit against Franklin Computer Corp. that resulted in the extension of copyright protection to computer software in either source or object code form. Franklin sold a computer that was compatible with the Apple II computer, but such compatibility was achieved by copying the code stored in the ROM (read-only memory) chip in the Apple II and using that same code in Franklin's computer. Years later, Apple further helped to extend copyright protection to the *user interface* of a computer program when it sued Microsoft and Hewlett-Packard for infringing copyrights in the Apple Macintosh operating system. This time, however, Apple lost, but not because a user interface couldn't qualify for copyright protection; the judge ruled that it could. Apple lost because Apple's user interface wasn't sufficiently original in comparison to the Microsoft Windows user interface (which was used in Hewlett-Packard's product as well). How could this be? Didn't Apple have the very best user interface at the time? Wasn't the Window's user interface very similar?

The application of copyright law is not an exact science, and in this case, it was further complicated by a rather unique set of facts. First, Apple had licensed its copyrights in the Apple Macintosh user interface to Microsoft for use in version 1.0 of Microsoft Windows. The license agreement was poorly drafted (I didn't do it), so the court ruled that the license extended to further uses of the same material in subsequent versions of Microsoft Windows. Because they were licensed, this decision removed a substantial portion of the original elements in Apple's user interface from being subject to infringement. The court then precluded additional elements from being protected because they were functional in nature and thereby inherently lacked originality. Purely functional elements, or arrangements of them for functional purposes, such as dials, knobs, and buttons for a television, the dials of a clock on a stove, and certain user interface elements, are beyond the scope of copyright protection. For example, file folder icons had been used in other programs, and while Apple's were different, they weren't original. Finally, the court looked at what was left, and there wasn't much. The court then compared the remaining user interface elements from Apple's product to Microsoft's product and said they weren't substantially similar, which is the basic test for infringement.

## Ideas

The most significant area of exclusion from copyright protection includes procedures, methods, systems, processes, concepts, principles, discoveries, or devices (which are all other ways of saying *ideas*). In 1880, the U.S. Supreme Court ruled, in a case involving a book illustrating a system of bookkeeping, that a book could be protected as the expression of the system, but the system itself was an idea and as such was a creature of patents, not copyrights. Thus, copyright protection does not extend to ideas, but it can extend to the particular expression of an idea. For example, you cannot get a copyright on the idea for a story about a fisherman chasing a whale throughout the seas, but you can copyright the literary expression of that idea, such as *Moby Dick* (first published by none other than John Wiley & Sons, my distinguished publisher). Likewise, you cannot get a copyright on the idea of using a computer to allow users to explore a mythical island and solve complicated puzzles, but you can copyright the computer program MYST, its images and its music. Copyright protection alone, however, will not prevent others from using the same idea as long as they create a program that involves different characters, explores a different place, and solves different problems.

Alas, it is much easier to say that copyright law does not protect ideas—that there is an actual dichotomy between an idea and the expression of that idea—than it is to apply such a rule in practice. When an idea merges with its expression, the expression cannot be protected by copyright. Instructions are a common example of the merger of ideas and expressions. If someone were allowed to copyright the instruction "put coin in slot and press button for selection," it would be very difficult for other vending machine operators to express to users the idea behind the basic operational use of the machine.

## Common Terms

A related concept is called the *scènes à faire* doctrine, which acts to exclude copyright protection where an expression is standard, stock, or common, or where the expression is dictated by *extrinsic* factors, or *externalities*, that limit or constrain choices of different expressions. Elements of a computer software program have been found to be outside of the scope of copyright protection because those elements were dictated by the following:

- Mechanical specifications for the computer on which the program was intended to run
- Compatibility requirements of other programs with which the program was designed to operate
- Computer manufacturing design standards
- Demands of the industry being serviced
- Widely accepted programming practices within the computer industry

### Digital Copies

Although copyright law has been tested, stretched and updated to accommodate new technologies in the past, more new copyright laws were established in the first 15 years of the computer industry than were established since the turn of the twentieth century. Since 1995, in order to accommodate the Internet, the degree of change has been even more substantial. Never before has a new technology provoked such fear and loathing on one side and radical cries for change on the other. What scares one side and enthralls the other side is that a digital copy of a digitally recorded song is as good as the original. That digital copy can be reproduced many times and distributed around the world in a matter of minutes via the Internet. Thus, the degree of risk and loss for copyright owners is high, but the elimination of distributors and music labels controlling the kinds of music available to people around the world is a significant and positive change for consumers. As you can imagine, the distributors and music labels are not too enthralled with losing this control. To further complicate matters, the original infringer is not the only party making copies of the song, although not all copiers can be treated as infringers. Balancing all of the interests involved is very complicated.

Most infringers who have copied songs on their host computers and distributed those songs on the Internet obtain access and hosting services from ISPs. Those ISPs make copies of the songs transmitted from the infringers' host computers and store those copies on the ISPs' servers. When the song is packetized to transmit it over the Internet, each of the packets representing the data comprising the song is again copied and very temporarily stored in the ISPs' routers—and every other router those packets go through on the way to their final destination. The packets are then reassembled, copied, and stored on either another server or on another host computer. To play the song on that host computer, the song is copied into dynamic memory. If the users of a particular ISP frequently access the originating site, that entire site might also be copied by that ISP to a cache server to cut down on traffic to the original site and speed up its users' access to the data. Thus, the *routers, servers,* and *host* computers making up the Internet also make copies of virtually every work transmitted to or through those devices, whether they are infringing or not. Copyright owners and bureaucrats have had a difficult time understanding how the Internet works, why so many copies need to be made, and why it is impractical to hold everyone who makes a copy along the way liable for copyright infringement. It is because of these views that stretching the law to accommodate the Internet has been a particular challenge.

## What Protection Do You Get under Copyright?

As previously mentioned, the owner of the copyright, who may or may not be the author, has the right to exclude others from doing the following:

1. Reproducing the work (scanning, faxing, photocopying, downloading from the Internet, etc.).

2. Preparing derivative works of the original work (translations or upgraded versions) or otherwise modifying the original work (creating a new work that incorporates the original work, such as a *framed* web site).

3. Distributing copies or phono records of the copyrighted work to the public by sale or other transfer of ownership (e.g., rental, lease, or lending).

4. Performing or displaying the work publicly if the work is literary, musical, dramatic, choreographic, a pantomime, a motion picture, or other audiovisual work.

5. Performing the work publicly by means of a digital audio transmission if the work is a sound recording.

As you can see, a copyright is actually a bundle of rights. This is a simple concept when one party owns all of the different rights, but it is much more complicated when different parties are involved. For example, for every musical recording, there are at least three sets of rights: rights to the master recording, rights to the lyrics and composition of the song, and rights to the performance. A record company typically owns the master recording. A music publisher typically owns the song. A performer or a group typically owns the rights to a particular performance or rendition of that song. While many people realize it is illegal to copy a song from a CD and sell copies of that song, the same people think nothing of using the lyrics in something they sell or performing the song in public for money.

None of these rights matter without the ability to enforce them in some way. Thus, when an exclusive right is infringed, the copyright owner can seek to have the infringement stopped and recover money. As a result of a successful lawsuit, a court can order a temporary or permanent injunction against further infringement and can have infringing goods captured and destroyed. A court can also award damages for the infringement to the owner, together with attorney's fees and costs associated with the suit.

Typically, an award of damages is based on the actual harm to the plaintiff, but the court can sometimes alternatively award *statutory damages,* a fixed amount awarded to the plaintiff regardless of damages. Statutory damages are fairly popular in copyright infringement cases because in the absence of statutory damages an owner must prove actual harm, which is much more difficult. For example, if you can prove only that the defendant copied three songs, how much is that worth? Later in this chapter, under the title What Happens When You Are Liable for Copyright Infringement, you'll find an explanation of these different damages and the statutory damage amounts. More important, the attorney's fees associated with any enforcement action can often exceed the statutory damage award, which may severely reduce the value of enforcement in many cases. A copyright holder can seek an award of statutory damages, attorney's fees, and costs only when the copyright holder has used a proper copyright notice on the infringed work.

## Copyright Notice Requirements

Prior to 1989, when the United States signed a treaty called the Berne Convention, a copyright owner could not enforce any of its rights if the copyrighted work did not have a notice, such as a © 1992 XYZ, Incorporated, on a majority of the legal copies of the work. While notice is no longer required, a court will deny the owner statutory damages and attorney's fees if the work isn't registered within a certain period of time, and in order to be registered, the work requires a notice. A copyright notice also serves to notify people that your work is protected and lets them know whom to contact to obtain permission to use one of the exclusive rights. The date is useful because it lets people know the age of a work. In addition, if a right is infringed and the defendant had access to a copy with a proper notice of the copyright, then the defendant will have a hard time proving innocent infringement, a defense that would mitigate damages, or getting a court-ordered license.

The form of notice depends on the type of work being marked. If the work can be visually perceived, the © symbol should be used, together with the year of first publication and the name of the copyright owner. If the symbol cannot be used, then it is okay to use the word *copyright* or *copy.* Phono records of sound recordings use a different symbol, a *P* in a circle. In addition to notice, a copyright can be registered with the Copyright Office at any time during the period of protection by depositing in the Copyright Office two complete copies of the best edition of the work, together with an application and a small fee ($30 or so at this time). You can even file copyright applications online with the Copyright Office at www.loc.gov/copyright/.

## Copyright Management Information

In addition to adding all of the liability limitation provisions associated with ISPs (as will be discussed in Chapter 3, *A Special Law for ISPs: The DMCA*), the Digital Millennium Copyright Act (DMCA) also added a number of new protections for copyright holders. One such protection relates to something called *Copyright Management Information* (CMI). CMI is defined as identifying information about a copyrighted work. This identifying information typically includes the copyright notice; the name of the author and, in certain cases, the performer, writer, or director of the work; and the terms and conditions for use of the work. The Register of Copyrights may include additional items in CMI as prescribed by regulation.

On its face, CMI does not look like a form of protection, but it becomes one because the DMCA prohibits the intentional removal or alteration of CMI without authority, as well as the dissemination of CMI or copies of works if one knows that the CMI has been removed or altered without authority. This means that you cannot purposely strip a copyright notice or other CMI from any work bearing such—for example, certain comment fields in a software program. Because future versions of the IP and TCP standards may include metadata that includes CMI associated with the payload of a TCP/IP packet, you will have to keep these provisions in mind, especially if you decide to process incoming packets in such a way as to remove any header data.

Criminal and civil liability can result from stripping or altering CMI. Criminal liability requires that the act be done with knowledge. Criminal penalties range up to a $500,000 fine or up to five years imprisonment for a first offense and up to a $1 million fine or up to 10 years imprisonment for subsequent offenses. Civil liability requires reasonable grounds for knowing that an act of stripping or altering CMI will induce, enable, facilitate, or conceal an infringement. The range of equitable and monetary remedies available for violations of CMI protections is similar to those generally available under the Copyright Act, including statutory damages.

## Side Law: Copyright Term Extension

What do you do if you are a major media company that has built itself around an animated character that was created many years ago and whose term of copyright protection is about to expire? You do what any average citizen would do—go to the U.S. Congress and get the term of protection extended for all copyrighted works. Thus, in 1998, in accordance with the Sonny Bono Copyright Extension Act of 1998, the term of protection for all works was increased by 20 years. The constitutionality of the Extension Act has been under attack on the grounds that it violates the "limited" term of protection that was authorized by the Constitution, but this attack is unlikely to be successful.

### Copyright Term of Protection

The length of time of protection depends on the author. For works created by a single author and published or registered on or after January 1, 1978, protection is automatic from the moment of creation until the end of the author's life plus an additional 70 years. Joint works use the last surviving author's death plus 70 years. Works made for hire (and anonymous and pseudonymous works, unless the author's identity is revealed in Copyright Office records) are protected for 95 years from publication or 120 years from creation, whichever is shorter.

## When Is a Copyright Infringed?

Copyright infringement can result whenever someone practices one of the foregoing exclusive rights without authorization from the owner. For the person or entity that directly performs the infringement (e.g., the one actually making the copy of the protected work), there is no knowledge requirement for civil liability. In this context, copyright infringement is often called a *strict liability offense*. This means, for example, that if you copy or distribute a protected work, whether or not you knew it was protected or knew it was illegal to make a copy, you may be subject to civil liability for copyright infringement. Criminal liability, on the other hand, requires knowledge, as do the two forms of indirect infringement that exist in the United States and some other countries, which I will discuss at the end of this section.

This strict civil liability rule exists for direct infringement because copyright owners have convinced lawmakers that people know or should know when they are committing an act of direct infringement, so it isn't fair to force copyright owners to have to prove knowledge. Copyright owners believe that people know when they are performing such an act (e.g., copying something) and that they know or should know whether they received someone's authorization before they committed that act. Obviously, any sane person knows when they have made a copy, but that same person doesn't always know that the work they are copying is protected by copyright or that they need an authorization to make the copy. Furthermore, most people take the term *copyright* literally, and therefore think that it only has to do with making copies. They don't realize that copyright law extends to distribution, displays, performances, and derivative works, so it never occurs to them that an authorization might be required. One of the most common types of innocent infringement is the creation of unauthorized derivations. But, even when people know that copyrights serve to prevent copying of certain works, they often do not think that the exclusionary rules apply to the type of copying they are performing.

# The 10 Mythical Defenses to Copyright Infringement

As a result of the general populace's ignorance of copyright law, it follows that the 10 most common justifications for infringement, which I call the "10 mythical defenses," are as follows:

1. *"I made at least seven changes to the copyrighted work" (the Seven Changes Rule).* No one is really sure where this mythical defense came from or why it won't go away. I even had a student reference this nonexistent defense during a law school exam, despite the fact that, during one of my lectures, I explained at length that this was not a defense. Anyway, as I stated earlier, copyright infringement could result whenever someone practices an exclusive right without authorization. To prevail in court, however, the copyright owner must be able to prove that the infringer had access to the copyrighted work and that the allegedly infringing work was substantially similar to the copyrighted work. By asserting that you have made seven changes to a work, you are admitting access to the copyrighted work. Such admissions are not good. Also, in the vast majority of cases, seven changes will be insufficient to avoid a finding of substantial similarity. Unfortunately, there is no reliable guide that exists regarding how much material you can copy from a work before infringing upon that work. For example, it is indeed possible that the Seven Changes Rule might operate as a defense where the copyrighted work had only ten unique expressions and you changed seven. In most cases, however, a work has thousands of unique expressions, so changing only seven makes little difference. This defense is mythical because it would be the very rare case indeed where it could possibly apply.

2. *"There was no copyright notice on the work."* As noted earlier, notice has not been required for many years. Although lack of notice used to be a legitimate defense— and still can be with respect to older works—it probably has applicability to only 0.1 percent of all present cases of infringement.

3. *"I attributed the work to the original author."* Attribution is important. Attribution alone is not a defense. Many people think that republication of a work with attribution should be viewed as a favor to the copyright owner. Not only does it generate listeners, viewers, or readers that the owner otherwise lacked, the attribution gives the owner due credit for the work. Owners don't really want due credit as much as they want money, so if all you give them is due credit, they aren't likely to be grateful.

4. *"My use was a fair use because I am a critical scholar, a teacher, or a researcher."* Fair use is a legitimate defense to copyright infringement and it can apply to criticism, comment, news reporting, teaching, scholarship, and research. It so rarely applies to *for-profit* companies, however, that I generally tell people to forget that the defense even exists. Nevertheless, if you assert the fair-use defense, a court is required to con-

sider four factors in determining whether the defense applies (see Side Law: Fair-Use Examples):

- *The purpose and character of the allegedly infringing use.* Noncommercial, productive, and transformative uses are more likely to be found to be fair use than any form of for-profit use.

- *The nature of the copyrighted work.* Copyrighted works that primarily consist of facts or limited expressions, certain types of compilations, out-of-print and otherwise inaccessible works, and utilitarian works have limited protection and are occasionally subjected to the fair-use defense. Fine art, fiction, and utilitarian works have greater protection and are rarely subjected to fair use.

- *The amount and substantiality of the portion used, from both a quantitative and qualitative perspective, in relation to the copyrighted work as a whole.* For example, in critiquing a book, you can use quotes from the book to illustrate points, but if you use so many quotes and include so much of the work that you replace the need to purchase the work being critiqued, fair use will not apply.

- *The effect of the allegedly infringing use on the market for or value of the copyrighted work, including natural potential markets for derivative works.* Again, supplanting the market for the original will severely cripple the applicability of this defense.

5. *"I am a hobbyist,"* or *"This was for my personal use."* The nature of your intended use of a work will hardly matter if the alternative to infringing the work was to buy a legitimate copy. Most copyrighted works are sold to people for their personal use in the first place.

6. *"I had to pay for the copies,"* or *"I made only a few copies for my friends and I did not charge them."* The fact that a criminal must incur some expense in order to carry out a crime does not forgive the crime. When you illegally copy a work, you are paying for only the cost of paper or magnetic tape and the use of a copier or duplicator. You are not paying the copyright owner for the copyrighted work. Likewise, the fact that you made only a few copies or did not charge others for the copies that you did make does not excuse the loss of funds to the copyright owner

7. *"I took the material from something that is out-of-print or no longer in production."* Just because an article or book is out-of-print or a record or movie is no longer in production does not mean that the copyright on such an article or book has expired. Many copyright owners intentionally pull their works from the market to build renewed interest in the works, so it is not safe to assume anything.

8. *"I found the material on the Internet or in a public library so the material was in the public domain."* There is a huge difference between works that are available to the public but still protected by copyright and works that are in the public domain and freely available for use by others. A work is considered to be in the public domain only if it loses its copyright protection, either through term expiration, legislative exclusion (government-funded works), or judicial decision (taking rights away from a copyright owner), or if it is dedicated to the public in writing by its owner. Many costly mistakes, however, have been made in this area by misjudging when protection for a work stops.

Numerous television stations learned this lesson a few years ago when they mistakenly thought the term of protection for the movie, *It's a Wonderful Life*, had expired, resulting in widespread use of the movie throughout the holidays. Without the loss of protection, a work is not considered to be in the public domain unless the legitimate owner has declared its intention in writing to dedicate the work to the public. This rarely happens. Thus, freeware and shareware, two types of software that are often distributed over the Internet for little or no cost, are not in the public domain and cannot be legally copied without authorization. The Free Software Foundation (FSF) provides a wide variety of software in object and source code format for free, but subject to restrictions in accordance with its GNU Public License (GPL), which is also called a *copyleft license.*

As best as I can tell, GNU is a play on words that stands for *GNU not Unix.* The GPL is called a *copyleft license* instead of a copyright license because it has the opposite effect of a typical copyright license. For example, if you incorporate FSF-licensed code (the *Program*) into your proprietary software, you can distribute the Program only in accordance with the terms of the copyleft license. In particular, the GPL states "[E]ach time you redistribute the Program (or any work based on the Program), the recipient automatically receives a license from the original licensor to copy, distribute or modify the Program subject to these terms and conditions. You may not impose any further restrictions on the recipients' exercise of the rights granted herein." See www.fsf .org/copyleft/gpl.html for more information. If the Program were truly in the public domain, FSF would not be able to enforce such restrictions, and people would be free to take the Program, copy it, modify it, and distribute it along with their own proprietary products for some fee. FSF wants the Program to be free of charge and doesn't want people claiming rights in it by incorporating it into their products. Thus, FSF uses copyright law, rather than the lack of protection, to ensure the free dissemination of its code.

9. *"The person who gave me the material said it was okay for me to use it."* This is a very common issue within many companies. Just because people verbally tell you it is okay to use a copyrighted work doesn't mean they had the right to do so, that they own the copyright, or that they will acknowledge their authorization later when it really matters. I know a number of people who have received verbal authorizations from people who didn't have the right to grant the authorization or who changed their mind and later denied ever providing one. Any time an authorization is received it needs to be in writing, even when the authorization is free. Certain facts also need to be stated. For example, the granting party should warrant that he or she is authorized to grant such rights. Many people are concerned that asking for written authorization will offend the offering party and blow the free deal, but this risk is often better than getting in trouble later.

10. *"I made changes to 20 percent of the work" (the 20% Rule).* There is no 20% Rule. The same issues that were previously addressed with respect to the Seven Changes Rule apply equally to the mythical 20% Rule. However, I have separated the discussion regarding these two mythical rules to more fully illustrate application of the access test and the substantial similarity test that follows. While it is fairly easy to recognize the similarity between an original work and one that includes only seven changes, it is much harder to perform this analysis when 20 percent or more of the original work has been changed.

## Side Law: Fair-Use Examples

There are a number of good examples that illustrate application of the four factors relevant to the defense. In the Zapruder film case, the author of a book about the Kennedy assassination included some sketches in the book that were based on frames from the famous Zapruder film of the assassination (*Time Inc. v. Bernard Geis Associates*, 293 F.Supp. 130 [1968]). While this was a for-profit use and the portion taken was fairly significant to the work as a whole, the court ruled that the film was largely a factual work. The court also found that there was an overriding public interest in having the information available (not subject to strong protection) and that there was little, if any, injury to the plaintiff. In *Sony Corp. of America v. Universal City Studios, Inc.*, 464 U.S. 417 (1984), the Supreme Court ruled that a VCR could be fairly used to record copyrighted works for time-shifting purposes as long as the VCR had some other noninfringing use.

There have also been a number of parody or satire cases. The most interesting one involved the song "Oh, Pretty Woman." The issue was whether the rap group 2 Live Crew's remake of Roy Orbison's song was a fair use. This case was interesting because it appears as though the parody defense was made up *after* 2 Live Crew was accused of infringement rather than before the infringement occurred. While intent is not an element, in my humble opinion, it seems that the defense should not apply unless one intended to parody or make satire of a work at the time the allegedly infringing work was created. Because 2 Live Crew intended to make money from the use, the allegedly infringing work was clearly for profit. Nevertheless, once the court bought into the idea that the second work could have been a parody of the first, the rest of the defense fell into place.

*First,* to parody a work, it is necessary to use some elements of the prior work in order to create a new one that, at least in part, comments on the original. *Second,* enough material must be used from the original in order to make the second work recognizable, which tends to be pretty easy because people parody only famous works. *Third,* the amount taken must be reasonable in view of the character of the parody. *Fourth,* there can be no adverse effect on the market for the original work. Given this case, it would be interesting to see what would happen if someone created Macrohard Porthole, a fully operational and compatible but parodied version of Microsoft's Windows product.

A copyright owner can typically prove that one of its works has been infringed if the copyright owner can show the following:

1. It owns a valid copyright in the work.

2. The defendant had access to the copyrighted work and copied that work.

3. The copyrighted work and the allegedly infringing work are substantially similar from the viewpoint of an ordinary observer.

It is often difficult for a copyright owner to prove that someone actually copied a work. After all, the copyright owner doesn't have a picture of you standing at a photocopier with a copy of his or her work in your hand and a sinister look on your face.

## Side Law: Coincidence?

My favorite, presumably true, example of coincidental similarity involved William Pene du Bois's book entitled *The Twenty-One Balloons* and F. Scott Fitzgerald's story entitled "The Diamond as Big as the Ritz." Shortly before *The Twenty-One Balloons* was published, Pene du Bois's publisher informed him of the similar nature of Fitzgerald's story. To his horror, Pene du Bois discovered that not only were the two plots of both stories quite similar, but they also contained many of the same ideas. In both works, a main character discovers a fabulous amount of diamonds, resorts to secrecy to protect the find, and ends up spending the billions in like ways, right down to being dumped from a bed into a bathtub. Pene du Bois stated, in an author's note to his book, that while he understood that there was but one obvious solution to hiding the discovery—secrecy—he had no explanation for the fact that he and Fitzgerald imagined spending the money in almost the same way.

The rules have therefore been structured to allow copyright owners to rely on circumstantial evidence. This makes it easier for copyright owners to win their cases without having to prove actual copying. Thus, when a copyright owner can show that the two works are so strikingly similar that any question of independent creation, coincidence, or the possibility of a common source can be precluded, access and copying will be inferred.

Even if two works are strikingly similar, without the existence of an identical or almost identical copy the copyright owner will still have to show that the two works are also *substantially similar.* While substantial similarity does not require word-for-word copying, it cannot be readily determined through use of a standard or bright-line (indicating yes or no) test either, such as the mythical 20% Rule. The 20% Rule appears to have been based on the facts in a particular lawsuit where a work was found not to be infringing because the defendant changed more than 20 percent of the work that was allegedly copied. The facts in that case made this a reasonable decision, but those same facts obviously do not exist in each case. Thus, it does not follow that changing 20 percent of any work always will or should avoid infringement.

For example, in Figure 2.1, Work A is composed of 25 percent new material that is original to Work A and 75 percent preexisting material in the public domain. Work B in Figure 2.2 includes 75 percent of the new material from Work A, with the remainder made up of new material. Because Work B includes less than 20 percent of Work A ($75\% \times 25\% = 18.75\%$), it isn't infringing under the 20% Rule. This result makes no sense, however, because Work B used a larger portion of what was unique about Work A. In Figure 2.3, Work C is made up of all of the preexisting material from Work A, but none of the new material. Nevertheless, under the 20% Rule, Work C would infringe Work A because it includes more than 20 percent of Work A. This result makes no sense, either, because all of the material copied from Work A was in the public domain and should not have been subject to protection.

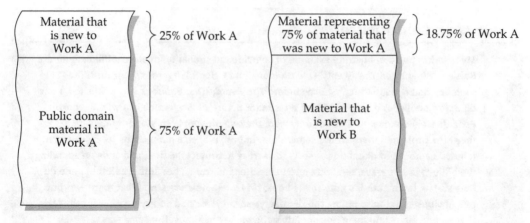

**Figure 2.1** Work A.

**Figure 2.2** Work B includes less than 20 percent of Work A.

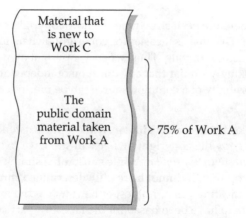

**Figure 2.3** Work C includes more than 20 percent of Work A.

It is obviously impossible to create a bright-line test that can be used in each case with different facts, so the courts have tried different approaches to assessing substantial similarity. The most widely accepted approach is a three-stage test involving abstraction, filtration, and comparison. In the first stage, the allegedly infringed work is broken down into its constituent structural parts (e.g., the different operational modules of a software program or the different portions of a web site). Each of those parts is then examined to remove all of the material that cannot be protected by copyright, such as ideas and preexisting or functional material. The resulting kernel or kernels of protected material from the allegedly infringed work are then compared with the allegedly infringing work to determine the level of similarity between the two.

For example, with respect to Figures 2.1, 2.2, and 2.3, the preexisting material in Work A would be abstracted and filtered out before the comparison between Work B or Work C was made to Work A. It would then be clear that Work B included a substantial portion of the unique material from Work A, and Work C included nothing subject to protection from Work A, so the correct results could be obtained. Some works, however, comprise unique combinations of old materials. The filtration stage of this test can wipe such works clean of material to be compared in the last stage. In such cases, courts have applied a *look-and-feel* test to determine if the overall work is deserving of protection. Attempts to take the look-and-feel protection approach beyond the scope of the overall work have met with little success.

Any time there has been a direct infringement there may also have been an indirect infringement, at least in those countries that recognize some form of indirect liability. The most common type of indirect infringement in the United States is contributory infringement. Contributory infringement can result when one supervises or directly financially benefits from the direct infringement of another. To prove contributory infringement, the copyright owner must first show that the accused contributory infringer knew or should have known about the direct infringement. Then the copyright owner must show that the accused materially contributed to the infringement in some way and directly benefited financially from the infringement.

A typical example involves infringing performances by musical groups at restaurants, nightclubs, and dance halls. The owner of the business provides the facilities and the audience for the performance and makes extra money as a direct result of the performance. Even though the owner doesn't necessarily know what music will be played, the owner has the ability to know in advance and to control the situation. Contributory infringement laws were developed to prevent such businesses from claiming they have no responsibility for the infringements committed by others.

## What Are Some Defenses to a Claim of Copyright Infringement?

In the event you are accused of infringing or you are concerned you might be infringing someone's copyright, what are your defenses? The best defense, of course, is to avoid infringement in the first place by making sure that you and all of your employees know the law and take prudent precautions to avoid problems. If you are an ISP and can show that someone else was the source of the infringement, you can take advantage of the protections of the Digital Millennium Copyright Act (DMCA) discussed in Chapter 3, which are limits on liability, not defenses. If you still can't avoid being accused of infringement, then the next best thing to do is to attempt to disprove what the copyright owners must prove in order to win their infringement claim, such as lack of substantial similarity. As a practical matter, there are not many defenses to copyright infringement. As previously stated, knowledge is not a requirement to proving infringement, so lack of knowledge is not a defense, although it is sometimes possible to show that your infringement was innocent, meaning you honestly thought the work wasn't copyrighted for some very good reason (e.g., the copyright notice includes the wrong date, such as 1889 instead of 1989). As illustrated in Figure 2.4, even this kind of mistake may not be sufficient to protect you if the work in question has to do with modern technology, because most people would know it was a mistake.

# © 1889 Microsoft Corporation

**Figure 2.4** Is this copyright notice correct?

The antitrust laws and other so-called equitable defenses, such as *estoppel* (an Old English way of saying "stopped") and *unclean hands,* can sometimes be relied upon if you can show that the copyright owner has misused a copyright or otherwise done something wrong and therefore doesn't deserve to have its rights protected. Estoppel can occur when the copyright owner, knowing that you are infringing, conducts itself in a way that it knows will be relied upon by you when you don't realize that you are infringing, and you do in fact rely on the copyright owner's conduct. In such cases, the copyright owner will be estopped from proceeding with a claim of infringement. The doctrine of unclean hands is a very rare defense. It typically succeeds only when the defendant can show that the copyright owner has committed some sort of fraud, criminal act, or other serious transgression that relates directly to the subject matter of the infringement, such as breaking into your business to gather evidence of infringement. Although I included fair use in the list of mythical defenses, it is indeed a legitimate defense for some types of defendants, but I remain committed to the belief that for-profit ISPs will rarely be included among such fair-use company.

## What Happens When You Are Liable for Copyright Infringement?

As an individual, unless you have been trafficking in pirated goods, you will probably avoid serious trouble because pursuing you will not be worth the effort to most copyright owners. Businesses are not treated so tenderly. Copyright owners stand a better chance of collecting damages, recovering costs, and making examples of businesses that infringe copyrights, even small businesses. A number of copyright owner trade associations, such as the Software Publishers Association (SPA), even provide

### Side Law: Content Delivery versus Content Access

Many ISPs are engaged in other aspects of electronic commerce, aside from content access services, that raise many different infringement issues. If your company, like America Online, has embraced the content delivery side of the business, your copyright experiences will be quite different from ISPs that simply provide access and transport. If you are or plan to get involved in content development and licensing, I recommend hiring counsel with experience in negotiating and structuring content-related agreements before doing anything else. This is a tricky business, and it is easy to make big mistakes. As a plain old ISP, however, you will still use content from other parties (for example, in your marketing materials, advertisements, web sites, business planning, training), so copyright disputes will be hard to avoid.

enforcement services and have paid bounties to employees or ex-employees who report infringing employers. As an individual, chances are good that you don't need to worry about your child-care provider pointing a finger at you.

If you are found guilty of copyright infringement, you could be subject to both criminal and civil liability. The content community routinely seeks legislation to increase the severity of criminal fines and punishment and the size of statutory civil damages. For example, legislation was passed in 1999 (the Digital Theft Deterrence and Copyright Damages Improvement Act) that amends the Copyright Act to increase the minimum statutory damages from a range of $500 to $20,000 to a range of $750 to $30,000. Additionally, the maximum statutory damages for willful infringement are increased from $100,000 to $150,000. Moreover, the bill directs the Federal Sentencing Commission to adjust sentencing guidelines for criminal copyright infringement to ensure the stringency of the penalties and to reflect the value of the infringed work(s). As a result, the numbers that follow cannot be relied upon forever, but they certainly establish a current floor. Statutory awards are ordered by the court and do not require any evidence of actual damage. If a copyright owner can show actual damage in excess of the statutory award, it is highly likely that an award equal to those damages will be ordered.

Willful copyright infringement that yields the infringer some financial benefit is a crime. The specific penalties depend on prior offenses and the number of copies made or distributed within a certain period of time. A first offense can result in a fine of not more than $25,000, imprisonment not exceeding one year, or both. Subsequent offenses for certain types of works, such as sound recordings and motion pictures, can result in a fine of $250,000, imprisonment not exceeding five years, or both. Courts can, and often do, also order seizure, forfeiture, and destruction or other disposition of all infringing reproductions and all equipment used in the manufacture of such reproductions. These are not good things and should be avoided.

On the civil side, a copyright owner can seek actual damages suffered by the copyright owner and any additional profits of the infringer, but if such damages are hard to prove (and they often are), then the copyright owner can elect statutory damages. In either case, the copyright holder can also recover its full costs, including reasonable attorneys' fees. For now, statutory damages for all infringements of any one work range from $750 to $30,000, although reductions to $200 and increases to $150,000 are available in some cases. The other remedies include injunctions against future infringements and the impounding and destruction or other disposition of any infringing reproductions and articles used to make such reproductions.

# Free Speech and Related Rights

Article I of the First Amendment to the U.S. Constitution states that "Congress shall make no law . . . abridging the freedom of speech, or of the press; or the right of the people peaceably to assemble, and to petition the Government for a redress of grievances." A strict interpretation of this language would lead one to believe that your right to speak freely or to publish information in the United States is protected from any federal law passed that would reduce those rights. But Congress makes laws all the time and has authorized federal agencies to pass regulations many of which could be argued to reduce your free speech and press rights, such as copyright law. Even though copyright law originates with the Constitution, not an amendment, Congress created the laws implementing copyright law. Because copyrighted works include words and other forms of expression, it is often argued that the enforcement of copyright law must result in the repression of speech and the press.

The Supreme Court, however, has not accepted this argument and has over time interpreted the Constitution and the First Amendment to prevent such conflicts. In particular, the Supreme Court has drawn a distinction between actions by private individuals and the government for the purpose of applying the rights guaranteed by the Constitution. A citizen of this country, for example, may be able to stand on a public sidewalk and freely express her views, but she cannot stand in your front yard and do the same. Furthermore, the action of a government official, a police officer, in removing her from your yard does not change the nature of the action. In this case, the government official is merely enforcing a private right at your request rather than forcing you to resort to violence to remove the woman from your property—at least *society* operates to prevent the use of violence in some instances.

## Filtering Speech and Other Content on the Internet

In contrast, an action by a library board to mandate the use of filters on all Internet terminals in public libraries in Loudoun County, Virginia, was held to be unconstitutional because the mandate abridged the free speech rights of all adults wishing to use those terminals. A number of people have told me that they didn't understand this decision because the filters did not prevent adults from freely expressing themselves (i.e., the filters prevented speech only from coming in, not going out). The filters did, however, repress the speech of anyone attempting to communicate with those adults, which was considered to be unconstitutional. The library board subsequently fixed this problem by requiring adults to sign an acceptable-use policy that allowed adults to use the terminals unfiltered provided they did not use them to view illegal material, such as child pornography. If tested in court, such a policy would probably be considered a minimal burden on free speech compared to the compelling public interest in protecting children from inappropriate material.

## All Speech Is Not Treated Equal

It is also important to keep in mind that not all speech or press (e.g., child pornography) is protected in the United States or in many other countries. For example, commercial speech is a form of speech that is subject to government restriction only under certain circumstances. Commercial speech is speech that is commercial in nature (i.e., speech that advertises a product or service for profit or that is used for some other business purpose). Commercial speech may be restricted only if the following apply:

- The government has a substantial state interest in restricting the speech.
- The restriction directly and materially advances that interest.
- The restriction is no more extensive than necessary to serve that interest.

In contrast, other types of speech, such as hate speech, defamatory speech, and speech that induces violence, are basically unprotected. These other forms of speech are not protected because the individual's right to speak is abridged by the government's overriding obligation to protect the public welfare. For example, when someone distributed a vulgarity-filled e-mail including racial slurs to 25,000 students, professors, and staff of Stanford University, the university could and did legally stop distribution of the e-mail because the speech contained in the message was not protected. Moreover, the university's e-mail system is a private network and the university is a private institution, so no governmental action was involved. The matter has also been subject to an investigation by the high-tech crime unit of the local district attorney's office.

## What Is Considered to Be "State Action"?

If the state takes action to prosecute the perpetrator, assuming the state can show that it has a compelling reason for acting, that person's free speech rights will not be violated because the speech was not originally protected by the First Amendment. Likewise, police units in Germany, the United States, Canada, France, Italy, Britain, Japan, and Russia have all been established to look for illegal activity on the Internet—for example, child pornography (illegal in almost all countries) and political extremism (which is illegal in Germany). These police units legally use nicknames to gain access to web sites or engage in conversations in newsgroups and chat rooms to root out illegal activity.

A court's enforcement of a subpoena in a private lawsuit provides a similar example. As with the earlier trespasser example, society has sought to prevent parties in private lawsuits, such as divorce proceedings or child-custody fights, from resorting to improper actions to collect information to support their cases. As a result, if you file suit against someone, you can seek to discover information about the opposing party that is reasonably related to your suit. If the party refuses, you can request the court to order that party or a third party who holds the information to provide it through a subpoena. For example, as explained in Chapter 3, if you receive a subpoena under the DMCA, you are obligated to disclose the requested information. You are not obligated to appear in court to defend the subpoena on the customer's behalf or to notify your customer that you have been served with the subpoena. The same general rule applies to private lawsuits under federal law, so most ISPs do nothing to protect customers without a contractual obligation to do otherwise. Most of the larger ISPs, however, have adopted policies restricting the release of customer information in civil actions and obligating the ISP to notify customers before releasing the requested information. In criminal cases, the ISPs release the requested material immediately and do not inform the customer.

Because the court's subpoena on behalf of a private entity is not considered a government action, the whole matter falls outside the scope of the First Amendment. This fact has not prevented people from arguing that the use of subpoenas to force ISPs to disclose customer information is a constitutional violation.

## Side Law: John and Jane Doe Suits

The pseudonyms John and Jane Doe are used in court documents when a party files suit against someone who cannot be named. Sometimes the plaintiff is required to protect the name of a defendant who might be a minor or a government witness. Other times, the plaintiff lacks the information necessary to name the other party. For example, you may know you have been wronged, but you may not know who was responsible. During the course of the litigation, the discovery of evidence may reveal the appropriate defendant. John and Jane Doe suits have recently been used by a number of companies seeking to enforce private subpoenas to force ISPs to identify their customers. Raytheon, a Massachusetts-based defense company, filed a trade secret lawsuit against John Does 1 through 21, then subpoenaed Yahoo! for the names of the individuals who had allegedly posted offending messages to a Raytheon-related message board operated by Yahoo! In this case, there were 21 unknown individuals. Once Raytheon had collected the 21 names from Yahoo!, it dropped the suit. This case has been used as an example of how a John Doe's constitutional right to free speech through anonymity is being abused through misuse of the legal process.

### Redressing Your Grievance or Libel?

The First Amendment to the U.S. Constitution also grants U.S. citizens the right to petition the government to redress their grievances. People have relied upon this right to speak out on unpopular subjects in public places and to write to government officials demanding action. In the course of speaking on a particular subject, an individual might allege that a government official did something wrong. Such statements, even when proven wrong, are typically protected from civil lawsuits by the accused government because doing otherwise would likely prevent people from ever saying anything bad (i.e., individuals would fear being sued if they spoke out). Arguably, the Internet could be used, primarily in the form of e-mail messages, but possibly through the use of web sites, to similarly petition the government. How far an individual can go (i.e., what they can say) in this regard is yet to be determined.

### Controlled Exposure

Because the Constitution acts to guarantee certain types of content and activities that many people still find to be harmful and offensive, especially to children, a number of tools are under development to enable people to better control their exposure on the Internet. The World Wide Web Consortium has developed the Platform for Internet Content Selection (PICS), which uses hidden metatags at the top of a web page to identify the content of that page and to enable users of the PICS system to filter out certain types of marked pages. The problem with this solution is, of course, that it relies on people to actually, and appropriately, mark pages. Other systems have been developed or are under development that will operate as an interface between the Internet and users of the system, allowing users to access only approved pages.

---

## Side Law: www.smalltownjustice.com

A lawsuit has been filed by a California Highway Patrol (CHP) officer against a woman who published a web site dubbed Small Town Justice. See www.smalltownjustice.com. Apparently, the CHP officer arrested the woman in rural Inyo County in 1993 for speeding and felony evading arrest after he initially tried to pull over her yellow Corvette. She subsequently published the web site to criticize the CHP officer and other law enforcement officials in Inyo County. The CHP officer claims the criticism is untrue and has sued the woman for libel, seeking $1 million in damages and removal of the site. The woman claims that removal of the site would violate her First Amendment rights, particularly her right to petition the government for a redress of her grievances. While the First Amendment does provide such a right, it is doubtful the Constitution drafters anticipated the Internet as the medium for such petitions, so this matter will require some interesting constitutional interpretation. In all likelihood, even if the CHP officer prevails, the court will probably require only that she modify the site to remove the libelous material rather than take down the entire site.

---

Finally, a number of filters have been developed or are under development that filter out pages on the basis of words or images, such as certain profane words or images that include a high percentage of flesh-colored skin, which allegedly works regardless of the skin tone.

# Trademarks and Unfair Competition in Cyberspace

Trademark and unfair competition issues are growing concerns in cyberspace and often accompany copyright infringement claims. For example, a number of ISPs have recently received letters from the head of a religious organization claiming that the church's copyright and trademark rights were infringed by anyone using the church's name on the Internet. So far, the church has singled out only alleged infringers who criticize the church. Because names cannot be copyrighted, the DMCA does not apply. Furthermore, the DMCA deals only with copyright infringement, not trademark infringement, so the provision of notice under the DMCA is the wrong way to go about putting people on notice of your trademark rights. Even if it were effective notice, however, it is unlikely that any trademark infringement occurred, because the church's name seems to be made up of a combination of other church's names. As I have mentioned before, complete details of the DMCA and its implications are covered in Chapter 3.

While the church's letter failed to provide any notice under the DMCA, had trademark infringement actually been involved, it is possible that the letter could have provided someone with notice under trademark law, because DMCA-type protections (that prevent defective notices from having any effect) have not been extended to trademark law. It is therefore important to understand trademark and unfair competition laws in the event you are ever pulled into an infringement action between a customer and another party. More directly, it is important to understand trademark and unfair competition laws because you are running a business. Trademark, unfair competition, and certain state laws enable businesses such as yours to distinguish themselves from one another and keep businesses from competing unfairly.

## What Is a Trademark?

A trademark is a *thing* that identifies the origin of a product or service in a particular trade. The term *service mark* is sometimes used to distinguish a trademark that applies to a service rather than to a product. This naming structure can be confusing, however, because most people use the term *trademark* regardless of whether they are applying it to a service or a product, and many people refer to services, such as financial services, as products. I recently explained to a senior executive that his company was a service company, not a product company, as he believed. He thought of his company as a product company, even though his company provided only services, because he had heard people within the company refer to the company's service *products* so many times that he had actually come to think of the company's services as products rather than actual services.

If you agree that this can be confusing, consider the fact that the names of many companies are not trademarks at all. Thanks to mergers, reorganizations, and other modern-day changes, company names are often used only as corporate identifiers and not necessarily as trademarks for any of the company's products or services. For example, Tricon Global Restaurants Inc., stock ticker symbol YUM, is the corporate name of the company, spun off from Pepsi, that owns Taco Bell, Pizza Hut, and Kentucky Fried Chicken restaurants. In addition to trademarks and service marks, *certification marks* (e.g., the Good Housekeeping symbol) are used to identify goods or services meeting certain qualifications. *Collective marks* identify the goods and/or services of members of collective organizations, such as the AFL-CIO for local union organizations. *Geographic marks* identify the geographic operation of a business or the geographic origin of a product—Napa Valley wine, for example. For the sake of simplicity, throughout the remainder of this book I will use the term *mark* when talking about any of these very similar rights.

Now, back to *thing*. A *mark* can be almost anything, thanks to modern law, that can be used to identify the source of goods or services and to distinguish those goods or services from those of a competitor. Long ago, marks were mostly common words and people's names. Sometimes those words and names would be used in combination with symbols and images, such as the image of a codfish in association with John's Fish & Chips. Over time, marks have become much more complicated as more people named John opened fish-and-chip restaurants. In this context, the evolution of marks is very similar to that of people's names. John was the only name needed by a fisherman in a small English village thousands of years ago. Over time, John had to identify himself as John, son of Robert, then John the Fisherman, then John Fisher from Avonmouth, and so on. As more words and names were similarly used as marks, however, people had to resort to using made-up words, such as Xerox, Exxon, and Intel, and acronyms, such as IBM, AT&T, and GE, and all sorts of other identifiers. Logos, such as Planter's Mr. Peanut and Apple Computer's rainbow Apple with the missing bite, and stars and whirls and stripes galore have become very important international symbols that allow companies to cross international boundaries as well as language and cultural barriers—although one has to wonder what people in some countries think about the connection between fruit and computers or, for that matter, a peanut with arms, legs, a cane, a top hat, and a monocle.

In recent years, the scope of mark protection has expanded to include other forms of identification, such as the pink color of Owens-Corning's fiberglass product and the sound accompanying the NBC peacock logo when displayed on television. Harley-Davidson has even tried to protect the exhaust sound of its motorcycles, but has so far been unsuccessful.

# How Do You Obtain and Keep Rights to a Mark?

The right to a mark in the United States is obtained through use. There is no requirement to first register the mark with a state or the U.S. Patent and Trademark Office (USPTO). You do not have to reserve a corporate name with the secretary of state for your state. You do not need to send yourself a letter that includes a copy of the mark inside a sealed envelope. (And before you ask, sending yourself a letter doesn't do anything to help you establish a copyright or prove you have invented something, either.) The right to a mark is automatically established, subject to preexisting rights, simply by using that mark on goods, in association with services, or in the sale or advertising of either. Once a right is established, it can be maintained through continued use, but it can also be lost through lack of use.

In contrast, the right to a mark can be acquired in many other countries by simply registering the mark with the trademark office of that country, even if the mark has never been used. Most of these countries require you to eventually use the mark as claimed in the registration in order to maintain your rights, but many years can pass before the mark will be taken away for lack of use. In an effort to conform U.S. practice to that of other countries, the United States now allows you to file an "intent to use" application to reserve the right in a mark, provided you have a bona fide intention to use it. Unlike in other countries, however, you must actually use the mark in the ordinary course of trade, not merely reserve the mark, before a registration can be issued. The fact that many countries do not require use or a bona fide intention to use a mark in order to register that mark has resulted in the piracy of many U.S. marks in other countries. Pirates look for U.S. marks on goods or services that are not yet available in a country and then register those marks in that country before the U.S. company thinks to do so. The pirates then contact the U.S. companies and offer to sell them the registrations for their own marks! A similar sort of piracy has cropped up on the Internet, called *domain name piracy*, which I will discuss later in this chapter under the heading Domain Name Piracy Battles.

Before you start using a mark or go to the effort and expense associated with obtaining an international registration, it is a very good idea to make sure no one else is using that same mark, or a very similar one, for a similar type of good or service. The process of checking for preexisting rights is called *clearing a mark*.

# How Do I Clear a Mark?

If you have come up with a new name that you would like to use as a mark, you can perform an initial search on the Internet to see if anyone else is using that same mark in the same way. The USPTO web site, www.uspto.gov, has a searchable database of registered and pending marks, but this won't help you identify marks that are being used but are not yet the subject of a registration or an application. General Internet search engines can also be used to search for names, but they cannot be used to search for logos because search engines do not yet allow you to search for images. Thus, an initial Internet search should be used only to eliminate widely used name marks or to establish that the mark you wish to use is a *descriptive* or *generic* name of a product or service and therefore available for use by anyone. If the initial search is even slightly ambiguous, or if your mark includes graphic elements that can't be searched, the next step is to have a trademark attorney order a search report through a specialized search company, such as Thompson & Thompson. The attorney will then interpret the report, which can also include logos, to establish whether anyone has already obtained rights to that mark via a federal registration or application, a state registration, an international registration, or just through use of the mark as evidenced by business records, domain name registrations, and many other sources.

You may also be able to determine the rights that another party has in a mark simply by noticing the symbol used in association with that mark. If a party doesn't use any notice symbol in association with a mark, such as ™ for an unregistered trademark, ℠ for an unregistered service mark, or ® for any type of registered mark, that party may have intended to indicate that it doesn't consider the mark to be protected. I tend to find that people overuse notice symbols rather than underuse them, so if you do not see one, it may be safer to assume it was a mistake than an indication of anything.

As noted, the ™ and ℠ symbols are informal ones that can be used by anyone to indicate a claim to common law rights in the mark with which the symbol is used. In this context, *common law* refers to state judge–made laws (i.e., case law that preexisted or exists outside the scope of federal statutory laws). The ™ symbol is supposed to be used with marks that identify the source of goods, and the ℠ symbol is supposed to be used with marks that identify the source of services, but I frequently see the ™ symbol used on both types of marks. Once a federal registration has been obtained, a party can use the symbol ®, or the phrases *Registered U.S. Patent and Trademark Office*, or *Reg. U.S. Pat. & Tm. Off.* The rules for indicating your claim to a mark are pretty much the same from country to country. In the United States, you do not have to use the ® symbol, but failure to use it can prevent you from recovering damages from an infringer. Because the ® symbol is intended to indicate your rights in a mark and to keep other people from using it, use of the ® symbol without a corresponding federal registration is illegal and can cause you to lose whatever rights you may legitimately have in the wrongly identified mark.

The more unique a mark is, the easier it is to protect and to clear for use. If you do not care to protect the mark, then you can use a descriptive term, such as "black rubber" for tires. The term *black rubber* would be considered descriptive of any tire product made out of black rubber. No country will allow you to protect that term as a mark because doing so would interfere with other people's right to use that term to properly describe their tires (i.e., they are made out of black rubber). If you used the term *black rubber* to describe a tire product made out of something other than rubber, however, you might get into trouble, especially if it turns out that your mark is deceptively misdescriptive. Generic names, such as *tire* for a tire product, are also easy to clear and hard to protect.

## How Do I Protect a Mark?

In the United States, once a mark has been used, the owner of the mark can seek to protect that mark in the state in which it is used, or federally if that mark is used in interstate commerce. Because federal protection is much more important than state protection, I will discuss the federal registration process first. Assuming your mark meets the necessary requirements (discussed subsequently), a federal registration can be obtained by filing an application with the USPTO. You can do this yourself by using a book of forms or a do-it-yourself book that you should be able to find at any large bookstore, possibly even at Amazon.com or barnesandnoble.com. You can even file an application online at the USPTO web site. I do not, however, recommend filing your own trademark application. Although trademark law is fairly simple, the use of the wrong description in an application, or some other mistake, could jeopardize your rights. In addition, once you have filed, you may need to respond to questions or challenges raised by the USPTO, and it will help to know what you are doing if that occurs.

It is almost always better to hire an attorney who specializes in this area to prepare and file the application for you and to respond to the USPTO on your behalf. True, those who should know what they are doing sometimes make mistakes, too, but at least they have malpractice insurance, whereas you are self-insured. The cost of the attorney's services will vary greatly with the uniqueness of the mark to be protected and the size of the law firm you choose. Bigger, more prestigious firms tend to charge more money. If the mark is unique and not descriptive or generic, the entire cost of obtaining a registration could be less than 1,000 U.S. dollars (USD). If your chosen mark is very similar to other marks in the same class of products or services or has some other problem, the cost of the service could be significantly more.

### Registration Requirements

Moreover, you may never even obtain a registration. Applications are examined first and are not automatically granted in most countries. Once an application has been filed in the United States, an attorney at the USPTO examines it for completion and legal sufficiency. To be complete, the application must include specimens, such as box labels or marketing collateral showing how the mark is used in commerce, a drawing of the mark, and a fee. If you file an intent-to-use application (described previously), the specimens are not required until you seek a registration based on your use. An applicant's mark will generally be granted a registration, in most countries, except in the following cases:

- The applicant's mark is merely descriptive or deceptively misdescriptive of the goods or services and has not otherwise obtained secondary meaning. A mark has obtained secondary meaning when it is recognized in the market as an indication of the source for the goods or services in question.

- The applicant's mark is generic (i.e., incapable of distinguishing the applicant's goods or services from those of others, such as "beer" for beer).

- The applicant's mark so resembles another registered mark, or a mark or trade name previously used by another and not abandoned, that it is likely to cause confusion, mistake, or deception when applied to the applicant's goods or services.

- The applicant's mark consists of immoral or scandalous matter, such as the silhouette of a naked person.

- The applicant's mark consists of a flag or coat of arms of the country or other governmental entity, such as the Olympic rings. Almost all countries have a rule similar to this for their flags and symbols.

- The applicant's mark consists of a name, portrait, or signature of a living individual without that person's consent.

In addition to actual use of a mark in commerce and a bona fide intention to use a mark, an application can also be based on a preexisting registration or application in the applicant's country of origin. If based on an application, the application must have been recently filed (i.e., within the last six months in the United States). To further conform U.S. law to the laws of other countries, the United States allows foreign-based applicants to file a statement of a bona fide intention to use a mark in commerce, and may allow that mark to be registered, even without proof of actual use.

## International Protection

To obtain international protection, you typically have to seek registrations in each individual country. The Benelux Treaty is one exception that allows for a centralized registration covering Belgium, the Netherlands, and Luxembourg. The European Union is considering a European Community registration. There is also the Madrid Agreement that allows applicants from member states to file a single application throughout much of Europe. The United States is not a member of the Madrid Agreement, but the U.S. House of Representatives just passed a bill to implement a Madrid Protocol, the name for the mechanism by which the United States becomes a member of the Madrid Agreement, and negotiations are under way for the Madrid Protocol that will meet both U.S. and Madrid Agreement member requirements.

Trademark piracy, outside of the context of domain names, is not a big problem under the U.S. system because the United States follows the first-to-use system, rather than first-to-file as in other countries. The first-to-use system is far from perfect and has its own set of unique problems. For example, because ownership is created by use, obtaining registration of a mark that was already in use by another does not necessarily improve your position—your rights may always be subject to this other use.

## Look before You Leap

In a lawsuit between Burger King and the owners of a couple of small restaurants, *Burger King v. Gene and Betty Hoots*, 403 F.2d 904 (7th Cir. 1968), Burger King found out that its federal registration for the mark *Burger King* on hamburger restaurants was subject to the preexisting rights of the Hootses to use *Burger King* for hamburger restaurants within the limited geographic territory of Mattoon, Illinois. An additional oddity of the U.S. system is that a mark cannot be sold without the goodwill of the business represented by the mark. Thus, McDonalds and Burger King could not merge, sell off the mark *Burger King*, and just adopt the mark *McDonalds* without also selling goodwill and assets associated with the mark *Burger King*. Of course, the merged companies could just abandon use of *Burger King*, but if they did, then a competing company could pick up the name and McDonalds wouldn't be able to do anything about it. It is therefore better to sell the mark, with a limited amount of goodwill, to someone like the Hootses who might be willing to agree not to expand their use of the mark beyond a two-state region involving only a couple of restaurants.

Many companies fail to consider such issues during the frenzy associated with big-business transactions (e.g., mergers or acquisitions), and these mistakes cost such companies, and much smaller entities, significant amounts of money to fix later, if the mistake can be fixed at all. When Volkswagen beat out BMW to buy Rolls-Royce, Volkswagen apparently failed to make sure that it was also acquiring the right to the *Rolls-Royce* mark, which was actually owned by a company that made airplane engines. BMW then arranged to buy the mark and certain assets from this other company at a significant discount from the price paid by Volkswagen. Of course, the aging manufacturing plant and other assets acquired by Volkswagen are worth very little without the right to use the *Rolls-Royce* mark on luxury cars. The lesson here: Don't assume your corporate lawyers know anything about intellectual property law.

## Federal versus State Protection

Trademark law developed from common law, so the right in mark technically exists at the state level in addition to the federal level, at least within the United States. State protection of a mark, however, applies only to the extent that the state protection does not conflict with federal protection. State protection is appropriate for purely local businesses, such as a neighborhood deli, that cannot qualify for federal protection. State protection, formally known as a *registration*, is almost automatic. Most states do not examine the registration applications, so they tend to be inexpensive and quick. A state registration can serve as constructive notice of a company's claim to statewide protection, so if the deli ever wants to expand into the northern part of the state, it won't be precluded from using the same name. Once you have obtained a state registration, your mark will be listed in computerized search report service databases, which may help to dissuade others from using the same or a similar mark if they search those databases when attempting to clear the mark they want to use. Finally, when it comes to enforcement, state registrations tend to be more valuable to local businesses than national ones. State court judges and juries tend to favor local businesses in disputes involving nonlocal businesses. There is no law that says you

## Side Law: Sage Advice for ISP Start-Ups

I have found that many companies, during the start-up phase, file for trademark protection within one state and then file for protection in subsequent states as they expand their business accordingly. While this can build a rather extensive portfolio of state registrations, it is usually better to get a federal registration as soon as your business expands into interstate commerce. In the old days, proving you were engaged in interstate commerce (a federal requirement) was sometimes tricky (you had to be able to show sales orders placed by out-of-state customers, out-of-state advertising, etc.). The explosive use of the Internet makes it easier for some companies, such as e-commerce-related businesses selling goods to out-of-state customers, to establish an early presence in interstate commerce. Such businesses might want to think twice about using evidence of doing business with a state that has adopted very aggressive Internet tax rules.

ISPs that provide access service to customers only within a state, however, might have a more difficult time establishing that the mark associated with their access service is being used in interstate commerce. Restaurants and other types of local businesses have gotten around this restriction in the past by showing that they have used the mark when buying goods and services from out of state. A similar approach might work for ISPs, especially if the ISP obtains banner advertisements, search engines, and other services from out-of-state suppliers for use on the ISP's access service home page.

can't have both a federal registration and one or more state registrations, but a federal registration typically provides a procedural advantage and generally takes precedence over a state registration.

Federal registrations typically take over a year to process and approve, and they are more expensive than state registrations because of higher filing fees, more complicated requirements, and the overall examination process, which typically requires you to pay for a professional to represent your interests. Nevertheless, a federal registration has the advantage of conferring nationwide protection that is effective from the date you file your U.S. application, thereby giving your operations in California and Nevada rights that are equal to those in Virginia and Puerto Rico, regardless of whether you have operations there. Like a state registration, federal registrations end up in search report service databases, but they are also published on the Internet by the USPTO and in a federal publication that is available in most major libraries. A federal registration is also evidence of the registrant's exclusive ownership rights, and anyone challenging those rights has the burden of proving otherwise. In some cases, a federal registration can even be incontestable, such as when a registered mark has been used for five years without challenge and certain procedural requirements have been fulfilled.

Furthermore, the ® symbol, or the phrases *Registered U.S. Patent and Trademark Office* or *Reg. U.S. Pat. & Tm. Off.*, can be used only to identify a federal registration. Pending federal applications and state registrations can use only the ™ and ℠ symbols. Remember to use the ™ symbol with marks that identify the source of goods and the ℠ symbol with marks that identify the source of services.

The final major advantage of a federal registration is that a federal court can hear both the federal claims of infringement (under subject matter jurisdiction) and any related state law claims. By contrast, a state court can hear only the state claims and can never adjudicate the federal claims. Thus, taking your case to federal court allows you to kill two birds with one stone. The related state claims can include state mark infringement, unfair competition, misrepresentation, fraud, and so forth. Generally, but not always, federal judges have more experience in dealing with marks than state judges and tend to be more qualified. Some rural states do not require certain types of judges to be lawyers. Even though such judges might be very bright, the lack of appropriate training in the law can result in some bizarre decisions. Once you have obtained a federal registration, the states are precluded from requiring any modification in the display of your registered mark because of any state registration. Federal registrations can also be used as the basis for obtaining registrations in other countries and to prevent the importation of infringing goods, neither of which is made possible by a state registration.

# When Is a Mark Infringed and What Can You Do about It?

A mark is infringed whenever someone uses the same or a confusingly similar mark, without authorization, on the same or closely related goods or services in the same geographical area. This is true whether the mark being infringed is federally registered or not, although, as previously noted, federal registration has many benefits. In some cases, the infringement protection of a particular mark may be allowed to naturally expand to include goods or services or geographic areas other than those specifically protected. For example, a mark on fresh produce may, over time, naturally expand to include canned or frozen produce or even ready-made frozen meals. Likewise, a registration on access service may readily expand into hosting services and communication-related services.

If a mark is infringed, a variety of civil remedies are available to you under U.S. law and in most states. U.S. trademark law is set forth in the Lanham Act. The Lanham Act is also known as the Federal Trademark Act of 1946, which demonstrates its age. It was renamed after former congressman Fritz G. Lanham, who was a big trademark advocate. Some states even have criminal laws covering certain forms of infringement, but enforcement of criminal laws requires governmental participation. Typical civil remedies include an injunction against future infringement, an award of damages equal to the infringer's profits or a reasonable royalty for past infringement, the destruction of materials bearing the infringing mark, the cost of the lawsuit, and even attorneys' fees in exceptional cases. Under the Lanham Act, however, attorneys' fees, costs, and damages will be awarded only if the infringer had actual notice of the registered rights in the infringed mark. Actual notice can be established only through use if the ® symbol is used. In other words, the requirement to use the registration symbol ® is a practical one, not a legal one. Thus, you can choose not to use the symbol if you don't care about collecting damages, costs, and fees for infringement.

Strangely enough, many trademark holders fail to use the ® symbol. Most people fail to use the symbol out of ignorance (i.e., because someone didn't like it or because someone didn't realize its use was important). Other people purposely choose not to use the symbol in certain cases. I know of a company, for instance, that does not use the ® symbol with its logo whenever it could be argued that the logo is being used to identify the company rather than to indicate the source of origin of the company's goods or services. The company has its logo painted on the fuselage of its corporate jets without the ® symbol because a senior executive thought it looked better that way. Because the company wasn't about to go into the airplane business and it was highly unlikely that anyone else would use the same logo on airplanes, the company thought the risk of not being able to get damages, attorneys' fees, and costs was worth taking to appease this one executive.

### What If the Infringer Is You or Your Customer?

If the mark possibly being infringed is not yours, but rather someone else's, and either you or one of your customers is to blame, then the situation is obviously different. The defenses applicable to claims of mark infringement are somewhat broader than those available to claims of copyright infringement. First, you can attempt to show that the marks are used in different classes of goods and services. If that doesn't work, you can attempt to show that there is no confusion among customers of the different goods or services because the disputed marks are not confusingly similar, or that the customers are very sophisticated and would not be confused, or some such argument. Failing any of these attempts, you could then attempt to claim that your use was fair use because you were comparing the disputed marks, or you were parodying the other mark, or something along those lines.

If your customer is the infringer, you cannot simply stand by and allow the infringement to continue once you know about it. As with copyright law, the notions of indirect liability apply equally to trademark law, but unlike copyright law, the DMCA does not apply to help limit your liability. In at least two lawsuits, bulletin board system (BBS) operators have been found indirectly liable for trademark infringement and unfair competition, for knowingly distributing infringing software and works. In one case, the infringed works were Sega video games. In the other case, the infringed works were trademarked Playboy material. Neither of these cases are good examples of what could happen to ISPs, however, because both cases involved situations in which the BBS operators were also acting as the direct infringers. In such cases, it is common for the court to rule in favor of every claim made by the mark owner and against the defendant. The situation could be different if an ISP knows about the infringement by a customer but does nothing. However, I wouldn't count on it.

## Unfair Competition and Related Claims

Most cases of infringement, whether for copyright, trademark, or patent, often include related claims associated with unfair competition. Infringement claims involving products and product packaging often include a trade dress claim as well. A *trade dress* is the unique characteristic of the packaging for a good or its container. A Windex glass-cleaner bottle is an example of a product with a unique trade dress.

Trade dress claims are supported by the "any container for goods" language in Section 43(a) of the Lanham Act, as subsequently discussed. Because ISPs don't sell products, you might wonder why trade dress is relevant to ISPs, but even ISPs package materials that are sent to their customers, such as the millions of compact discs sent out by AOL and other ISPs. The design of a web site might also eventually qualify for trade dress protection, although this hasn't happened yet.

While state unfair competition and related laws exist and are frequently used, Section 43(a) of the Lanham Act was specifically developed to provide a federal cause of action for trademark-related unfair competition injuries, including trade dress claims. State unfair competition–related laws cannot interfere with the rights granted under federal law, and the few states that do have unfair competition laws tend to focus on fraud, misrepresentation, and other consumer protection–related themes.

This language can be used to prohibit someone from using your trademark in competition with you. It can be used to prohibit someone from making a product or service that looks or sounds like yours (i.e., *passing off* ). And, whereas Section 43(a) is supposed to be for trademark-related injuries, courts have applied it regardless of whether trademarks were even involved in the dispute. For example, courts have found products and packages to be infringing a mark even though those products and packages did not include that mark. Courts have also found confusing descriptions and misrepresentative advertisements to be a sufficient connection for the Lanham Act to apply. As a result, many non-trademark-protected products and packages have been protected under the Lanham Act, such as teddy bears, sport shoes, and restaurant decors.

If someone copies the trade dress of your packaging, you will have to prove three elements in order to win a trade dress claim under Section 43(a). First, to be valid, unless a trade dress shape is inherently distinctive, you must be able to show that the shape is recognized by customers to identify and distinguish the source of the particular good or package. Next, functionality cannot dictate the shape of the object to be pro-

## Side Law: Lanham Act Definition of Unfair Competition and Trade Dress Infringement

Any person who, on or in connection with any goods or services, or any container for goods, uses in commerce any word, term, name, symbol, or device, or any combination thereof, or any false designation of origin, false or misleading description of fact, or false or misleading representation of fact, which, (1) is likely to cause confusion, or to cause mistake, or to deceive as to the affiliation, connection, or association of such person with another person, or as to the origin, sponsorship, or approval of his or her goods, services, or commercial activities by another person, or (2) in commercial advertising or promotion, misrepresents the nature, characteristics, qualities, or geographic origin of his or her or another person's goods, services, or commercial activities, shall be liable in a civil action by any person who believes that he or she is or is likely to be damaged by such act.

tected, such as a disc-shaped package for a compact disc. Finally, you must prove that customers or others will likely be confused about the source, relatedness, or sponsorship of the product or package because of the similar design or shape.

# The Clash between Trademarks and Domain Names

In some ways, the creation and existence of domain names has been one of the most exciting things to occur in trademark law in many years. A *domain name* is an identifier that is used by the Internet to identify individual hosts (i.e., computers). The Internet Protocol, also called *IP* like intellectual property, is the communications protocol responsible for making sure packets are sent to the right destinations on the Internet. This protocol relies on IP address information to deliver mail and other data from computer to computer. An *IP address* is a 32-bit number that can be represented as a sequence of four decimal numbers, each ranging between 0 and 255 (e.g., 127.48.132.98). As far back as 1969, users of the ARPANET (a predecessor to the Internet) used names to identify end locations in the ARPANET. Because there were relatively few ARPANET users, it was possible to map names to corresponding ARPANET end locations by using a single table called *host.txt*. Even in 1983, when the Internet was first up and running, a similar table was used to associate simple host names with IP addresses. When it became apparent that this naming system would not scale well to a large number of users, the Domain Name System (DNS) was invented. DNS uses a distributed database of domain name/IP address pairs. DNS was designed in the mid-1980s by Paul Mockapetris, together with the late Jon Postel and others, to keep track of these domain names, subdomains, and so forth through a hierarchical system in which each upper-level domain maintains a list of addresses of the domain just beneath it. Thus, every individual host connected to the Internet has a domain name that is tracked by a higher-level domain.

## IP Addresses and the DNS

Assume user A wants to send an e-mail message to user B using user B's Internet address red@foo.bar.com. As illustrated in Figure 2.5, a domain name lookup message is prepared and sent to a root domain name server. The lookup message contains the entire domain name foo.bar.com. The root server then sends that lookup message to the DNS server responsible for all domain names ending in bar.com. The DNS server looks up the domain name and returns to user A's computer an IP address, such as 127.48.132.98, that corresponds to the domain name foo.bar.com. In this case, because I am talking about the transmission of an e-mail message, the IP address is actually associated with an Internet mail server (e.g., user B's e-mail host). The e-mail application running on user A's computer then opens a *transmission control protocol* (TCP) connection with user B's e-mail host.

The e-mail host validates the mailbox that is intended to receive user A's message (i.e., a check is performed to make sure there is a *red* at foo.bar.com). Once the mailbox is validated, the message is sent. User B can thereafter connect to the e-mail host and retrieve the e-mail message. The actual process is somewhat more complicated and can vary depending on the nature of the message to be transmitted. The basic

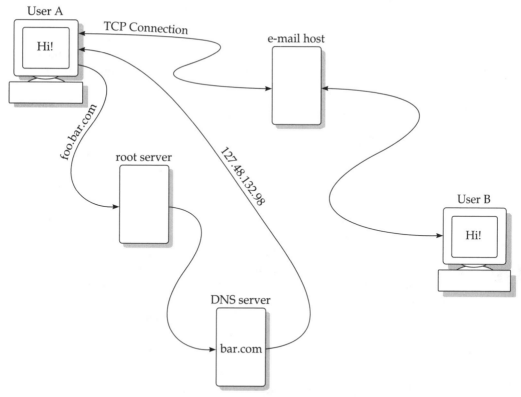

**Figure 2.5** Illustration of the Domain Name System in action.

point is that the DNS creates a logical way of making sure each message has some-place to go and that the domain name associated with it has been resolved into an IP address before a message can leave its source.

An *Internet address* is an IP address. Most people refer to their e-mail address, such as tim.casey@wcom.com, as an Internet address, but that isn't true. Technically, only the por-tion of the e-mail address to the right of the @ (*at*) sign (the domain name) identifies a com-puter (a host) and can be converted into an IP address. The user name to the left of the @ sign in this case corresponds to a particular e-mail account or mailbox on that host. An Internet address can be expressed in many different ways. For example, lib.mcix.wcom.com identi-fies a particular host (lib). In this case, lib identifies a computer that runs an internal library site within a network of computers (mcix), within a larger network of computers (wcom), within the domain of commercial sites (com). Well, actually it doesn't—you wouldn't expect me to give you a real address, would you?

When communicating with computers located outside of the United States, you may also see a domain name with characters on the far right, such as .de or .tm, which identify a *country code top-level domain*, or ccTLD. The ccTLD is reserved for individu-ally recognized countries or territories, as determined by ISO 3166-1:1997, where ISO stands for International Organization for Standardization (see www.iso.ch). The .com domain and other domains such as .net and .gov are called *generic top-level domains*, or gTLDs. A gTLD identifies different classes of domains that have been reserved or used for different purposes. For now, 13 so-called root name servers, located in different places around the world, are used to provide the top-level hierarchy for the DNS database. Figure 2.6 illustrates the hierarchical delegation of domains under a root.

### It Was a Good Idea at the Time . . .

As already noted, the DNS was developed as a scalable way to identify computers through use of IP addresses. As the Internet was commercialized, however, people began to use ccTLDs and gTLDs with other identifiers in ways that were never anticipated by the initial developers. Commercial users began to create domain names that referenced companies, organizations, products, services, concepts, and just about anything else. When used in such a manner, a domain name is identical to a mark and is subject to the same types of disputes typical to marks—with one major exception: Whereas many different entities can use the exact same mark for different classes of products and services without conflict, such as *MCI* for communication services, *MCI* for buses, and *MCI* for a home-improvement contractor, there can be only one mci.com. This exception largely has caused the dilution disputes between mark owners and registrants mentioned earlier, but it has also caused mark owners to demand a review of the domain name registration process and caused some domain name holders to register their domain names as trademarks.

The domain name registration process was originally run by SRI International under contract to the Defense Advanced Research Projects Agency (DARPA). As a result of a number of changes, including the development of NSFNET, the National Science Foundation (NSF) inherited management responsibility for certain top-level domains. NSF then later competitively contracted with Network Solutions, Inc. (NSI) to manage the registration of domain names in those domains. While initially performing such ser-

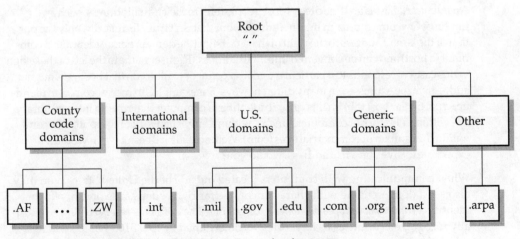

**Figure 2.6** Hierarchical delegation of domains under the DNS.

vices, NSI did not process domain name applications according to the criteria used by the USPTO to register marks. Instead, NSI registered domain names the way the trademark offices of certain countries register mark applications—on a first-come, first-served basis. This practice has led to the same type of piracy problems that previously existed around the world, but magnified by the ubiquitous nature of the Internet. After some initial panic during which some companies paid pirates to recover domain names that included marks, many mark owners quickly learned that this was a losing battle because of all of the domain name variations that were possible. Trademark owners started suing pirates, as well as NSI, in an effort to block the use of identical or similar-sounding-looking domain names. Initial efforts by trademark owners produced mixed results, but in recent actions, and as evidenced by even more-recent legislation in the United States, mark owners have begun to score some victories around the world.

# Trademark Dilution

Trademark dilution is a particular type of trademark infringement that was added to Section 43 of the Lanham Act by the Federal Trademark Dilution Act (FTDA). The FTDA was passed to provide an extra measure of protection for famous marks that are being used by other people in a commercial context without permission, but not necessarily in a confusingly similar fashion. For example, the use of the IBM logo on a drain-cleaning product may not result in regular trademark infringement because it is doubtful that IBM has trademark protection for that class of goods. Under the FTDA, the IBM logo may be protected from that use anyway because using the possibly famous logo on a drain cleaner may be considered to tarnish IBM's mark.

If you own a *famous* mark, you are entitled to an injunction against another person's commercial use of any other mark in commerce that dilutes your famous mark. This is true even if the diluting mark is not confusingly similar to your famous mark and even if the other party's use of the diluting mark began after your mark become famous. *Dilution* is defined in two ways: tarnishment and blurring. *Tarnishment* occurs when a famous mark is linked to lower-quality goods or services or is otherwise displayed in a derogatory manner, such as the use of a famous mark in association with a vulgar saying on a T-shirt. *Blurring* involves the whittling away of the value and selling power of a famous mark because of unauthorized uses. For example, the use of a famous tire mark (as in a trademark rather than a rubber deposit on the road) for a roadside restaurant guide might be considered a blurring because of the identical nature of the marks and the related nature of the products.

The FTDA does not define *famous,* so proving that a mark has become famous is the most difficult aspect of gaining protection under the FTDA. Some of the factors that have been applied by courts in trying to make this determination include the inherent or acquired distinctiveness of the mark, the duration and extent of use in connection with the goods or services, the advertising and publicity associated with the mark, and the degree of recognition of the mark. To further complicate matters, some courts have interpreted the FTDA to also require proof of actual harm. Thus, in *Ringling Bros. and Barnum & Bailey Circus v. Utah Division of Travel Development,* 107 F.3d 449 (4th Cir. 1999), the federal Fourth Circuit Court of Appeals dismissed a dilution claim by Ringling Bros. against the state of Utah for use of the phrase *The Greatest Snow on Earth* to describe Utah snow. The court ruled that Ringling Bros. wasn't actually harmed by Utah's use of the similar-sounding slogan.

## Famous Goes Only So Far on the Internet

Although the FTDA has been used to prevent a number of famous marks from being used as domain names without permission, some trademark owners have not been as successful. For example, Hasbro, Inc., successfully enjoined the continued use of the domain name candyland.com held by an adult-entertainment provider because it diluted Hasbro's famous trademark *Candyland* (a children's board game). Although this result was not particularly surprising, the situation might have been different if candyland.com had simply been acquired, but not used in this fashion, by someone else, such as a domain name pirate. As noted earlier, the FTDA requires that the disputed mark be a "commercial use . . . in commerce." A number of people have wondered what would happen if someone had just reserved the domain name and done nothing more (i.e., not used the domain name in commerce). Thanks to the late-1999 passage of the Anticybersquatting Consumer Protection Act (ACPA), which will be discussed shortly in great detail, that question is likely to be answered fairly soon.

In the meantime, Dennis Toeppen (who runs an ISP in Illinois) "decided to see what would happen" if he registered a number of domain names that included other people's marks. Toeppen apparently made this statement in a post to a Usenet newsgroup called chi.internet. What happened was that Toeppen was promptly sued for infringement under the FTDA. So far, Toeppen has lost two different dilution suits because he not only registered the domain names, but he also established web pages corresponding to the domain names and attempted to sell the domain names to the mark holders. Both courts found such actions to be commercial in nature and used in commerce, even though the material on the web pages was innocuous and had nothing to do with the mark owners.

The FTDA was also successfully used by Planned Parenthood Federation of America, Incorporated, to stop the continued use of plannedparenthood.com by an anti-abortion web site. In this case, the defendant wasn't interested in selling the domain name. Rather, the defendant wanted to keep Planned Parenthood from using the name and wanted to try to influence anyone going to the anti-abortion web site by mistake. Nevertheless, the court found that the defendant's use was in commerce because the Internet is interstate in nature and because the activities of a multistate business were blocked by the defendant's use of the Planned Parenthood mark. In the event the court's reasoning was attacked on appeal, the court also applied a section of the Lanham Act that does not specifically require use *in commerce*, just likely confusion, mistake, or deception, and held that the defendant's use was commercial in nature because of the effect it had on Planned Parenthood's activities.

Playboy Enterprises has also won injunctions prohibiting the continued use of the domain names playboyxxx.com and playmatelive.com and the continued use of a famous mark that could not even be seen. In the latter case, Playboy was granted an injunction prohibiting the continued use of Playboy marks in metatags. *Metatags* are visually hidden code words in a web page that can be read by search engines. In the Playboy cases, the defendant used famous Playboy marks as metatags in pornography sites to attract visitors looking for Playboy products. While it is hard to imagine one such product being tarnished by the other, blurring does seem to be a distinct possibility, so Playboy prevailed.

### In-Porsche

Despite numerous victories, the owners of famous marks, such as Ringling Brothers, have not always prevailed in dilution cases, even when their marks were famous. For example, Porsche Cars North America, Inc. (Porsche) recently failed to get an injunction under the FTDA against the continued use of 128 different domain names, such as porsch.com (notice the missing *e*) and porsche.net. The problem in this case had nothing to do with the famous nature of the Porsche marks. Rather, Porsche chose to sue the domain names themselves, in what is called an *in rem action* (*in rem* is Latin for "against the thing"), rather than suing the people who registered them, which would have been an *in personam action* (*in personam* is Latin for "against the person"). Although Porsche could not identify a number of the domain name registrants because of anonymous registrations, the real issue was that Porsche wanted to deal with all 128 offending domain names in one suit rather than having to file numerous separate suits. Although the court had sympathy for Porsche's predicament, created by the first-come, first-served domain name registration process adopted by Network Solutions, Inc. (NSI), the court also felt that the various registrants had a right to adjudicate their interests in person under the due process clause of the Constitution.

# *In Rem* Actions against Domain Names under the Anticybersquatting Consumer Protection Act

It will be interesting to see if other defendants accused of violating trademark rights under the Lanham Act, including the FTDA, latch onto this due process clause argument, because the number of *in rem* actions against domain names is likely to increase after passage of the Anti-cybersquatting Consumer Protection Act (ACPA). Among other things, the ACPA gives trademark owners the right to file *in rem* civil actions against domain names under certain conditions. Such actions can be filed in the judicial district where the domain name registrar, domain name registry, or other domain name authority (registrar/registry/other) that registered or assigned the domain name is located.

The conditions that apply to such actions include the following:

- The domain name must violate a trademark right in a mark registered in the U.S. Patent and Trademark Office or otherwise protected by the ACPA.
- The court must find that the owner of the trademark could not have obtained in personam jurisdiction over any person.
- The court must find that the owner of the trademark, through *due diligence,* was not able to find the person who would have been the defendant in an in personam action.

Due diligence can be shown by sending a notice of the alleged violation and an intent to proceed under the ACPA to the registrant of the domain name at the postal and e-mail addresses provided by the registrant to the registrar and by publishing a notice of the action as the court may direct. The remedies available to a trademark owner in an in rem action are limited to the forfeiture, cancellation, or transfer of the domain name. The obligations of the registrar/registry/other are discussed in greater detail in Chapter 5, *What Is an ISP to Do (or Not)? Content and Activity Regulations to Live By.*

Porsche and other trademark owners were not the only entities that found themselves at odds with the domain name system and the domain name registration process—which brings us to our next topic.

## Domain Name Piracy Battles

An Australian court recently issued orders prohibiting a number of different parties in Southport, Queensland, from using three Internet domain names they had registered in the United States and were subsequently offering for sale or rent in Australia. The Italian soccer equipment and clothing maker Umbro also recently won a default judgment for trademark infringement against a domain name registrant identified as 3263851 Canada, Inc. The judgment was in default because 3263851 Canada failed to appear from Canada to defend itself. Because the defendant remained in Canada, Umbro stood little chance of collecting on its default judgment. Umbro therefore filed a successful claim under Virginia law, where NSI is located, to garnish the domain names registered to 3263851 Canada, just as wages can be garnished to fulfill a child-support payment default. NSI has appealed this decision on the grounds that the domain names are licensed rights from NSI, not property rights of the domain name registrants, and therefore cannot be garnished.

In a similar action, PaineWebber, Inc., recently succeeded in getting the domain name wwwpainewebber.com (note the lack of a dot after www) taken away from Rafael Fortuny, who ran a pornography site, and also got an injunction against NSI to keep it from registering any similar domain name to anybody else. Fortuny registered this domain name in the hope that some people trying to find the PaineWebber web site might accidentally type the wrong Universal Resource Locator (URL) into a World Wide Web browser and thereby end up at Fortuny's pornography site instead. In a plea similar to those of ISPs faced with monitoring for copyright-infringing material, NSI appealed on the grounds that it isn't capable of reviewing all of the different domain names it registers for mark infringement. By mid-1999, NSI had issued more than 4 million second-level domain (SLD) names in the .com, .net, and .org gTLDs and was registering over 7,000 additional SLDs every day. Taking this into consideration, a number of courts have ruled that NSI doesn't have liability for mark infringement issues resulting from its registration activities.

Nevertheless, this issue (i.e., what to do about the clash between trademark rights and domain names) is far from settled, and how it is resolved will be important to ISPs. If NSI or other registrars are held liable for mark infringement for registering marks, any ISP could potentially find itself being accused of infringement. ISPs who become registrars, help customers register SLDs, or park SLDs for customers on their servers to help reserve an SLD might find themselves implicated in the infringement. This would be especially true if the ISP knew a customer was using an infringing name to attract business to a web site hosted by that ISP.

## The Rise (and Fall?) of Domain Name Dispute Resolution

An international effort has been under way to bring greater certainty to this area of the law, to help stop domain name piracy, and to hopefully restructure the domain name registration process in a way that puts innocent users and trademark owners on even ground. NSI's monopoly is gradually being taken away, and the registration process is being opened up to competition and regulation via ICANN (Internet Corporation for Assigned Names and Numbers), which was awarded the contract by the U.S. government to perform such services. At the request of ICANN, the World Intellectual Property Organization (WIPO) put together a report recommending that famous marks be given special protection in the domain name context and that an alternative dispute resolution process be established for resolving domain name disputes. After a number of meetings on this issue, ICANN established a small working group to review the WIPO proposals.

The working group was directed to better define cybersquatting, to define reverse domain name hijacking, to develop a uniform dispute resolution policy, and to develop corresponding procedures to be followed by all ICANN registrars when confronted with disputes involving such issues. ICANN then considered the input from this working group and developed a Uniform Dispute Resolution Policy (UDRP) for consideration by all Internet users. The UDRP has now been approved by ICANN, and all ICANN-approved registrars have adopted the procedures. The WIPO, which provides alternative dispute resolution services, has even heard its first dispute involving an Australian registrar.

ICANN's successful efforts in this regard may have been short-lived. Within two months of ICANN's adoption of the UDRP, the United States passed the Anticybersquatting Consumer Protection Act (ACPA). The ACPA was included in omnibus appropriations legislation passed at the close of the 106th session of Congress. Although the Clinton administration noted that it did not think the ACPA was necessary in view of ICANN's UDRP, the president nevertheless signed the spending bill. In other words, no matter how much the administration didn't like the ACPA, this matter wasn't important enough to justify vetoing a spending bill that otherwise gave the administration what it wanted—which is exactly why the ACPA was included.

The administration considered the ACPA to be unnecessary because it established hard law where ICANN's UDRP had attempted to establish soft self-regulatory practices. More significantly, the UDRP defined cybersquatting, bad faith, and other elements in ways that tended to balance the interests of both sides of the debate (i.e. the trademark owners and the innocent registrants of domain names who had suddenly been accused of being cyberpirates). The ACPA, on the other hand, tends to favor the interests of trademark owners and individuals who have their names appropriated as domain names. Both efforts, however, were aimed at so-called cybersquatters who prey on the well-known marks of others by registering them as domain names with the intent of selling the domain names to make money or otherwise cause mischief.

## The Anticybersquatting Consumer Protection Act (ACPA)

The ACPA amends good old Section 43 of the Trademark Act of 1946 once again by adding an entirely new Section 43(d). This new section provides for an explicit trademark remedy for cybersquatting and protection against the domain name registration of names of living persons.

Under the ACPA, a civil cause of action can arise due to the registration, trafficking in, or use of a domain name that is identical to, confusingly similar to, or dilutive of a mark or a name of another that is protected as a mark under the Trademark Act at the time the domain name was registered. This provision requires trademark owners to demonstrate the domain name registrant's bad-faith intent to profit from the goodwill of the trademark owner's mark. The provision does not extend to cases in which the domain name registrant was unaware of another's use of the name or in which the registrant registers the domain name for purposes other than bad-faith intent to profit from the goodwill of a mark.

A nonexhaustive list of factors defined by the ACPA is intended to be used by a court to measure the bad-faith intent of a registrant. These factors attempt to balance the property interests of trademark holders with the legitimate interests of Internet users and others. The factors listed in the ACPA include the following:

- Whether the registrant has any trademark or other intellectual property rights in the name
- The extent to which the name consists of a legal name of the registrant or a name that is otherwise commonly use to identify that person
- The registrant's prior lawful use of the name in connection with bona fide offering of goods or services
- The registrant's bona fide noncommercial or fair use of the name in a site accessible under that name
- The registrant's intent to divert consumers from the trademark owner's site to the registrant's site using the name
- The registrant's offer to transfer, sell, or otherwise assign the name to the mark owner or another party for financial gain (based on the registrant's prior conduct)
- The registrant's provision of false information when applying for or maintaining the registration of the name
- The registrant's historical use of other names that incorporate the marks of others
- The extent to which the mark incorporated into the name is distinctive and famous within the meaning of the Trademark Act

While the ACPA states that Section 43(d) of the Trademark Act does not limit the application of other statutes and remedies to cybersquatting cases, it does limit the application of the UDRP with respect to disputes that can be resolved within the United States. Most large mark owners are not going to take the chance of losing a domain name battle just because the provisions of the UDRP are more balanced. Mark owners are also going to want to take advantage of the federal remedies for damages and injunctive relief. The ACPA extends statutory damages to cybersquatting cases. Amounts of not less than $1,000 and not more than $100,000 per domain name could be awarded to mark owners. The amendment also provides that in any civil action under new Sec. 43(d), A court may also order the forfeiture, cancellation, or transfer of a domain name to the owner of the mark.

With respect to personal names, a cause of action is available against anyone who registers a domain name without consent where the following occur:

- That domain name consists of, or is substantially and confusingly similar to, another living person's name.
- The registrant had the specific intent to profit from selling that domain name.

There is an exception for good-faith registrations of names used in, affiliated with, or related to a copyrighted work, where the domain name will be sold in conjunction with the exploitation of the copyrighted work. This exception, of course, is the work of the movie and publishing companies. While they wanted to make sure no one else could profit from the use of an actor or actress's name, they wanted to preserve their right to profit from those same names when used in association with their movies and book titles.

The ACPA became effective on November 29, 1999, but infringement damages apply only to the registration, trafficking, or uses of domain names in violation of the ACPA after its date of enactment. The other aspects of the ACPA are discussed in Chapter 5.

## Cybersquatting

*Cybersquatting* has generally been defined, including within the ACPA and the UDRP, as any registration of a domain name that is similar to someone else's trademark (or personal name), where the registrant has no legitimate right to the domain name and there is some evidence that the registrant registered the name solely to take advantage of the trademark holder or individual owner of the name. Every major corporation has been subject to numerous cybersquatting attempts. One MCI WorldCom attorney, after being approached at church (not the same one mistakenly sending ISPs notices under the DMCA), politely refused the offer to buy a domain name from a grandmother who had registered a domain name (at the suggestion of her son) similar to an MCI WorldCom mark.

## Reverse Domain Name Hijacking

*Reverse domain name hijacking* occurs when the holder of a trademark discovers that its trademark has been legitimately incorporated into a domain name registered by someone else and then brings a suit or administrative action against the domain name holder to try to take away that domain name. For example, Clue Computing registered the name clue.com and was subsequently sued by Mattel for infringing the trademark for Clue, which is the name of a board game. Mattel was attempting to argue that its trademark for a common term in one narrow area—games—usurped anyone else's right to use that common term in any other way on the Internet. Rightfully, Clue Computing won this suit, because it has a completely legitimate right to use the word *clue,* and it was not using it in a way that would create confusion between itself and Mattel.

### It Would Be Nice to Finish What Was Started

WIPO's involvement in this entire matter and the ultimate adoption of the UDRP had some added significance to me, and I remain rather interested in seeing fair and appropriate rules and laws established with respect to domain names. Before ICANN was officially ICANN, the WIPO was casting about for ways to get involved in the domain name dispute battle. It was during this period that I suggested to WIPO's general counsel, Francis Gurry, that WIPO undertake a worldwide effort, using the Internet, of course, to gather people's input on how to resolve the domain name/ trademark issue. With the subsequent support of the U.S. government (WIPO effectively cannot do anything unless at the request of a member state) and ICANN's request, WIPO was selected to put together the report that ultimately led to the adoption of the UDRP. Although I would have liked to have been more heavily involved in the development of WIPO's report, it was important not to have too many Americans involved in the effort, so I voluntarily backed away from being involved. It was also nice not to have the spend the time such involvement would have required.

Later, when ICANN established its small working group tasked with negotiating the terms of the UDRP, I was invited to participate in a few of the meetings that were held to work through the issues. Although it is sometimes very difficult to overcome entrenched positions and fear of the unknown, I was impressed by how hard everyone honestly tried to understand the other parties' positions and develop solutions that were in the Internet's best interests. The resulting UDRP did not satisfy all of the parties, especially because some of the people involved in this matter are not, in my opinion, in the least bit rational, which is why the ACPA was passed into law. However, if the UDRP is given a chance, it should help to resolve the vast majority of domain name disputes around the world in an appropriate fashion.

## Patents, Trade Secrets, Antitrust, and Standards

The most important thing that anyone can learn about patents is what they are and why they exist—historically and today. Once the history of the patents is understood, many damaging misconceptions about patents can be readily corrected. One such misconception involves the application of patents to the Internet. Recent news stories would lead one to believe that patents had not applied to the Internet until 1999, but this is far from the truth. Patents have applied to many aspects of the packet-switched networks from the first day a packet was sent and received. "Okay," you say, "but that was just to the hardware, not the software or the protocols or the businesses on the Net." But you are wrong. Patents applied to software long before there was a single legal decision confirming that fact. The same is true with respect to protocols and business methods, but before we get into those issues, let's start with a description and history of patents.

# Patent Ideology

Today, a patent is an intangible right, granted by a government, to exclude others from making, using, or selling (or, in the case of the United States, importing) the patented invention in that government's territory. In this context, a patent is referred to as a *negative right* because it only includes the right to *exclude* others from making, using, or selling the invention and does not grant the owner the positive right to make, use, or sell (collectively, to *sell*) the patented invention. This rather confusing distinction is based on the idea that most inventions, in some way or another, are improvements on prior inventions. A patent on an improvement carries no right to sell the improvement in violation of the rights of the owner whose patent it improves. If you were to grant a positive right to the improvement inventor, you would take away preexisting rights from the original inventor. Hence, the basic patent (the original patent) is a blocking patent to the improvement patent because the latter cannot be sold without the authorized use of the former.

For example, with reference to Figure 2.7, Skyler owns patent X, which comprises the elements A, B, and C. Jacquelyn owns a different patent, patent Y, which also comprises the elements A, B, and C and which adds element D. In this case, Jacquelyn's patent is considered to be a patentable improvement of Skyler's patent because of the addition of element D. However, Skyler's patent blocks Jacquelyn's patent because Jacquelyn's patent comprises all of the elements of Skyler's. If Jacquelyn were to be given the positive right to sell her invention, she would necessarily take away rights from Skyler. Thus, Jacquelyn cannot sell her own invention without getting Skyler's authorization to sell his. In the converse, Skyler cannot use Jacquelyn's element D just because Jacquelyn's invention is based on his.

Any other system would effectively encourage people to steal the inventions from all of those who came before. Some people might argue that this would be good because it would encourage improvements. It would also discourage people from disclosing their inventions in the first place, a major goal behind the patent system, because the inventor would only get ripped off. To encourage disclosures and improvements, Jacquelyn

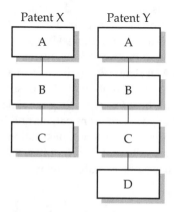

**Figure 2.7** Distinguishing different inventions.

has the right to exclude Skyler from selling her improvement in patent Y, and Skyler has the right to prevent Jacquelyn from selling his patent X. Thus, if Skyler really wants to use patent Y, he can ask Jacquelyn for a license in exchange for money or a license to use patent X (a *cross-license*) or vice versa. This structure forces patent owners to share patent rights in order to get rights they need, which is also good for competition.

## Patent History

The patent system, however, was not always this way. As my eight-year-old son recently discovered on a field trip to historic Williamsburg, Virginia, the United States was essentially an underdeveloped country during its early years. In order to encourage the establishment of settlements and manufacturing facilities, the colonies offered legal monopolies, not patents, to entice development and industry, such as mills and factories. Massachusetts was the first state to offer such monopolies, in 1641, followed by Connecticut, both starting with saltworks. Massachusetts also granted the first patent, in 1646, for an improved scythe and the right to exclusively manufacture it for a period of seven years, although the inventor asked for fourteen. However, the colonists were concerned that the granting of exclusive favors would lead to the same abuses that ended up strangling the economies of the countries from which they had fled. Thus, Americans adopted the principle that the inventor of something new and useful was entitled to a patent as a matter of right rather than favor. This principle was first incorporated into general patent legislation in South Carolina in 1784. Other states soon followed and also began to require that inventors disclose and publish their inventions so that others might use them after the patents expired. This requirement forced patent owners to share knowledge rather than maintain it as a secret, which helps to enhance innovation and, as a result, economic growth and competition.

### Sinking the Boat

Due to conflicts resulting from different states granting the same patent rights to different inventors, the states ended up abrogating the right to grant patents to the federal government. For example, in 1784 James Rumsey was awarded patents in Virginia and Pennsylvania for a boat that could be easily moved against rapid waters. In 1786, John Fitch built a steamboat for use on the Schuylkill River in Pennsylvania and applied for patents in a number of states, resulting in his own Pennsylvania patent in 1787, as well as patents in all other states except Maryland (where Rumsey managed to get it blocked). Rumsey's and Fitch's efforts won the attention of the Constitutional Convention, whose members even boarded Fitch's boat for trips along the Delaware River, resulting in a proposal to give Congress the power to grant patents and issue copyrights. Thus was born the patent and copyright clause of the Constitution, which I quoted earlier in this chapter. Congress never officially took the right to grant patents away from the states, but interestingly, no state has a patent statute today.

### From Steamboats to the Internet

At any rate, Congress was not prepared for the onslaught of citizens seeking patents. Apparently, so many people were petitioning Congress for patent protection on different inventions (Congress had no process set up for granting patents) that Congress was literally overrun for a number of years. In response to George Washington's plea to do something, Congress finally passed the Patent Act of 1790 in an attempt to correct the situation. Unfortunately, the 1790 Patent Act still did not provide a procedure for dealing with conflicts between different applicants claiming rights in the same inventions, which is what happened when four different inventors, including Rumsey and Fitch, applied for patents on steamboat-related technology. The Patent Board proceeded to grant patents to all four inventors. Because Fitch's patent apparently had priority, the other two inventors eventually acknowledged Fitch's rights, but Rumsey did not. He went on to get six patents of his own and continued to do battle with Fitch for many additional years. I have used this example to illustrate an important point: Patents are controversial issues for every new industry that comes along, whether it is software, the Internet, or steamships, with many conflicts over who owns what before everything settles down as the industry matures. Over the last hundred years, many people have argued that patents shouldn't apply to cars, steelmaking, drugs, semiconductors, computers, biotechnology, or software, yet each of these industries has thrived—and to the extent they had problems, it wasn't because of patents. What makes people think the Internet should be different?

# The Development of Modern Patent Law

Although the Patent Act was amended in 1793 to arbitrate conflicts between inventors, it also did away with the requirement to examine patent applications before granting patents, and it allowed the states to continue granting patents, resulting in even more conflicts. The granting of patents on just about everything by different states and the federal government eventually led to the passage of a new patent law in 1836. This law created the Patent Office and the requisite examination of patent applications and established the basic requirements for a patent (that are still followed today), such as a detailed specification, a drawing, and an oath of inventorship. Design patents were added by amendment in 1842, and the whole thing was redone in 1952. The Patent Act of 1952 was largely written by Judge Giles S. Rich, who was in private practice at the time and went on to become the first patent attorney appointed to the U.S. Court of Customs and Patent Appeals (CCPA). He was also one of the first judges appointed to the Court of Appeals for the Federal Circuit (CAFC). Regrettably, Judge Rich (really the dean of the modern patent bar) passed away on the very day I was writing this section.

## The Modern Patent

Under the 1952 Patent Act, an invention was still required to be new and useful, but a new requirement was added. Now the invention also had to be *not obvious* to a person of ordinary skill in the relevant art. We will talk about this standard later. Furthermore, inventors was required to set out what they regarded as the particularly patentable aspect of their invention (that which they had a right to exclude) in a claim. Hence, the claims, which are the numbered paragraphs that appear at the end of every patent, are the most important part of the patent. Whereas the first part of the patent describes the invention in great detail, the claims establish the scope of protection to be granted to the inventor.

Although I mentioned the CAFC in relation to the 1952 Patent Act, it is important to note that the CAFC was not created until 1982. Prior to that date, appeals from the federal district courts related to patent infringement lawsuits were first heard by the various U.S. circuit courts of appeals within their territorial boundaries, such as the Second Circuit or the Ninth Circuit. Appeals from these courts could be heard only by the Supreme Court. The CCPA heard appeals only from the Board of Appeals at the PTO, as when an inventor was protesting a patentability decision, but could not hear infringement cases. Because the Supreme Court rarely gets involved in patent cases, choosing to spend its time on more interesting subjects like the First Amendment (go figure), the courts of appeals were largely left on their own to interpret the patent laws. Some courts of appeals seldom enforced patents, interpreting the Patent Act to match their opinions, while other courts of appeals did just the opposite. With little intervention by the Supreme Court to settle the disputes between the courts of appeals, chaos ensued.

This arrangement also encouraged forum shopping. *Forum shopping* is the process by which the first party to file a suit makes sure the suit is started in a district court within the jurisdiction of an appellate court that favors its case. Thus, people wishing to enforce patents picked courts that upheld patents, and people wishing to defeat patents picked courts that would not. Forum shopping severely undermined the value of patents, because whenever a patent holder offered to license a patent to a potential licensee, that potential licensee would run to the court of its choosing and seek to have the patent invalidated.

## The Patent World on Its Head

The establishment of the CAFC changed everything. The CAFC sits between the courts of appeals and the Supreme Court and hears patent infringement–related appeals, among other things, before they can be further appealed to the Supreme Court. If the CAFC did not enforce some patents, the CAFC would almost cease to exist, because the patent system would self-destruct. (If you can't enforce a patent, why bother getting one?) Given this outcome, the CAFC obviously began to enforce patents. By the late 1980s, patents went from being enforced less than 20 percent of the time to being enforced more than 80 percent of the time. It also began to normalize the decisions of the courts of appeals. As a result, forum shopping dropped dramatically. Both steps made patents much more valuable, so it became cost-effective to litigate patents. Litigation increased by 50 percent by the end of the 1980s as well. On top of all of that, damage awards in patent cases skyrocketed, exceeding $800 million in numerous cases, thereby significantly enhancing the value of patents overall.

The CAFC, however, is far from perfect. While the CAFC has many judges, only three typically hear any one case. As a result, some three-judge panels issue opinions that conflict with other three-judge panels. Once in a great while, all of the judges will hear a case, called *en banc,* to come up with a consensus opinion, but that is pretty rare, so the Supreme Court still has to intercede from time to time. Many other aspects of the patent system, aside from the CAFC, also require further corrective attention. Accordingly, efforts continue today to craft more effective patent laws. The latest effort is called the American Inventors Protection Act of 1999 (AIPA). The AIPA introduces new regulations that seek to do something about protecting inventors from disreputable invention promoters ("We'll help you get a patent and make millions!"), changes the term of protection for patents, introduces a new defense, and changes a number of other aspects of the U.S. patent system. I will discuss the AIPA at appropriate places throughout this section of the chapter.

## Why Patents Really Should Matter to You

Although it has always been considered an honor to get a patent—I am even honored to have my own application pending on behalf of MCI WorldCom—patents have not always figured heavily in the operations of many companies, but that is changing rapidly. Certain components of the communications industry, for example, were more focused on competing for customers than on anything else for many years (and still are). Others have been more focused on preserving monopolies (and still are). That is another subject entirely, but it helps to explain why local services and international calls can be so expensive. Over time, many of the long-distance companies have learned that competition comes in many different forms, including customers, employees, stock analysts, benefit plans, technologies, brand names, and even patents.

While AT&T had been collecting patents for many years, companies like MCI and Sprint had not. In addition to being a big service company, AT&T was a large equipment manufacturer, so its competitors figured AT&T's thousands of patents related to the nonservice side of the business. Like many Internet companies of today, they might have even assumed that patents did not really apply to their service businesses. Imagine their shock when AT&T came around with a number of patents allegedly covering the basic provisioning of 800 and 900 services. Sprint eventually took a license, provided that AT&T agreed to sue MCI if MCI did not also take a license. MCI decided to beat AT&T to court, so it sued AT&T, seeking to have the patents invalidated. AT&T countersued for patent infringement—and off they went. Many years later the parties settled the litigation (something I actually helped negotiate), but in the intervening years of battle, MCI and many other companies in the communication services business came to realize that it was important to have patents as well—which led to the creation of my job at MCI WorldCom. Thanks, AT&T!

Why did all of these companies decide it was better to have patents than to not have them? Well, consider this. Even a "small" long-distance company can produce a billion dollars a year in revenue. If you worked for such a company and it infringed a patent and was ordered to pay a small royalty, maybe 1 percent on the last six years of revenue, say $4.5 billion, your company would owe $45 million. This would cover only past damages, not future royalties. In the future, you might be enjoined from continuing to offer the service, or you might have to pay an even higher royalty for the continued privilege. However, if *your* company owned a patent that the *other* company infringed, the situation might be very different. You might be able to avoid paying anything, or you might even get some money back. If the other company was bigger, you could infringe many of its patents for every one of your own that it infringed, due to differences in revenue applied to the patents.

## To Fight or Switch?

Now which would you rather do, fight the other party on the basis of your litigator's truly wonderful skills and bargain-basement fees, or wave your own patents around in the other company's face, eventually resulting in a cross-license between the companies? What if I told you that for around $1 million you could defend yourself in a fairly serious patent infringement suit. With that same money, you could also apply for, issue, and maintain as many as 80 decent patents of your own? Which is the better investment? Money is literally wasted on defending yourself just so you can avoid having to pay more money in the future if you lose or else having to settle and take a license anyway. Money spent developing a patent portfolio will help keep other companies from suing you and possibly force them into a license.

These issues have nothing to do with the patent system's philosophical benefits or detriments to society. Tim Berners-Lee, one of the developers of the World Wide Web, recently stated that patents are ruining the Internet and encouraged people not to apply for them. Whether you agree with him or not, taking his advice wouldn't make sense unless you are certain everyone else in the world would do so as well. In short, it is a simple matter of business economics and reality—not personal opinion. A patent is an economic weapon that many of your competitors are going to use. No matter how much you don't like them or understand them (many ISPs fall into both categories), they exist. They are part of our Constitution, and they are not going away.

So what if you get a patent, then what? You have several options. A good defense usually requires more than a single shield, so it makes sense to have more than one patent. In fact, it makes sense to have quite a few of them, even if only for the purpose of preventing other people from getting them and using them against you. Also, once you get a patent, you don't have to do anything with it until you feel compelled to do so. But, if you are interested, you can do quite a bit. Many companies are interested in paying money for the right to sell your patents in areas you are not—and will even approach you and offer you money! Patents can also be used to generate business opportunities: exchanging a license for something else you might want but cannot buy, securing a bigger discount, improving the time to market for a product or service, and so on. You can get a patent on unused technology and license it to other people to recover the research and development dollars you expended. You can even get a patent on some standard technology you want to promote. For example, rather than use the patent to get money from the companies that implement the standard, you can charge them nothing and use the patent's enforcement rights to make sure those companies continue to conform to the standard in the future.

## Keeping Your Options

In other words, patents are all about options. The only limit is your imagination, and I have a pretty vivid one at times (my wife often wonders why my imagination seems to bloom only at work), so I have done some pretty wild things with patents, much to my employer's benefit. If you have applied for a patent, you have the option of pursuing it through to issuance. I will explain what "issuance" means shortly. If the patent issues, you have the option of deciding what to do with it. You don't have to do anything if you don't want to, or you can be as passive or as aggressive about licensing it as you want. The choice is yours. If you don't apply, or fail to take the steps that are necessary to prevent the loss of your patent rights by mistake or foolishness, then all of the options are gone, and you have no choice and no rights. So, what do you do?

Maybe you spend money for a relatively cheap and long-lasting insurance policy and the optional right to do other things. Maybe you just sit around complaining that you don't like patents, arguing that they shouldn't apply and/or will ruin the Internet, and musing about how life would be so much better if they just went away. Maybe you just wait until you get sued and then decide what to do. Only you can make these decisions for your own company, but MCI WorldCom went from 8 issued patents and 23 pending applications in the United States in 1995 when I joined the company to over 300 issued patents and more than 800 pending applications in the United States by the end of 1999. That gives you an idea of my company's opinion on the subject.

## What Are the Different Types of Patents?

One type of patent covers most inventions—the *utility patent.* There are also patents called *design patents* and *plant patents.* A plant patent protects new varieties of cultivated asexually reproduced plants, such as roses or grafted fruit trees, but not tuber-propagated plants (e.g., potatoes) or plants that can be found in an uncultivated state (i.e., naturally occurring). These won't be of much use to you. Design patents are for new, original, and ornamental designs of an article of manufacture. I once tried to get a design patent on some computer icons, but failed. The USPTO ultimately decided that icons were functional, not just ornamental, and therefore could not be protected by design patents. Design patents, along with copyrights (they cover different aspects of the design) can be used to protect things such as the shape and appearance of a computer housing, a water fountain, a lamp fixture, and so forth.

Apple used to file design patents on all of its computer housings. I don't know if it still does, but I noticed that Apple chose to sue a number of companies who produced designs similar to the iMac for trade dress infringement rather than for design patent infringement. I always thought of design patents as being of limited value because the claim of a design patent is the drawing of the design itself. If you include all of the vent lines and other detailed features of the design in your drawing, an infringer can adopt the same basic shape, but vary some of the other details and avoid infringement. Although I will more fully explain how infringement can be proven or avoided, for now suffice it to say that if you don't perform all of the elements or steps in a claim, you can't infringe that claim.

As it turns out, however, patent types are not mutually exclusive, so the same object that is protected with a design patent can also be protected with a utility patent, provided that different inventions, the ornamental and the functional, are covered by each. A copyright or trademark or trade dress might also apply. For example, a computer housing (such as Apple's iMac design) could be protected by a design patent because it has a new, original, and ornamental design, and a trade dress, but that same housing could also have utilitarian aspects, such as superior air-cooling capabilities, that separately qualify for protection.

## What Can Be Patented?

"[A]nything under the sun that is made by man" can be subject to patent protection, according to the Supreme Court. This quote comes from a 1980 decision called *Diamond v. Chakrabarty*. Diamond was the commissioner of the USPTO at the time, and Chakrabarty was an inventor whose patent application had been rejected by the USPTO. Chakrabarty sued the commissioner to get the USPTO decision overturned (this is the way it is supposed to work). Because the subject matter of the patent involved a man-made living organism, a certain type of bacteria, the Court ruled that the invention was patentable subject matter. Likewise, under the belief that there are certain "manifestations of . . . nature" that should be "free to all men and reserved exclusively to none," the Court also ruled that three categories of subject matter were not patentable—laws of nature, natural phenomena, and abstract ideas.

## Patenting Software and Computer-Implemented Inventions

I will leave the discussion about patenting bugs, and I don't mean the software variety, for some other venue, but believe it or not, this discussion about laws of nature and natural phenomena ended up being of critical importance to software. Here's why. In *Diamond*, the Court was interpreting the portion of the patent statutes that has to do with patentable subject matter, Section 101, which states that a patent may be issued for *any new and useful process, machine, manufacture, or composition of matter.* Despite the Court's rather simplistic ruling, the lower courts (and even the Supreme Court itself) have had a difficult time applying it to software-related inventions. Part of the reason for this is that the Supreme Court had previously ruled, back in 1972 (*Diamond* was decided in 1980), in a decision called *Gottschalk v. Benson*, that a certain type of computer program could not be patented. The program converted numbers from a binary-coded decimal form into a pure binary form. The Court ruled that the program was not patentable because the naturally occurring algorithm used to do the conversion had no application other than in connection with a digital computer and that granting of a patent on this program would completely preempt the use of that algorithm by others. Although the Court stated it was *not* holding computer programs to be unpatentable, it was setting a pretty high bar because virtually all programs used algorithms.

### Is Software a Fruit or Vegetable?

Based on *Gottschalk*, the USPTO Board of Appeals took the position that all computer software–related claims were naturally occurring, nonstatutory subject matter and therefore could not be patented. The Board of Appeals reached this conclusion because computer software was based on math (mathematical algorithms), and math was considered to be a manifestation of nature, so computer software must be a product of nature. Math was considered a manifestation of nature because math simply illustrates naturally occurring states (e.g., $E = mc^2$). In other words, math is discovered, not invented. The Board of Appeals stated that it thought this decision was in conformity with *Diamond*.

## The Freeman Test

Fortunately, the CCPA established a different test. This test stemmed from an appeal to the CCPA by an inventor named Freeman. The decision on the appeal is known as the *Application of Freeman*. The test developed in *Freeman* was to be used when determining whether a patent covered nonstatutory subject matter (e.g., a mathematical algorithm). The first part of the test involved determining whether the *patent claim* in question was a direct or indirect recitation of an algorithm, based on the theory that if the patent claim failed to even recite an algorithm, it clearly could not preempt one. The second part involved ascertaining whether, in its entirety, the patent claim wholly preempted that algorithm. In *Freeman* itself, the CCPA stopped before getting to the second part of the test because its application of the first part convinced it that the patent claim did not recite an algorithm.

Shortly thereafter, the Supreme Court got involved again (didn't I say they didn't like patent cases?) in a decision called *Parker v. Flook*. The patent claim involved in *Parker* was a method for updating alarm limits in the catalytic conversion of hydrocarbons. The claim covered a process having the following three steps:

1. Measuring a variable related to the alarm limit.
2. Using a mathematical algorithm to compute an updated alarm limit.
3. Adjusting the alarm limit accordingly.

Because the USPTO had concluded that only the second step was different from *prior art* methods used for this process, the patent application was originally rejected as nonstatutory. *Prior art* generally includes relevant documents within a particular field of science (the *art*) that were published before a patent application was filed on an invention. The Board of Appeals agreed, but the CCPA reversed on the grounds that *Benson* applied only to claims that entirely preempted an algorithm, and because this claim involved postsolution activity, step 3, it was distinguishable from *Benson*. In *Parker*, the Supreme Court rejected these arguments and went on to state that the proper way to analyze such a claim was to treat the algorithm as though it were part of the prior art, in which case all of the elements were in the prior art. As a result, the Court found the claim to be obvious and therefore unpatentable.

## The Freeman-Walter Test

In view of *Parker*, the CCPA went back and modified the second portion of the Freeman test in an appeal called the *Application of Walter*. This modification, called the Freeman-Walter test, attempted to draw a distinction between algorithms simply being incorporated into claims versus algorithms actually being used in claims to produce some physical thing or result. This distinction clarified nothing, so in *Dia-*

*mond v. Diehr*, the Supreme Court tried once again. This time the claims at issue involved an improved method for curing rubber, which involved the continual measurement of the temperature inside a press and then feeding that information back to a computer to calculate the temperature and time needed to determine the best time to open the press. The Court admitted that the claims actually recited a well-known equation and implementation in a programmed computer. Nevertheless, the Court held that the issue was whether that equation was being claimed in the "abstract" or as "applied" in a claim when viewed as a whole to create a statutory invention under Section 101. The Court found that it was an applied algorithm, and thus the claims were allowed.

## The Freeman-Walter-Abele Test

The CCPA then tried again in an appeal called *In re Abele* to apply the Court's direction by further modifying the Freeman-Walter test as follows: (1) Does the claim recite an algorithm either directly or indirectly? (2) If so, is the algorithm applied in any manner to physical elements or process steps, provided that the application is limited by more than a field-of-use limitation or nonessential postsolution activity? This new test was called Freeman-Walter-Abele.

## Enough with the Tests Already!

At this point, the CCPA was dissolved and rolled into the CAFC. The CAFC went on to rule, in a series of additional cases not worth mentioning specifically, that the Freeman-Walter-Abele test wasn't very good and that in fact software claims that did something more than just claim the algorithm, as well as computer-implemented apparatus claims, were patentable.

Despite my heading that says "enough," I *will* mention two more cases. The *Warmerdam* appeal, a post-*Abele* decision, was particularly entertaining because the CAFC found that the method claims in *Warmerdam,* which were for generating a data structure representing a set of artificial circular boundaries, or bubbles, for a collision-avoidance system, were unpatentable. But, the CAFC found that the single apparatus claim, for a machine with a memory that contains the exact same data structure representing the bubble hierarchy generated by the method claims, was patentable subject matter. In other words, almost anything found to be unpatentable subject matter, such as a data structure, could be turned into patentable subject matter if simply claimed in the memory of a computer.

## Patented Memory

This decision led to the idea that any form of memory, such as a floppy disk, could be protected if the data stored therein met other patent criteria, such as novelty. Because the PTO had been denying applications for "storage medium(s) claimed as an article of manufacture," a test case was put forth called *In re Beauregaurd. Beauregaurd* involved appeals by several applicants, including IBM. During the course of litigating this appeal, the USPTO cut the matter short by stating that "computer programs embodied in a tangible medium, such as floppy diskettes, are patentable subject matter under 35 USC Section 101." As a result, the CAFC dismissed the case because the USPTO and the appellants were in agreement, so there was no dispute. Even though *Beauregaurd* resolved itself in a strange way, it was still an important decision to the software industry. Here's why.

### Who Do You Sue?

Patented software is generally sold on CDs and floppy disks, but patent claims are generally written to cover the function of the software, not the disembodied form of the software stored on some medium. Because the patent claims covered the use and function of the software, and a CD including the patented software did nothing on its own, prior to *Beauregaurd* it wasn't considered an infringement of the patent simply to sell the CD. Thus, if a software company wanted to enforce its patent rights against a competitor selling software covered by its patents, it had no choice but to sue that competitor's customers, the entities actually using the software or making and using the machine programmed with the software. I'm not sure what they intend to do about software downloaded over the Internet, because this was not really addressed by *Beauregaurd.* Maybe we will start to see patent claims directed to software stored in the memory of a router. Either way, the patent owner is not really interested in suing the users of the software, who are often its customers as well, because each user typically represents only one infringement out of millions.

At any rate, as a result of all of this, it is now very clear that software is patentable if a patent claim to that software meets all of the other requirements of patentability, which we'll discuss shortly.

## Patenting Business Methods

Turning now to the patentability of methods of doing business, we see a similar mess. When I went to law school, it was well settled that methods of doing business were considered to be nonstatutory subject matter, but unlike software and computer-implemented inventions, there has been no case law on this direct subject. For example, Ronald B. Hildreth authored a book, *Patent Law: A Practitioner's Guide,* published by the Practicing Law Institute in 1993, which stated that "[a] patent cannot be secured for a system of doing business." This changed, however, when the Supreme Court let stand the CAFC's 1998 decision in *State Street Bank & Trust Co. v. Signature Financial Group, Inc.*

Signature had obtained a patent that covered the method of operating a pooled mutual fund as well as the data processing system that permitted multiple mutual funds with the same investment objectives to pool their funds in a common portfolio. Signature's data processing system calculated the daily value of assets held in the common portfolio and allocated those assets, and any gain or loss, to each individual fund based on the fund's partnership interest at the end of each trading day. State Street Bank sought to license the data processing system, but when negotiations broke down, it sought to invalidate Signature's patent on the basis of the algorithm exception (they lost this one, too) and the business methods exception. State Street Bank initially won a summary judgment ruling on the basis of the business method exception, but the CAFC (in an opinion authored by Judge Rich) reversed that ruling. The CAFC, finally, specifically rejected the Freeman-Walter-Abele test in favor of determining whether the invention produces a "useful, concrete, and tangible result," which could include the singular output of a number. The court also stated that "since the 1952 Patent Act, business methods have been, and should have been, subject to the same legal requirements for patentability as applied to any other process or method."

Because the USPTO had been holding onto a number of Internet-related business method patent applications pending the outcome in *State Street*, a large number of business method patents issued shortly after the *State Street* decision. Some of those making headlines include Cybergold's patents (5,794,210 and 5,855,008) for paying consumers to look at advertisements on the Internet, Netcentives Inc.'s patent (5,774,870) for an online frequency award program, Amazon.com's patent (5,960,411) for 1-click purchase technology, and Priceline.com's patent (5,897,620) for reverse seller's auctions on the Internet. Copies of any of these patents can be obtained from the USPTO's web site (www.uspto.gov). A copy of the front page of the Priceline patent appears in Figure 2.8. In addition to a fairly significant public outcry relating to the *extension* of patent rights to business methods, the American Inventors Protection Act (AIPA) included a new defense that is applicable only to business method inventions—perhaps signaling Congress's discomfort as well. The new defense is discussed subsequently under the heading The First Inventor Defense.

## *The Anatomy of a Patent*

Because all modern patents are processed for electronic printing and storage, the information in a patent is assigned different section numbers. With reference to Figure 2.8, the patent number (Section [11]) appears in the upper right-hand corner, right above the patent's issue date (Section [45]). The last name of the first listed inventor is shown in the upper left-hand corner. The title of the patent is listed in Section [54]. The title is intended to provide only a very general description of the field of the invention. All of the inventors, if more than one, are listed in Section [75], followed by the assignee in Section [73]. If the inventor(s) did not assign ownership of the patent to anyone before the patent issued, when the patent was first printed, no assignee will be listed. Most inventors work for someone else, so the assignee is usually the company the inventor(s) worked for at the time of the invention. Patents are often assigned after they are printed, so if you really want to know who owns the patent now, you will do an assignment search of the Patent Office's records.

Section [22] lists the filing date, which is the date the application that resulted in the patent was first filed with the Patent Office. Many patents will also list historical information about that patent application under the filing date. When you see that the patent application was a continuation, a division, or a continuation-in-part of other patent applications, you know that it took the inventor(s) a while to get the patent issued and that the actual filing date may be as early as the earliest date in the

# United States Patent [19]

## Walker et al.

[11] **Patent Number:** **5,897,620**

[45] **Date of Patent:** **Apr. 27, 1999**

[54] **METHOD AND APPARATUS FOR THE SALE OF AIRLINE-SPECIFIED FLIGHT TICKETS**

[75] Inventors: **Jay S. Walker**, Ridgefield; **Thomas M. Sparico**, Riverside; **T. Scott Case**, Darien, all of Conn.

[73] Assignee: **priceline.com Inc.**, Stamford, Conn.

[21] Appl. No.: **08/889,304**

[22] Filed: **Jul. 8, 1997**

[51] Int. Cl.⁶ ...................................................... G06F 17/60

[51] Int. Cl.$^6$ .................................................. G06F 17/60
[52] U.S. Cl. ...................................................... **705/5**; 705/6
[58] Field of Search ................................. 705/5, 6, 7, 9, 705/28; 707/1, 2, 3, 102, 104

[56] **References Cited**

### U.S. PATENT DOCUMENTS

| | | | |
|---|---|---|---|
| 4,775,936 | 10/1988 | Jung | 705/5 |
| 4,845,625 | 7/1989 | Stannard | 705/5 |
| 4,931,932 | 6/1990 | Dalnekoff et al. | 705/5 |
| 5,237,499 | 8/1993 | Garback | 705/5 |
| 5,253,165 | 10/1993 | Leiseca et al. | 705/5 |
| 5,270,921 | 12/1993 | Hornick | 705/5 |
| 5,331,546 | 7/1994 | Webber et al. | 705/6 |
| 5,483,444 | 1/1996 | Heintzeman et al. | 705/5 |
| 5,570,283 | 10/1996 | Shoolery et al. | 705/5 |
| 5,797,127 | 8/1998 | Walker et al. | 705/5 |

### OTHER PUBLICATIONS

Richard Carroll, *Hitch a Flight to Europe*, p. 1, <http//travelassist.com/mag/a69.html>. not dated.

*Airhitch Your Way To Low Cost Travel*, pp. 1, 2, <http://www.vaportrails.com/Budget/BudFeatures/Airhitch/Airhitch.html>. not dated.

Sue Goldstein, Airhitch, p. 1. not dated.

Miles Poindexter, *Airhitch: Myth or Fact*, pp. 1, 2. not dated.

*Frequently Asked Questions about Airhitch*, pp. 1–5, 1995, <http://www.isicom.fr/airhitch/ahfaq>.

*Across the Atlantic Anytime for $169!!!*, pp. 1, 2, <http://www.isicom.fr/airhitch/index.html>. not dated.

*Airhitch, General Information, New!!! Target Flights Update*, pp. 1–6, <http://www.isicom.fr/airhitch/info.htm>. not dated

*Target Flight(R) Quote Request Form*, pp. 1, 2, <http://www.isicom.fr/airhitch/tf_qrf.txt>. not dated.

*Working For/With Airhitch*, pp. 1–5, <http://www.isicom.fr/airhitch/jobs.htm>. not dated.

(List continued on next page.)

Primary Examiner—Stephen R. Tkacs
Attorney, Agent, or Firm—Morgan & Finnegan LLP; Jeffrey L. Brandt

[57] **ABSTRACT**

An unspecified-time airline ticket representing a purchased seat on a flight to be selected later, by the airlines, for a traveler-specified itinerary (e.g., NY to LA on March 3rd) is disclosed. Various methods and systems for matching an unspecified-time ticket with a flight are also disclosed. An exemplary method includes: (1) making available an unspecified-time ticket; (2) examining a plurality of flights which would fulfill the terms of the unspecified-time ticket to determine which flight to select; and (3) providing notification of the selected flight prior to departure. The disclosed embodiments provide travelers with reduced airfare in return for flight-time flexibility and, in turn, permits airlines to fill seats that would have otherwise gone unbooked. Because of the flexibilities required of the unspecified-time traveler, unspecified-time tickets are likely to attract leisure travelers unwilling to purchase tickets at the available published fares and, at the same time, are likely to "fence out" business travelers unwilling to risk losing a full day at either end of their trip. Moreover, the flexibilities required of the unspecified-time traveler need not be limited to a departure time; the flexibilities may also include the airline, the departing airport, the destination airport, or any other restriction that increases the flexibility afforded the airline in placing the traveler aboard a flight. The disclosed embodiments thus permit airlines to fill otherwise empty seats in a manner that stimulates latent and unfulfilled leisure travel demand while leaving their underlying fare structures intact.

**101 Claims, 20 Drawing Sheets**

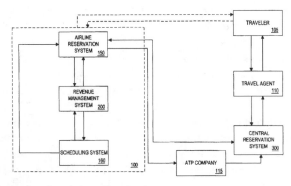

**Figure 2.8** Example of an Internet patent.

historical listing. Section [56] lists the references (also called *prior art*) that were cited by the Patent Office during the examination of the patent application. There is almost always at least one reference cited, sometime hundreds of them, which will be listed on the next page or two of the patent. As a general rule, if you are trying to invalidate a patent and the prior art references you have found are no better than any reference listed on the face of the patent, you don't stand a very good chance of succeeding. A court will usually defer to the examiner's decision to allow the patent to issue over the listed prior art references, especially if that prior art is better than your prior art.

Section [57] includes an abstract of the patent. An abstract is just a general description of the patented invention. The same person that wrote the patent application usually

## Side Law: International Protection

Almost every country has its own patent laws, although there are a few exceptions where some smaller countries, such as Liechtenstein, have basically adopted the laws of other countries. A patent issued in any one country, however, is enforceable only in that country and no others. Accordingly, if you want worldwide protection for an invention, you theoretically have to apply in every one of the more than 220 countries around the world. Before you let yourself get talked into this by a patent attorney, let me explain why it isn't necessary. First, many countries are closed societies, use few modern technologies, and/or have virtually nonexistent economies. Even if you could obtain a patent in one of them, it is unlikely that anyone would infringe it, unlikely that you would be able to enforce your rights, and even more unlikely that you would be able to collect sufficient damages even if you did. Furthermore, the judicial systems in many countries highly favor the citizens of that country over any foreigners, so it is often naive to assume that you will be treated fairly. As a result, the vast majority of all patents around the world are issued by a handful of industrialized countries where people have learned to trust the results of their courts.

Even in these few countries, the cost of international patent protection is still a big deterrent. In the United States, all patent applications must be filed in English, regardless of the country of origin. If you are a Japanese applicant, you must have your application translated from Japanese. The same is true for U.S. applicants filing applications in non-English-speaking countries. The cost of these translations can be astronomical, and they are not always very good, which can compromise the quality and enforceability of the resulting patent. I once had a Japanese patent translated three different times by three different translators. Each translation was significantly different from the next, so I ended up using the one I liked best, regardless of whether it was accurate. Thus, if you want patent protection in Western Europe, North America, and parts of Asia, you might have to have your patent application translated into 10 or more different languages. The United States does not charge any additional standard fees once your application is filed until a decision is made regarding its patentability, but many countries charge a standard fee every year just to maintain your application. As a result of all of this, while it may cost only $10,000 to $15,000 to obtain a U.S. patent, it generally costs $25,000 to $50,000 per country to obtain patents outside the United States, meaning that worldwide protection for a single patent can easily exceed $250,000. It better be good!

wrote the abstract. The abstract is intended to attractively describe the invention and must be no more than 250 words long. Don't be fooled into thinking that the abstract accurately describes the legal coverage of the patent. Only the claims, which are the numbered paragraphs at the very back of the patent, set forth the basic legal scope of the patent. Even then, the scope of the claims is subject to all sorts of limitations based on what the inventor said in the remainder of the patent application and during the process of getting the patent, so don't rely solely on the wording in the claims, either. If you really want to understand the scope of a patent, get a patent attorney to help you. At the bottom of the right-hand column, the number of claims and the number of drawing pages will be listed, right above an exemplary drawing of the invention.

# When Does an Idea Become a Patentable Invention?

Once you have determined that an idea could be subject to patent protection in the United States because it conforms to the basic subject matter analysis just discussed, you still have to figure out whether that idea is in fact a patentable invention. I mention the United States because patents are territorial by nature. (See Side Law: International Protection.)

## The Invention Must Be Novel

In most countries, however, an idea is considered to be patentable when, at the time of its invention, it is novel, useful, and not obvious to a person of ordinary skill in the art (i.e., the field of the invention). Basically, an invention is considered to be *novel* when no one else has previously invented the same thing. This means that the invention was not already known in that country prior to the alleged date of invention. Because it can be very difficult to prove what people knew at a particular time, patent systems generally rely on the following types of evidence, called *prior art*, for proof of prior invention:

- A description in a patent or printed publication by someone else anywhere in the world before the date of invention

- A description in a patent or printed publication by anyone (including the inventor) more than one year prior to the application filing date

- Proof of use or sale by anyone (including the inventor) in the country more than one year prior to the application filing date

I cannot overemphasize the importance and significance of such prior art when attempting to prove that a patent is invalid because it isn't novel. I have been confronted with many controversial patents over the years. Every time I would ask the engineers and programmers about prior art that existed at the time of the invention, which is usually presumed to be one year before the first application filing date, I would invariably get the same response: They first look at the patent issue date and exclaim: "How could they get a patent on that? Everybody was doing that five years ago." Because the application filing date is often many years before the patent issue date (see Figure 2.8), proof of something that happened after the application filing date isn't much help. Furthermore, when you ask for proof of what everyone was doing, it often doesn't exist. As the year 2000 remediation effort has taught us, programmers did not always do a very good job of documenting or commenting in their software code. Hence, I willingly believe the programmers when they tell me a patent is invalid, but I don't put much faith in their statements, either, because they can rarely find the proof needed to prevail in court. Neither the patent office nor the courts will just believe what you tell them—you have to have proof. Accordingly, you might want to consider archiving software, documentation, HTML code, and anything else that might prove useful in a future defense to a claim of patent infringement.

## The Invention Must Be Useful

Presuming an invention is novel, you must also figure out whether it is *useful* before it can be patented. This rule seems rather silly in the context of software and business method patents, but it can be quite important in other contexts. For example, certain drug combinations, such as steroids, are rejected under this rule if the patentee cannot state what the new compound could be used to cure or prevent (illness, injury, etc.). Perpetual-motion devices are also rejected as not useful because no patentee has ever been able to demonstrate that any such device actually works. Inventions are also considered not to be useful if they are frivolous, illegal, or immoral, such as a marijuana cigarette–rolling machine (which is illegal).

## The Invention Cannot Be Obvious

Even if an idea is novel and useful, to be patentable, it cannot be *obvious*. The test for obviousness is pretty much the same around the world. In the United States, the test is set forth in Section 103 of the patent statutes, which states in part that "[a] patent may not be obtained . . . if the differences between the subject matter sought to be patented and the prior art are such that the subject matter as a whole would have been obvious at the time the invention was made to a person having ordinary skill in the art to which said subject matter pertains." The easiest way to apply this rule is to pretend to lay the prior art out in front of a hypothetical person of ordinary skill in the art and ask whether the invention would have been obvious to that person at the time of the invention. If the invention is merely what one would expect of a person in that field, or is a mere rearrangement of parts, steps, and/or proportions, it would be considered obvious. On the other hand, if application of the invention creates some disproportionate, unexpected, surprising, or unusual result, or suddenly causes the product or service to obtain market success where there was none, then the answer might be different.

To apply this concept to any of the recently issued Internet-related patents, such as Priceline.com's *name your own price* patent (U.S. Patent No. 5,794,207), you must first look at a representative claim of one of the patents and break that claim down by its constituent parts. For example, claim 1 of Priceline.com's 5,794,207 patent defines a method of using a computer to facilitate a transaction between a buyer and at least one seller, including the following steps:

- Inputting into the computer a conditional purchase offer which includes an offer of price
- Inputting into the computer a payment identifier specifying a credit card account, the payment identifier being associated with the conditional purchase offer

- Outputting the conditional purchase offer to the plurality of sellers after receiving the payment identifier
- Inputting into the computer an acceptance from a seller, the acceptance being responsive to the conditional purchase offer
- Providing a payment to the seller by using the payment identifier

To analyze the patentability of this claim, think of all of the prior art references that might have existed at the time the patent application was first filed—September 4, 1996. Because the general rule is that an inventor is presumed to have first invented something up to one year before the inventor's filing date, eliminate any reference that does not predate the filing date by more than one year (true only in the United States). Then ask yourself, "Is every limitation stated in each paragraph of the claim shown by some prior art reference that was published before September 4, 1995 (in the case of the Priceline.com patent)?" If the answer is yes, then claim 1 may be invalid in view of that reference, but that is only one of many different claims, and you will need to perform the same analysis for each of the other claims. There are 44 total claims in the Priceline.com patent.

It is more likely that no single reference includes all of the claim limitations, so you must then begin to look for the missing limitations in other references. For example, prior to September 4, 1995, people unquestionably used e-mail to transmit offers to buy goods from other parties. I am sure an article could be found that includes this information. Remember that the USPTO and the courts will generally consider only published references as prior art, which tends to reduce fraud. The described activity would probably be equivalent to *inputting into the computer a conditional purchase which includes an offer of price.* But it is unlikely that those who sent such an e-mail also sent their credit card number along with their conditional purchase offer, or that they communicated the same offer to multiple sellers, for fear of having their offer accepted multiple times. If you can't find all of the missing limitations, and the limitations are not otherwise trivial, then the claim may be valid over those references.

Even if you find all of the limitations in all of your different references, you still have to ask yourself, "Would it have been obvious to someone of ordinary skill in this field of science at the time of the invention (approximately one year before the filing date) to have combined the missing limitation together to get the patented invention?" For example, say you found an article describing a pork bellies commodity exchange that used a computerized system for bidding on futures contracts that operated by sending the same bid to multiple parties. Would it have been obvious to combine the teachings of the pork bellies article with your e-mail article? If SEC rules prohibited the use of e-mail (I have no idea about this fact, I am just making all of this up), then it might not have been obvious to someone in either field to combine the two ideas. As a result of this type of obviousness analysis, the answer to the preceding question is often, "I'm not sure."

When you aren't sure about the answer, you apply what is called the *John Deere analysis.* This analysis comes from a famous case called *Graham v. John Deere Co.* In *Graham,* the U.S. Supreme Court established the following process for determining the obviousness of an invention:

1. Determine the scope and content of the prior art.
2. Ascertain the differences between the prior art and the claims at issue.
3. Resolve the level of ordinary skill in the pertinent art.
4. Determine the obviousness or nonobviousness of the subject matter against that background.
5. If necessary, secondary considerations, such as the commercial success, long-felt but unresolved needs, failure of others, and so on can be utilized to give light to the circumstances surrounding the origin of the subject matter sought to be patented.

Considering all this, I usually break down the analysis of the obviousness of a particular claimed invention by first separating the claim into elements. For example, a claim covering a coffee cup might include element A as the handle, element B as the cylindrical container, and so on. I then try to determine whether any of the prior art describes one of these elements and, if so, in what way and in what combination with other elements. If in the end one of the elements (provided that element isn't trivial or insignificant to the invention) isn't described by any of the prior art, or if the combination of elements isn't shown by the art, then I will probably consider the invention not to be obvious. Most people consider obviousness only in the defense of a claim of infringement or in the prosecution of a patent, but rarely go through this analysis when deciding whether to file a patent application, because of the subjectiveness of the analysis. With respect to whether to file or not file a patent application, the USPTO and its examiners are most skilled at making obviousness determinations, so it is generally better to let them earn the filing fees you have to pay for this decision. Once they decide, if you disagree, you can always argue the decision—all the way to the Supreme Court if you like.

## Patentability Bars

In the same manner that possession of such evidence can present a problem for other patent holders, it can also present a significant problem for you when you want to patent something. Generally, you will be barred from obtaining a patent on an idea if you have previously described your idea in a publicly available document, or used that idea in public, or offered that idea for sale. In the United States, you have a one-year grace period from the time that you have committed an act that is considered to *bar* you (prevent you) from being able to get a patent application on the idea on file with the USPTO. In the rest of the world, there is no grace period, so if you want patent protection, you need to seek it before you commit any one of those acts. The grace period in the United States has caused many problems and may eventually be eliminated, so even a grace period should not be relied upon. (See Side Law: First to Invent versus First to File.) It is always advisable, if patent protection matters to you at all, to make sure you have filed for patent protection before disclosing your invention publicly (such as in a technical paper), using your invention publicly (even if no one could have seen it), or offering to sell anything that incorporates your invention to anyone. With respect to this last condition, it is very important to realize that an actual sale is not required and that the thing you are selling need not exist either. As long as you know how you would create or operate whatever it is that you intend to sell, and believe you could deliver it as promised, even if you never do, the mere offer to sell will be considered a bar to patentability of any underlying idea.

## Side Law: First-to-Invent versus First-to-File

An invention always has to be filed in the country in which it was first invented, regardless of the nationality of the inventors or the country of origin of the inventor's employer. Hence it is very important to understand the basic patent laws of each country in which you operate your business. The United States presently follows what is called a *first-to-invent* patent system. The rest of the world, for the most part, follows what is called a *first-to-file* system. Because the United States gives its inventors a one-year grace period, during which the invention could be disclosed and claimed to have been invented by someone else, the United States also attempts to make sure it awards the resulting patent to the real first inventor—the "first to invent." Most other countries, however, do not provide such a grace period and will award a patent to the first party to file a patent application on the invention—the "first to file." Thus, if you invent something in the United States and want international protection, you must file for protection in the United States before committing a barring act, or you will lose your legal right to seek protection in other countries. You can, of course, always file for protection in the other countries, but if anyone ever finds out that your application was illegal, any resulting patent will be taken away, and you might get into legal trouble. If any of these barring acts occurred more than one year before your U.S. filing date, you will likewise lose your right to seek protection in the United States.

# Term of Patent Protection

As previously mentioned, a patent grants its owner the right to exclude others from making, using, or selling the claimed invention in the country of grant for a limited period of time. Most of the world grants a term of 20 years from the original filing date of the subject matter claimed in the patent. For many years, the United States granted a term of only 17 years from the date of issuance, but this caused many problems, especially with regard to intercountry harmonization and so-called submarine patents. A *submarine patent* is a colloquial term for a patent that has remained pending ("submerged") in the USPTO for many years (at least 10 or more) and that issues ("emerges") with claims covering technology that has become widely used during the intervening period.

A now-deceased inventor named Jerome Lemelson was particularly famous for a number of submarine patents that he kept submerged within the USPTO for decades through continuation applications and other tricks of the trade, then emerged with claims broadly covering things like bar-code-automated assembly lines. In an interesting twist on this, one of Lemelson's former employers, a mining company, has now claimed that Lemelson invented these ideas while working for the company and that it now owns the rights to the patents and all of the royalties paid to Lemelson over the years. Gilbert Hyatt also became famous when his patent on the basic semiconductor microprocessor emerged from the PTO after about 40 years. After briefly adopting a system whereby patents were protected for a term of 20 years from the date of filing or 17 years from issuance, the United States adopted a new system in 1999. Now a diligent applicant is guaranteed at least a 17-year term from the date of issuance because the U.S. patent laws automatically extend (day for day) the term of any patent not granted within three years of filing. Such extensions are intended to compensate only those inventors who have had the issuance of their patent delayed by the USPTO, and they cannot be used by inventors to purposely manipulate the patent system to delay the issuance of their patents.

## The Pending Patent Application

Historically, a patent application was confidentially maintained by the USPTO until any resulting patent issued. In accordance with the American Inventors Protection Act (AIPA), an applicant can request that his or her application be published, or alternatively, the USPTO will publish the pending patent application 18 months after the earliest filing date unless the application is:

- Abandoned
- Subject to a secrecy order
- A provisional application
- A design patent application
- Subject to a request not to publish

The decision to publish as well as the actual information to be published is determined by the USPTO. An applicant can avoid publication upon request and certification that the application has not been filed in any other country that will require publication of the application 18 months after filing. An applicant who has requested that an application not be published must rescind the request if the foreign filing situation changes. An intentional failure to comply with the rescission requirement will result in abandonment of any resulting patent.

Historically, a pending patent application had no exclusive right associated with it (other than a trade secret right prior to publication) and could not be used to prevent infringement while pending. The AIPA changes this rule somewhat by offering inventors whose applications were published by the USPTO before issuance a new provisional right to obtain a reasonably royalty from an infringer. The right exists only between the time the application was first published and issuance of the patent. If someone uses, offers for sale, sells, or imports the invention as a result of the application being published before issuance, the patent owner can go back and collect royalties, under very limited conditions, for such pre-grant usage after the patent is issued. For now, however, applicants aren't totally helpless to discourage their inventions from being used.

Once a patent application has been filed, an applicant can mark a product or service (usually the marketing, advertising, and billing associated with it) that incorporates the invention claimed in the patent application as "patent pending." Since patent applications are maintained in secrecy until either issued or otherwise published, the "patent pending" notice effectively puts a competitor on guard, but without any details about the nature of the alleged invention. Because any part of the product or service could be subject to the pending patent, this can operate as a significant deterrent to some competitors. Be careful: Improper use of this notice can result in a fine and possible civil liability.

# The Transfer of Patent Rights

While a patent application cannot be enforced, it can be assigned (sold) or licensed, as can a patent. In fact, both patents and patent applications (which I will refer to as patents) can be assigned or licensed in a myriad of ways. The exclusive rights to make, use, or sell can be assigned or licensed in whole or in part. Thus, a patent owner could sell the exclusive right to manufacture to Company A, license Company B and Company C to use the patent, and sell the exclusive right to sell to Company D and Company E. The patent owner could also assign or license the exclusive rights with respect to different territories within the United States. I made up an unusual license agreement myself years ago when I purchased an option to exercise the right to acquire the exclusive right to nonexclusively license or enforce a portfolio of patents to or against a particular company. As you can see, a vivid imagination is one of the requirements. Another is that an assignment must be in writing and recorded at the USPTO or else the assignment is void against a subsequent bona fide purchaser for value. Licenses, on the other hand, do not have to be in writing or recorded, but they do have to be carefully constructed by both parties, which I will talk about later.

# What Is the Process for Getting a Patent?

Now that you know why patents exist, what can be patented, and what you can do with one, how do you go about getting one? First and foremost, hire a patent attorney or patent agent who is registered to practice before the USPTO or appropriate patent office. A patent agent is someone who is licensed to write patent applications and work them through the USPTO, but is not otherwise licensed to practice law in any state. As you can see, patent law is so complicated and subject to such frequent changes that even skilled practitioners have trouble staying current with the law and making sure they are doing the correct thing at all times. Assuming you have hired a patent professional, it is now safe to at least walk you through the process.

The patent attorney or agent (the "attorney") will want to talk to the inventors or have them fill out an invention disclosure form. Either way, the attorney is seeking to collect certain details about the inventors and the idea that will enable the attorney to determine if the idea is patentable. A thorough description of the invention, including drawings, will help explain it and enable the attorney to write a draft of the patent application. A description and copies of any prior art will help determine the patentability of the invention. It will also help if the inventors can explain why their invention is different from or better than the prior art and to know whether there is any evidence of secondary considerations. The attorney will also try to find out if there has been or will soon be a barring event, such as an offer for sale or public disclosure. A disclosure pursuant to an appropriate nondisclosure agreement is not considered a public disclosure.

## *Avoiding Bars—the Bad Kind*

Inventors frequently wait until the last minute to tell the patent attorney about an invention. This frequently results in many late nights, increased expenses, and mistakes—all in an effort to avoid the quickly approaching one-year anniversary date of a disclosure or an offer for sale (the one-year anniversary is called a *bar date* because you are barred from seeking patent protection after that date). Inventors should always be encouraged to make the patent people aware of an invention as soon as possible. A patent application of average complexity typically takes 20 to 30 hours of billed attorney time to prepare, depending on the efficiency of the attorney and the complexity of the invention. I have written some 450 patent applications, some in as few as 10 hours and one that took over 120 hours. At almost $300 per hour, you didn't want to be the one paying that bill (over $35,000).

## Drafting the Application

Keep in mind that it takes about three days to bill 20 hours. It is mentally tiring to work all day long writing a single patent application, so most attorneys spread the time out over a larger number of days. If you have a complex invention and leave the attorney only a few days to write it, you will probably get a poorly written application. Also keep in mind that the attorney cannot always drop everything else to help you because you delayed. Inventors are sometimes frustrated by the length of time it takes to get a patent application drafted, but they forget that the attorneys are often working on a large number of different inventions in different fields of art for different clients. That attorney might spend every week, or even days in the same week, immersed in completely different technologies. The attorneys often have other priorities as well and frequently have to spend time, or should, researching the technology associated with your invention. This enables them to be better informed when they try to write your draft application, but it takes time. It is therefore not realistic to expect the attorney to be as knowledgeable about a given technology as you might be or to be able write a patent application as quickly as you think it should be written.

Once a draft has been written, the inventor will be asked to review it and make corrections. There may be a number of iterations of this process as the draft is improved. Once the application is ready for filing, a number of forms will be created, such as a declaration and an assignment. The declaration is a written oath to the government that is submitted with your patent application in which you swear that you are the first true inventor of the invention. If you work for someone else, it is highly likely that your invention really belongs to them, because it relates to your job, or because you invented it at work, or because you used your employer's equipment and facilities to invent it. In such cases, you will be expected to assign the invention to your employer, who will then file the application on your behalf. Most employees sign a form when they first start a new job requiring them to assign their inventions to their employer, so most patent applications are filed by companies. If you think that you and not your employer own the invention, I encourage you to seek legal counsel to establish ownership before doing anything else.

## Prosecuting the Patent Application

Once the patent application has been filed, it is prosecuted through the patent office. *Prosecution* is the term of art that has been adopted, I don't know why, to describe the process of arguing with the patent office regarding the patentability of the invention and, if you win this argument, negotiating with the patent office over the scope and patentability of the invention. Each patent application is assigned to a patent examiner on a FIFO (first-in, first-out) basis. It can therefore frequently take more than a year or two to get a first response from the patent office, especially in the software and Internet-related fields, so be patient. The vast majority of patent applications are initially rejected, for some reason or another, by the patent office. Any rejection that is received should be analyzed for accuracy and to determine whether it can be overcome. Many entry-level patent examiners are recent undergraduates and often lack the level of training obtained by the inventors, who often have master's and/or doctorate degrees in the field.

If it is deemed appropriate to argue the examiner's rejection, the attorney will prepare and file a response. If the examiner rejects the application again for the same reason, despite your arguments, the rejection is usually final. The examiner can reconsider a final rejection (unlikely), or it can be appealed to the Board of Appeals, or the entire application can be refiled as a continuation of the original. By paying an additional filing fee, you effectively buy the right to continue arguing the application. You can also add some additional matter, for example, if you have since improved your invention, in which case the application is called a *continuation-in-part* because part is new and part is old. The new part gets a new filing date and the old part keeps the original filing date. The submarine patents mentioned earlier were created by refiling the applications over and over again in response to rejections, thereby keeping them pending for years and years, until they finally wore down an examiner's resistance.

If the examiner, Board of Appeals, or a court agrees that your invention is patentable, it is *allowed*, which means you will receive a notice of allowance from the USPTO telling you that it has decided to grant you a patent covering the finally claimed invention. I say *finally claimed* invention because most applications are not allowed with the claims as originally filed. To get the examiner to agree to allow the application, you will frequently have to amend the claims, often more than once, to narrow the scope of the claims and to avoid prior art. Once the application is allowed, it is sent to the printing office. Although the USPTO has stated that it intends to speed up the printing process, in 1999 it took more than nine months on average to get a patent printed. Once the patent has been printed, the USPTO will assign an issue date and inform the inventors. New patents are issued every Tuesday, except on holidays.

# The Content of the Patent

The reason patent applications take so long is that they have to have a specification, including an abstract, a drawing (when necessary, and usually more than one is necessary), and a claim (at least one). The specification must include a complete and enabling description of the invention that sets forth the best mode of practicing the invention known to the inventors at the time the application was filed with the USPTO. Some attorneys will include only the minimal amount of information necessary to meet the statutory requirements of a disclosure, or rely on references to other publications to fill in background information, but this can be a big mistake, especially with complex technologies. The attorney sometimes forgets that it is his or her job is to write a patent application that can some day be litigated if necessary before a judge and jury who are not skilled in the technical field of the invention. A highly complex specification may impress the inventors, but it will only confuse the judge and jury. Despite the fact that the inventors may get annoyed with a lengthy layperson's discussion of well-known technology (to the inventors, at least), it is necessary to establish a basic understanding of the invention and will help to make the resulting patent much more valuable.

The drawings are pretty basic, although time-consuming, but it is the claims (the numbered paragraphs at the end of the specification) that take the most thought and are of the greatest importance. The best way to think of claims is to compare them to a deed of land. Like a deed of land, a patent claim sets forth the meets and bounds (or the four corners) of the property right. It is the claims, not the specification, that someone will infringe—or not. Over the years, I have had hundreds of employees come to me, concerned about somebody else's patent, after having read only the abstract of the specification. You have to read the claims to understand what the patent protects.

## Understanding Patent Claims

It is easy to understand why these people haven't read the claims, however, because at first blush the claims don't seem to make a lot of sense. Patent attorneys don't write claims like the following:

**Claim 1.**   A cup for holding beverages. The cup has a handle.

Rather, a claim for a coffee cup might look more like this:

**Claim 2.**   A beverage container, comprising

A hollow cylinder having an integrally closed end, said closed end being shaped so as to allow said cylinder to be placed in an upright position on a planar surface; and

A rigid, elongated, looped handle fixedly attached to said cylinder substantially perpendicular to said planar surface, thereby forming a container that can be filled with a beverage while positioned on a tabletop or like surface and lifted with said handle to a user's mouth.

Claims are written like claim 2 rather than claim 1 because the USPTO will reject a claim written like claim 1. Why? Doesn't claim 1 make more sense than claim 2? It might, at first glance, but remember that there are over 200 years of history behind the U.S. patent system, and many decisions have been handed down by the courts over the years interpreting what different words or claim structures mean. For example, to avoid any misunderstanding about where a claim begins and ends, it has been determined that each claim must be numbered (when there is more than one) and must be a single complete sentence—no matter how long. The claim must have an introduction for the claimed subject matter, called a *preamble,* to illustrate what the claim is about and to enable reference back to the claim in other claims. The claim must include a transition that bridges between the preamble and the body of the claim, such as *comprising* to establish whether the elements in the body of the claim are open-ended or closed-ended. *Comprising* is considered to be an open-ended transition, meaning that the claim can be infringed by something that includes at least the listed elements. The phrases *consisting of* and *consisting essentially of* are considered to be closed-ended transitions, meaning that the claim can be infringed only by something that includes solely the listed elements, nothing more and nothing less (in the case of *consisting of* ).

Claim 2 is actually clearer than claim 1 because it very carefully establishes the limits and scope of the claimed invention. For example, while claim 1 states that there is a handle, it doesn't state where the handle is located and how it is attached to the cup. Each element of a claim must be exact in order to distinguish each element, and the claim overall must be exact in order to allow anyone reading the claim to figure out what it covers and what it does not. For example, I know that a cup with two bulbous protrusions on opposite sides of an irregularly shaped bowl does not infringe claim 2, but I am not so sure about claim 1.

## The Issued Patent

Even though a patent has issued, it isn't free of the patent office. Because the USPTO follows the first-to-invent system, it can issue something called an *interference*. Most patent offices also issue reexaminations and will reissue patents. A patent interference results when the USPTO determines, on its own initiative or as the result of a petition, that two different inventors have claimed rights to the same invention. If your patent has issued, the USPTO can declare the interference only with someone else's pending application, because disputes between two issued patents have to be resolved through civil litigation and not within the USPTO. The purpose of the interference is to determine who was the first inventor.

A reexamination results when the patent office decides, on its own initiative or as the result of a petition, that a substantial new question of patentability has been raised about an issued patent. The present reexamination process in the United States is fatally flawed, because the requester is allowed to provide his or her arguments only in an initial request and is then cut out of the process. If the USPTO grants the request, the patent owner can then argue the case with the examiner (usually the one who examined the patent in the first place and who is very disinterested in admitting that he or she might have been wrong). As a result, most reexams merely serve to strengthen the patent in question, which results when the patent is again allowed over the newly cited art. Pending legislation is seeking to correct this problem.

A reissue results when a patent owner seeks to correct a patent as a result of an error, lacking deceptive intention, that causes the patent to be wholly or partially inoperative or invalid. Thus, if the patent owner becomes aware of new prior art that would have invalidated the patent, the patent owner can seek to narrow the scope of the patent to avoid any such later result. Likewise, if a patent owner discovers, but only within the first two years from issuance, that the patent covers less than the inventor had a right to, then the owner can seek to have the patent broadened.

## Patent Notice and Ownership

Once a patent has issued, the *patent pending* notice can be replaced with *patent* or *pat.* and the number of the patent. This notice is not required, and misuse can result in problems, but failure to use it can limit the damages obtainable from an infringer.

As with copyrights, the ownership of an invention originally belongs to the inventor(s), and only the inventor(s) can apply for a patent. However, as previously described, most inventors work for companies who have agreements (or hopefully do, anyway) with their employees that cause any employment-related inventions to be assigned to the company. The company then files for the patents on behalf of the inventors. If the company is a large company (over 500 employees) or a nonprofit organization, then the company has to pay the full amount of all of the various fees that will be charged. If the inventor applies on his or her own behalf or is with a small entity, the fees are significantly reduced. Generally, however, the government fees are small in comparison to the attorney's fees. Whereas the attorney's fees might be $8,000, the total cost of the application may be only $9,500.

## Patent Infringement

A patent has to be valid and enforceable in order to be infringed. To be valid, of course, the patent has to continue to meet the basic criteria for patentability. This is frequently an issue because, in the course of litigation, the defense often comes up with prior art and arguments to make before the court that were never considered by the examiner. A patent is presumed valid once issued, however, so the burden is on the defendant to prove otherwise, although newly discovered prior art that is more relevant than that considered by the examiner may be sufficient to overcome that burden. To be enforceable, the patent owner or applicant cannot have misused the patent or engaged in inequitable or unlawful conduct. Again, the patent is presumed enforceable, so the defendant has the burden of proving these facts as well.

Patents can be either directly or indirectly infringed, and such infringement can be either literal or equivalent. *Direct infringement* occurs when one defendant, or a group of defendants acting together, performs each and every element or step of one claim of one patent. Multiple claims of multiple patents may often be the subject of an infringement action, but only one claim of one patent needs to be infringed for some liability to result. If there is a direct infringer, there can also be *indirect infringers,* which are third parties who might also be liable because of inducement or contributory infringement. An *inducer* is someone who knowingly aids and abets someone else in the direct infringement of a patent. The knowledge requirement for inducement is pretty high, so the inducement must typically be purposeful and intentional.

*Contributory infringement* occurs when there has been a sale of a component of a patented item, where the component is a material part of the patent item and is not a staple article suitable for a substantial noninfringing use. Furthermore, the seller must have knowledge that the component was especially made for use in something (such as an apparatus, composition, or method) that would infringe a claim of the patent.

To *literally infringe* a claim, the infringer must perform each element or each step of the claim exactly as recited in the patent. Provided the claim does not use *consisting of* instead of *comprising,* as discussed earlier, the infringer can perform additional elements or steps without consequence. If the alleged infringer performs fewer elements or steps than appear in the claim, the claim is not infringed. The distinction between *comprising* and *consisting essentially of* is a bit more complicated. A claim of either *consisting essentially of* or *comprising* elements A, B, and C would be literally infringed by

---

## Side Law: Patent Infringement Applied to Internet

All of the rules that define different types of patent infringement apply to software, services, and hardware related to the Internet just as much as those rules apply in any other industry. For instance, with respect to the contributory infringement rule, if you sell a general-purpose search engine, and someone buys that search engine and builds it into a web site that then infringes a patent, which includes a search engine as a material part of the infringed claim, you probably won't be liable for contributory infringement. However, if you sell a search engine that is used as an after-market addition to the web site, in competition with the producer of similar search engines, with knowledge of a patent on the combination of that search engine with a web site, you could be liable for contributory infringement. A different rule applies to replacement components, which may exclude you from liability provided the parts are used to repair, but not to reconstruct, the originally patented item.

---

an invention performing nothing less than elements A, B, and C. As discussed earlier, however, an invention performing elements A, B, C, and D would literally infringe a claim *comprising* elements A, B, and C, but *not* a claim *consisting essentially of* elements A, B, and C, if element D was material.

Given the way claims are written, one typically does not see literal infringement in every case of infringement. The *Doctrine of Equivalents* was developed to prevent a defendant from getting out of infringement by arguing form over substance. If the defendant's device or process merely differs from the claim in name, form, or shape, or if one element was omitted and replaced with an equal substitute, there would still be infringement. The test for *equivalent infringement* is whether the defendant still performs substantially the same function in substantially the same way to obtain substantially the same result, despite the substitution. The Doctrine of Equivalents has come under significant fire over the years because it was considered to extend the scope of patents beyond what was originally intended by the inventors, and it is getting harder to prove infringement using it, but it hasn't been and probably will not be lost.

## Patent Defenses

So far, we have discussed most of the defenses that are available to any assertion of patent infringement, such as nonstatutory subject matter, lack of novelty, obviousness, fraud, and misuse. The most important defense, of course, is lack of infringement. Assuming you infringe the patent and none of the defenses so far mentioned are available, there are still more defenses. Other defenses include improper inventorship, failure to maintain (which I will talk more about), inoperability, lack of title to assert the claim of infringement, implied or explicit license, and *laches* (otherwise known as *sitting on your rights*). A significant defense that often goes unused, or at least isn't properly applied, is that of antitrust, which I will also discuss.

### The First Inventor Defense

The newest defense to claims of patent infringement, as well as a defense with particular application to the Internet, is called the First Inventor Defense. This defense applies only to methods of doing business and was created in 1999 as part of the AIPA. Prior to the AIPA, the fact that someone had been using a method as a trade secret, for example, did not protect that individual from a claim by another person who later obtained a patent on the same method. This forced people to get patents on technology that they would have preferred not to disclose—just so they could defend themselves from other people subsequently patenting it. This defense is available only against patented claims to a method and requires the following:

- Actual reduction to practice of the subject matter of the invention at least one year before the earliest filing date of the patent
- Commercial use of the subject matter of the invention at least one day before the earliest filing date
- Establishment by clear and convincing evidence

Application of this defense does not result in the invalidity of the subject patent. The defense is personal and can be used only by the party asserting it or by the customers or recipients of a useful end product produced by such a party. In addition to many other restrictions and limitations, the defense can be transferred only to another where the enterprise or business to which the defense is related is transferred as well.

## Patent Remedies

Unlike copyright law, there are no criminal penalties for patent infringement. The civil remedies available include injunctions from future infringement and some form of compensatory damages. In the unlikely event the plaintiff can show that every sale by the defendant would have otherwise been the plaintiff's sale, the plaintiff can get the infringer's profits. Typically, the compensatory award is one of reasonable royalties, which can be increased (up to triple the original amount) in cases of intentional infringement. What is considered reasonable varies greatly by technology and industry. I have heard of royalty rates as low as $0.0025 per chip for patent licenses in the semiconductor field and as high as 50 percent of revenue in other very high margin businesses. In general, license rates, and therefore what are considered reasonable royalties, range from 1 to 5 percent of actual or like-kind revenue for the licensed product or service. When a court is forced to determine damages on the basis of reasonable royalties, it will try to imagine what two parties would have negotiated in an arm's-length transaction executed prior to any knowledge of the infringement.

## Patent Maintenance and Annuities

The failure to maintain a patent can result in the loss of your exclusive rights. Most people think that once a patent has issued, that's it, but that is far from true. To increase revenue and to make sure patent owners are encouraged to either commercialize their inventions or turn them over to the public before the end of their normal term, all patent offices have instituted maintenance or annuity fees. In the United States, maintenance fees are due at 4, 8, and 12 years after issuance, although the fees actually have to be paid at 3.5, 7.5, and 11.5 years to avoid an extra surcharge.

As previously stated, other countries have annuities that are due while patent applications are pending in addition to fees due once the patents have issued. Some annuities are due every year. In almost all cases, the fees increase each time they are due to ensure that the patent owner really wants to maintain the exclusive right to the invention.

# Trade Secrets

One of the few areas of intellectual property law still primarily reserved to the states is that of trade secrets. Trade secret law has evolved from *action servi corrupti*—the Roman action for corrupting a slave. Apparently, because one could not recover money from a slave, it was common practice to entice another's slave to divulge the secrets of his or her owner. The Romans developed trade secret law in order to have recourse against the enticer.

Every state now has laws that protect trade secrets in some way, and most states have now adopted the Uniform Trade Secrets Act (UTSA). The UTSA defines a trade secret as information, including a formula, pattern compilation, program, device, method, technique, or process, that:

- Derives independent economic value, actual or potential, from not being generally known to the public or to other persons who can obtain economic value from its disclosure or use
- Is the subject of efforts that are reasonable under the circumstances to maintain its secrecy

The most famous example of a trade secret is the alleged formula for Coca-Cola. Only three people in the world are said to know the formula, and the Coca-Cola Company has gone to great lengths to protect it. For example, although Coca-Cola is made all over the world, the syrup is made only in Atlanta under tight security control. Nevertheless, I wouldn't be at all be surprised to find out that there either isn't a secret formula or it isn't anything special. Whether Coca-Cola could have patented the formula is also a mystery, but just because something is patentable doesn't mean that it has to be patented. Patent protection lasts only for a limited period of time, but trade secret rights can theoretically last forever. Had the formula for Coca-Cola been patented instead of protected as a trade secret, Coca-Cola's protection would have run out years ago, so trade secret protection was obviously the better choice.

Because a patent requires disclosure of only the best mode of practicing the invention and not every other mode or modes that are developed after the invention is filed, the remaining modes can be maintained as trade secrets. Such trade secrets can last indefinitely, provided reasonable steps are taken to keep the secret and somebody else doesn't independently discover it. One does not need to operate one's business like a nuclear weapons facility to keep a trade secret, however. Courts recognize that you must share some secrets with others (employees, vendors, consultants, etc.), but you should have them sign nondisclosure agreements to protect that information. Employees should have identification badges, access to facilities should be controlled, and other normal security precautions should be taken.

## Employee Issues

With respect to corporations, the most common trade secret disputes involve the raiding of employees from competitors, departing employees, and the submission of unsolicited ideas. All of these things are frequently occurring in the ISP industry right now. Raiding occurs when another employer quickly hires a number of employees, sometimes in groups, from your company on the basis of trade secret information. The trade secrets in these cases might include detailed information about the capabilities and pay of the raided employees, but could also include additional information those employees took with them to their next job. In each such case that goes into litigation, the court's decision will largely turn upon the perceived fairness of the raider's actions rather than the specific details of the trade secrets.

To best protect yourself and your company, it is a good idea to do two things:

1. Include a nonsolicitation, or *antiraiding,* provision in the standard confidentiality and intellectual property assignment agreement that you have employees sign when they begin employment with your company.

2. Conduct exit interviews with departing employees to remind them of their obligations to maintain confidences and to return any materials that they might have taken home.

It is also a good idea to make sure such agreements contain provisions to protect your trade secrets and that you take reasonable steps to protect those secrets during the normal course of your business. Once a trade secret is gone, through your own fault, it is gone forever.

The retained knowledge of a departing employee is always one of the biggest issues, especially when that employee has been working on a highly secret or unique project. An employer cannot, under the guise of protecting its trade secrets, prevent an employee from obtaining gainful employment in his or her profession. However, under the emerging doctrine of *inevitable disclosure,* it is sometimes possible to enjoin a former employee from taking a new position that is so similar to his or her former job that disclosure of your trade secrets would be inevitable. In general, though, employees are permitted to retain and subsequently use the general knowledge and skill they acquired during the course of their specific employment.

## Unsolicited Submissions

Unsolicited ideas and inventions can be the boon or bane of a corporation's existence. The research and development departments of corporations are not always responsible for every new idea developed in the world, so they must come from somewhere, and that somewhere is often in the mail. When an unsolicited disclosure of an idea shows up in your office in a hand-addressed envelope with "SECRET" written on the back flap and a poorly written cover letter that demands $100 million, you may wish it hadn't come to you. Companies need to have procedures for dealing with unsolicited ideas and inventions from their own employees and from people outside of the company, and then they need to make sure these procedures are followed.

If it is possible to detect the existence of an unsolicited submission without opening the envelope or having a meeting or phone conversation about the idea, the envelope should be returned. The submitter should then be told that such ideas will not be accepted without a waiver of trade secret rights or some other agreement regarding the exact position of the parties. If the idea has already been disclosed, it is best to return the material received and/or to otherwise state that the idea was submitted without any prior agreement regarding its confidentiality. In such cases, it is best to explicitly state that your company will not regard the submitted idea as a secret, but it would be okay to state that you would be willing to review it if resubmitted under a waiver agreement. In such cases, you should include a copy of a standard waiver agreement for the submitting party to sign.

# Antitrust

I have put the discussion regarding antitrust laws toward the end of this section because I do not intend to go into great detail about them and because antitrust laws frequently come up in the context of intellectual property laws, especially patents. Antitrust laws were developed to prevent people, usually corporations, from manipulating markets or otherwise using their dominant position in a particular market to adversely impact competition or prices. This principle is best illustrated in the U.S. government's antitrust lawsuit against Microsoft and in the European Commission's (EC's) similar investigation of Microsoft's practices in Europe. Almost any newspaper article about the lawsuit or the investigation will provide you with more information than you want to know about antitrust law in the software and Internet context. Nevertheless, here are some examples of illegal activities that have been at issue in the Microsoft case:

- Horizontal restraints, usually agreements, that affect the parties in a horizontal relationship (a direct competitor) from competing fairly with one another
- Resale price maintenance that seeks to control the price of commodities that have passed into the channels of trade and that are owned by dealers
- Tying arrangements whereby the sale of one item is conditioned on the purchase of another if (1) the seller has market power in the tying product, (2) the arrangement has an adverse effect on competition in the relevant market for the tied product, and (3) efficiency justifications for the arrangement do not outweigh the anticompetitive effects
- Certain forms of exclusive or discriminatory dealing

The recent antitrust trial was not Microsoft's first brush with the U.S. Justice Department. In 1994, Microsoft settled allegations that it had engaged in monopolistic practices by using unfair contracts to choke off competition and preserve its monopoly position. Under the terms of the settlement, Microsoft was barred from entering into per-processor licenses, obligating licensees to purchase any minimum number of products, entering into licenses with terms longer than one year, requiring licensees to pay on a *lump-sum* basis, requiring licensees to purchase other Microsoft products as a condition for licensing a particular operating system, and requiring developers of applications software to sign unlawfully restrictive nondisclosure agreements. The 1994 matter does not appear to be that far removed from the present case.

In early 1999, Microsoft was again in the antitrust news, this time with respect to European ISPs. Apparently, Microsoft maintained some provisions in its Internet Explorer agreements with ISPs that gave it the right to terminate the agreements if the ISP failed to attain minimum distribution volumes or percentages of the Microsoft browser and that prevented the ISPs from promoting or advertising competing browsers. In exchange for dropping these provisions, the EC issued a letter to Microsoft stating that it otherwise had no anticompetitive objections to Microsoft's licensing agreement with ISPs.

On November 5, 1999, U.S. District Judge Thomas Penfield Jackson issued comprehensive findings of fact in the first determinative stage of the U.S. antitrust trial against Microsoft. Judge Jackson determined that Microsoft was a monopoly that had used its monopoly power to stifle competition and harm consumers. There were three main facts that indicated to Judge Jackson that Microsoft enjoyed monopoly power:

1. Microsoft's share of the market for Intel-compatible personal computer operating systems is extremely large and stable.
2. A high barrier to entry protects Microsoft's dominant market share.
3. Largely as a result of that barrier, Microsoft's customers lack a commercially viable alternative to Windows.

Although the Justice Department was quick to claim victory, the findings of fact represent only a partial conclusion of the trial phase of the lawsuit. The findings-of-law component of Judge Jackson's decision is expected to come sometime in 2000. Because an appeal by Microsoft of any component of the court's findings could take several years, and Judge Jackson's decisions have been reversed by higher courts in the past, it is fair to say that this matter is far from over. On the other hand, many experts believe it is unlikely that an appellate court would significantly alter the court's sweeping findings of fact. Furthermore, the EC's investigation is far from concluded. Unless the parties settle the dispute first, of which there have been many rumors, this matter is likely to remain unresolved for many years. Absent a complete reversal of the Judge Jackson's findings of fact, any final decision or settlement will likely seek to change Microsoft's ability to control the personal computer operating system market. Possible remedies include the breakup of Microsoft, much as MCI was able to get the U.S. government to break up AT&T many years before. Although Microsoft bemoans any such possible action as being bad for the economy, one would be hard put to argue that AT&T's break up was bad for either the economy or the investors in its former components, including AT&T, Lucent, Bell Atlantic, BellSouth, and Southwestern Bell.

Finally, antitrust laws are often raised in the context of intellectual property laws because the two bodies of law appear to be contradictory to each other. A patent, for example, grants the patent holder a limited monopoly, whereas antitrust laws promote competition by making monopolies illegal. The U.S. government, at least, sees this matter differently. The Department of Justice and the Federal Trade Commission issued guidelines in 1995 that stated that they consider the intellectual property laws and antitrust laws to work in cooperation. Both laws share the common purpose of promoting innovation and enhancing consumer welfare. Intellectual property laws provide incentives for innovation and dissemination and commercialization by establishing enforceable property rights for the creators of new and useful products, more efficient processes, and original works of expression. In the absence of intellectual property rights, imitators could more rapidly exploit the efforts of innovators and investors without compensation. Rapid imitation would reduce the commercial value of innovation and erode incentives to invest, ultimately to the detriment of consumers. Antitrust laws promote innovation and consumer welfare by prohibiting certain actions that may harm competition with respect to either existing or new ways of serving consumers. Or so they say.

## Internet Standards

A large number of organizations are generating standards and protocols relating to the Internet. These include broad-based organizations such as the International Telecommunications Union (ITU), a United Nations–sponsored organization, and the Internet Engineering Task Force (IETF), a voluntary association of Internet engineers. These groups largely attempt to adopt standard protocols that promote interoperability between different hardware and software components incorporated into Internet Protocol (IP) networks around the world. Individual companies promote their own technology to these organizations in the hope that the technology will be adopted as a new standard, or they may team up with other companies to push some commonly agreed-upon technology outside of the normal standard bodies.

For example, RealNetworks' proposal for a Realtime Streaming Protocol (RTSP) was ratified by the IETF as a standard protocol for streaming media over the Internet. This is an example of a single company pushing its technology and a standards organization adopting that technology as a standard protocol. The Future I/O Alliance formed by Compaq, IBM, Hewlett-Packard, and Adaptec to help define standards for handling data inside server computers is an example of companies pushing for a commonly agreed-upon standard. This alliance is actually in competition with a Next Generation Input/Output technology proposed by Intel and supported by Sun Microsystems, Dell Computer, Hitachi, NEC, and Siemens. The Intel-sponsored standard is, of course, based on Intel microprocessor technology, whereas the Future I/O Alliance allegedly seeks to promote a standard that offers more opportunity to companies adopting it to differentiate their products.

Another interesting dispute involves instant messaging. IETF is now working on the development of the Instant Messaging and Presence Protocol (IMPP) to create a messaging standard that would require software to conform with publicly available specifications. This dispute arose after Microsoft introduced its own version of instant messaging software that could communicate with AOL's Instant Messenger and ICQ software users. AOL promptly jammed messages sent using the Microsoft software because it claimed that Microsoft's software compromised its members' privacy and security, unfairly hijacked its network resources, and automatically appropriated unwitting AOL subscribers. Whether the IETF will be able to develop interoperability between the existing competing systems remains to be seen, but if it does succeed, it would be nice if it took authentication and privacy into consideration as well—two areas that were not included when e-mail was first standardized.

## What's Open Source?

Intellectual property laws impact all standards, and antitrust laws can impact some corporate alliances. Patent issues are most prevalent, but trademark and trade secret issues also arise. Trademarks are implicated when there is a desire to protect the name of the standards body itself or the name associated with a particular standard. The Open Source Foundation (OSF), for example, has attempted to register the mark *open source* as a certification mark. A certification mark is a type of mark that is used to indicate that the goods or services bearing such a mark have been certified in some way. The *BBB On-Line* mark, like the *Good Housekeeping Seal* of the past, is an example of a certification mark in that it identifies web sites that comply with certain fair business practice guidelines established by the Better Business Bureau.

The *open source* mark is intended to be used to certify software programs that comply with the criteria established by the OSF to designate what it considers to be true open source software. The issue here is that the term *open source* is descriptively used to identify any product that has open source code. Hence, *open source* has become a generic term to describe a large class of software, not just software that conforms to the OSF criteria. This is also a good example of the types of abuses that can result when someone asserts trademark rights over descriptive or generic terms. Early in the 2000 U.S. presidential campaign, Al Gore's web site included a section that described how Gore's campaign was "open source" and actively encouraged people to join the campaign and add their *code* (ideas) to his *project* (the campaign). Shortly thereafter, the OSF criticized the Gore site as infringing upon its *registered* trademark rights. As it turned out, the OSF didn't have a registered trademark on *open source* at the time. Its application had been rejected because it failed to show that the mark had ever been used to certify anything as open source. Even if OSF can correct that problem, I would hope they would be denied protection for the mark because of the already distinct, generic, and descriptive characteristics of the term.

## Other Intellectual Property Issues in the Standards Context

Trade secrets are less frequently an issue because most people know that anything submitted to a standards body for review will necessarily have to be disclosed to other members of that standards body, including your competitors. Hence, it is rare when an attempt is made to protect a trade secret associated with any material submitted to any such organization. In the same context, however, private-alliance organizations may seek to protect key aspects of the technology upon which a standard is based as a trade secret, even after the standard is developed. The members of the alliance may therefore be required to sign some sort of confidentiality agreement that specifies the terms and conditions regarding when certain types of information can be released.

Copyright and patent issues also arise in the standards arena. Because any writing, but especially software source code, submitted to a standards body is subject to copyright protection, the issue occasionally arises of whether the submitted information can be copied without fear of allegations of copyright infringement. A number of standards organizations and private alliances resolve this dilemma through the adoption of policies that require copyright ownership in anything submitted to the organization to be assigned to that organization. Other policies allow the submitter to retain ownership but require an express license to anyone in the organization or alliance adopting the standard. In this context, copyrights sound like a nuisance, but many standards organizations have found them to be useful, especially where the standard to be adopted relates to the implementation of an idea, rather than to the idea itself. Where it is necessary to specify the standard in writing to require people to use the standard only as written, then those wishing to adopt the standard must first obtain a license to the underlying copyright. In doing so, they obligate themselves to the terms of a contract with the standards organization, thereby giving the standards organization some greater degree of control over the standard than it might otherwise have had.

Because patents can have much broader applicability than copyrights (a patent can actually cover the idea, not just its implementation), patents are treated in a similar, yet more circumspect fashion. Many different aspects of a new technical standard could be subject to patent protection, and although patents give standards organizations and alliances the ability to better control the implementation of a standard than would a copyright, patents can also be subject to more serious abuse. For example, most standards organizations have now adopted policies requiring patent owners wishing to participate in the standards-adoption process to disclose any patent rights that could be infringed by anyone practicing that standard. This disclosure requirement stems from an incident involving Dell Computer. Apparently, a Dell engineer involved in the development of a standard did not disclose the existence of a Dell patent covering that standard. Once the standard was adopted and other companies began to implement it, Dell attempted to collect royalty payments from those companies. A court subsequently decided that Dell had misused its patent by failing to disclose its existence, and Dell was forced to dedicate the patent to the public using the standard.

As a result of this incident, the standards bodies have also adopted policies governing what happens to patents that are not disclosed by their owners. The most common policy requires the patent owner to disclose the patent and to specify whether the patent will be dedicated to the public upon adoption of the standard or whether it will only be licensed. If it isn't disclosed, the patent owner agrees in advance to dedicate it to the public as a penalty for failure to disclose. If it is disclosed and it is to be licensed, the patent owner has to specify whether it will be licensed royalty-free or for a price. Because few will vote in favor of a standard that is subject to patent protection *and* unreasonable licensing terms, most standards organizations specify that the price charged and the terms and conditions must be reasonable. Many companies will refuse to vote in favor of any standard subject to a patent license fee to implement. This position makes sense, however, only where the cost of adopting the standard subject to the patent, including the cost of the patent license, exceeds the cost of implementing any comparable technology. If the patented standard is actually more efficient and cost-effective to implement, even with the patent fee, then it may make more sense to adopt it. Most standards bodies seem to have concluded that patents are a necessary evil and that as long as anyone voting for or adopting a standard knows the patent exists and the terms for its use, and they agree to adopt the standard anyway, then so be it.

## Antitrust and Standards

As for antitrust concerns, the mere promotion and adoption of a standard is not an issue. Matters get complicated, however, where competitors get together and agree to cut off other competitors through use of a standard or the assertion of some other form of market power. For this reason, most private alliances are said to be *open* standards groups, meaning that any company can join the group and have some say, usually according to published bylaws, regarding the adoption of a particular standard that might affect it. A closed standards development group that includes a number of competitors with the collective power to affect competition in a particular market will be subject to very careful antitrust scrutiny and is probably a very bad idea on its face.

# CHAPTER 3

# A Special Law for ISPs: The DMCA

T he development of copyright law has always been in response to challenges raised by new technologies, such as the original printing press, that enable the reproduction and distribution of works. In this regard, the Internet, or any digital network for that matter, presents some very difficult challenges. Digital networks result in many automatic copies. Routers make temporary copies of data packets for timing and alignment purposes. Cache servers make complete copies of works in order to place them in physical locations closer to users in order to improve the speed and efficiency of the network. Browsing software and personal computers make copies of works that are downloaded from the network and/or displayed or played by the computer. Users also make copies, lots of them, and any of these copies that are made are perfect; that is, they are not degraded like an analog copy of an analog recording. These copies can then be distributed around the world in a matter of moments at almost no cost, potentially creating exponential losses for copyright owners.

## History of the DMCA

You may have wondered, while reading Chapter 2, *Intellectual Property and Other Laws Made Simple*, what nightclubs and dance halls had in common with ISPs. The answer is, quite a bit actually—at least from the copyright owners' perspective. Analogous to the dance hall situation, the copyright owners figured that the ISPs had helped to provide the facilities (the network and access) and audience (users) for the direct infringers (more users), and arguably financially benefited from the traffic and service fees generated by popular infringing bulletin boards, newsgroups, and web sites.

Copyright owners also strongly believed that ISPs knew or could have known, had they bothered to look, that infringing works were being transmitted over their networks and stored on their servers. So after years of finding infringing *perfect* copies of their music and software on bulletin boards and web sites, and frustrated by not being able to find the infringers, copyright owners turned to the rules they knew best and attempted to apply them to ISPs.

## The Infamous White Paper

Since ISPs are easier to find and have deeper pockets than most direct infringers, it made perfect sense to focus on the responsibilities of the ISPs to prevent copyright infringement on the Internet. Thus, the Clinton administration responded to the complaints from music, software, and movie (content) companies in 1995 by proposing legislation as part of a white paper report entitled *Intellectual Property and the National Information Infrastructure* (NII) (see www.uspto.gov/web/offices/com/doc/ipnii/ for a copy). The White House Information Infrastructure Task Force on behalf of the Patent and Trademark Office and the Department of Commerce produced this report.

The Department of Commerce's accompanying press release explained that the "mission of the Department is to make our economy grow, to promote science and technology, and to increase our international trade." The late commerce secretary Ronald Brown stated, "This Report will help ensure that the NII [sic] is a favorable environment for the development of an electronic marketplace for commerce." He also stated, "Unless we provide legal protection of [intellectual property] on the NII, people won't be able to reap the benefits of these new technologies" (see www.uspto.gov/web/offices/com/speeches/95-27.html for a copy). While the administration and Secretary Brown may have truly believed that the proposed legislation (the NII legislation) fulfilled this mission and would have helped to create a favorable environment for the development of e-commerce, it could have had quite the opposite effect. If implemented, the NII legislation would have made ISPs strictly liable, with no actual knowledge required, for any copyright infringement resulting from a customer's use of the ISP's service. Imagine trying to run a profitable business in that environment. All a copyright holder would have to do is show that a copyright infringing work was transmitted across your network and you would be liable. Application of such laws also would have had an incredibly chilling, if not throttling, effect on communications as ISPs attempted the impossible task of monitoring transmissions for infringing works.

## A Dangerous Lack of Attention

Unfortunately, ISPs and their industry associations were not paying the slightest bit of attention to the task force's report or the resulting NII legislation and initially had no one advocating a different solution. The only real exception was the Computer and Communications Industry Association (CCIA), which had one person, Gregory Gorman, monitoring and reporting on the progress of the report. Since I worked at Silicon Graphics, Inc. (SGI) until May of 1995, I normally wouldn't have paid attention to this matter, either. One of my tasks while at SGI, however, had been to advise Chairman Ed McCracken, who served on the task force that produced the report. SGI made workstations with strong graphical processing capabilities and had been involved in an interactive television joint venture with Time Warner. The joint venture was called Road Runner. Because SGI was not an ISP and was heavily involved with a major content company, SGI generally went along with the content industries' interests in this regard, even though the possible impact was pretty apparent. I then moved from California to Washington, D.C., to work for MCI, a major ISP. Having had my hands in the development of a monster, the NII legislation, I felt an obligation to help tame it and, if that wasn't possible, to kill it. But first, in order to get people to understand why the NII legislation was bad, I had to explain, to what later seemed like half of the world, how the Internet worked.

## You Mean ISPs Can't Do That?

An ISP, of course, has no way of knowing what is inside every one of the billions of data packets transmitted over its network every day. Even if the ISP could look inside a packet and get around any encoding or encryption that was utilized, the amount of data would be too small to have any discernable meaning to anyone attempting to look at it. But even if a number of related packets could be combined to reveal more of the content, the ISP would still know very little about the copyright status of the content or whether it was infringing. For example, if you pulled a number of packets off the Net and recombined them to reveal a picture of a red ball resting on a table, what have you learned? You still don't know whether the picture is subject to copyright protection or whether it is infringing. The content companies insisted that this was a bad example because it was more likely that the packets would represent a scene from a famous movie or music from a popular song. Even if such a ridiculous proposition were true, the ISP would still have no realistic way of determining whether the packets were being distributed by someone who had the right to do so.

There is no national, online database of all of the copyrighted content in the world that can be checked to verify copyright protection and authorizations. The European Union (EU), by the way, is still considering legislation that would exempt from copyright law only temporary copies of works made on the Internet, even if automatically made by routers or cache servers, if the copies were first authorized by the copyright owners. Even if there were such a requirement and a copyright/authorization database existed, attempting to use that database in real time to perform a copyright protection and authorization check on all data packets going through each router on the Internet would bring the Internet to a screeching halt. As you will read, the battle to prevent this result was won in the United States, but the war continues throughout the rest of the world because many countries are just developing their copyright laws to accommodate digital technologies. Hopefully, efforts like those of the EU will be defeated, but the very fact that the EU legislation received serious consideration goes to show you how naive people can be when it comes to understanding the Internet.

Although content companies have recently changed their opinion—and their investments—with regard to the Internet, many originally viewed the Internet as an intolerable threat to their existing distribution mechanisms. Furthermore, the proponents of the NII legislation, like many of those in the EU, were completely ignorant of how the Internet worked. The technological naiveté of the proponents is best demonstrated through a comment made by a content company representative. She publicly stated that ISPs could monitor for infringements being transmitted to the United States from overseas sites if ISPs simply looked at everything coming across the fiber-optic lines strung across the oceans. When I asked her how she suggested ISPs perform such a task, she recommended that we cut the fiber-optic cables open so we could see the stuff as it was going past. "After all," she said, "they are optical, so you must be able to see what's inside." Many congressional members, staff, and news reporters knew about as much as she did, so she was not alone in her ignorance.

## A First-Round Victory

The NII legislation ultimately failed to pass, thanks to the efforts of a group called the Ad Hoc Copyright Coalition (AHCC), which Gregory Gorman and I helped to start. The AHCC was formed from a number of ISPs and their associations, telecommunication companies and their associations, and additional associations representing universities, colleges, and libraries. The NII legislation, as previously stated, was just the first skirmish in a big battle of a long war. As soon as it appeared that the NII legislation was losing ground, the administration proposed adding similar language to a draft treaty that was being considered by the World Intellectual Property Organization (WIPO). This was an excellent tactic because the NII legislation had been killed while still in the House of Representatives. Treaties, however, are ratified by the Senate and implemented only in the House. Thus, if the content companies and the administration could get the same basic language into a treaty and get that treaty ratified by the Senate, they stood a much better chance of getting it through the House. Given these events, the AHCC had no choice but to try to get the treaty stopped or changed before it made its way back to the Senate.

## The WIPO Treaty Negotiations

The WIPO (pronounced "double-yew eye pee oh," not "wipe-o"; they get quite offended by the latter) is a United Nations standing body that is responsible for the establishment of international intellectual property laws. The U.S. proposal was made during the last WIPO meeting, after more than five years of meetings, to consider the technical terms of the treaty. After this meeting, the treaty would be drafted and then introduced for negotiation and vote at a WIPO diplomatic conference in December of 1996. Since the AHCC was focused on the NII legislation and didn't realize the administration would go to such lengths, only Gregory Gorman and Marc Jacobson of Prodigy attended the WIPO meeting to protest the adoption of the U.S. proposal— and two voices did little good. We did find out, however, that a Finnish bureaucrat was responsible for drafting the treaty and its comments, so Gorman and I and a few other AHCC members flew to Helsinki to press our case. Working with an attorney and an engineer from Sonera (which was called Telecom Finland at the time), we explained to the bureaucrat, in Finnish, what was wrong with the proposed language and asked him to fix it. This bureaucrat, like many of the WIPO diplomats, was responsible for copyright policy in his country and was primarily interested in doing what was necessary to establish strong copyright laws. He also patiently explained to us that his job was limited to drafting what was proposed at the technical meetings. Because our positions had not been officially stated by a country, there was little he could do. He did, however, offer to put some helpful language in the comments, which was the hook we needed.

Since MCI was partnered with British Telecommunications at the time, I flew from Helsinki to London to try to convince BT to work with Sonera to tackle this same problem in Europe. BT and Sonera then got together with an attorney in Brussels named Thomas Vinje and established what is now called the Alliance for a Digital Future (the Alliance) to perform such a function. The AHCC and the Alliance then began to attend a number of meetings, leading up to the 1996 Diplomatic Conference, to try to convince representatives from the different countries to support our cause. The most successful meeting in this regard was the African Regional Conference in Morocco in 1996. Masanobu Katoh of Fujitsu, Gregory Gorman and I from the AHCC, and some Alliance members attended this meeting. In addition to explaining how the Internet works and why the draft treaty was defective (and getting lost in the Casbah), we also sought to convince the Africans that they should support our position as a bloc of votes, because doing so would give them the ability to more directly influence the outcome. The Africans agreed with these suggestions and came to our aid, along with a number of other countries, during the Diplomatic Conference to force the United States and a number of European countries to agree to more reasonable language. As an aside, the Africans have since used similar bloc votes to get an African, Kamil Idris, elected as director general of WIPO, and another African, Kofi Annan, elected as secretary-general of the United Nations.

# The Birth of the DMCA and the E-Commerce Directive

When the WIPO treaties did make it back to the United States for ratification, Congress was beginning to understand the complexity of the situation involving ISPs and had generally agreed that the treaties needed to be implemented in view of the ISP liability issues. This led to a long series of congressionally sponsored negotiation sessions between the two sides, during which I was the primary representative of the communications companies. The outcome of all of this work was the truly revolutionary Digital Millennium Copyright Act (DMCA) of 1998, which was signed into law in the United States in 1999. In accordance with the terms of this law, ISPs generally have no monetary liability for copyright infringement when they are operating as a conduit for communications, in other words, as a backbone or access provider. Under the law, ISPs could also avoid monetary liability for copyright infringing material that was stored on the ISP's network if the ISP removed or blocked access to the infringing information when it knew it to exist or appropriately responded to a statutorily compliant notice regarding that infringing material. This latter provision has become known as *notice and take down*. A similar legal structure was introduced in the Proposal for a European Parliament and Council Directive on Certain Legal Aspects of Electronic Commerce in the Internal Market (the E-Commerce Directive).

To illustrate the importance of the DMCA and the E-Commerce Directive, consider the alternative. Given a fundamental lack of understanding about how the Internet works and what is reasonable to expect of an ISP, it is fairly easy to see how a court could find ISPs liable for their users' infringement. After all, the provision of access and web hosting services appears to be material to the infringing use of a hosted site. If a court believed that the ISP knew or should have known what was on the hosted site, liability was sure to follow. For example, a Dutch court recently ordered a Dutch ISP to remove copyright infringing material from a site it was hosting and even found hyperlinks to that site from other sites in Holland to be an infringement of the same copyrighted material. The court is now considering the damages to be assessed for the infringement. Under the DMCA, the Dutch ISP might still have to take down the infringing material, but it is unlikely that the Dutch ISP would have been subject to monetary damages.

# Basic Legal Rules of the DMCA

The DMCA implements the WIPO treaties and therefore includes many different provisions aside from those directly applying to ISPs. Some of these provisions relate to sound recordings, computer maintenance and repair, copyright protection systems, and copyright management information. With respect to copyright protection systems, such as those that have been incorporated into digital videodiscs (DVDs) and DVD players, the DMCA establishes rules regarding the circumvention of such protections. This means you cannot legally create and sell a device that was designed for the purpose of allowing users to make copies of works incorporating technologies intended to prevent people from making such copies. With respect to copyright management information, such as the copyright notice and related information that appears in this book or on software or other works, the DMCA establishes rules to prevent that information from being removed or altered and to punish violators of such rules.

## Structural Composition

The most important provisions of the DMCA obviously relate to ISPs or service providers as they are variously defined therein. One section establishes very broad limitations on service provider liability for material that is simply online. Another section addresses limitations on liability for system caching. A third section covers the storage of information on systems or networks at the direction of users, in other words, hosting. A fourth section covers information location tools, which is another name for search engines and hypertext links. A fifth section establishes special rules for nonprofit educational institutions, which effectively operate as ISPs for all of the on-campus users of an institution's network. Additional sections deal with elements of the notice-and-take-down provisions that were created to help prevent abuse and to protect free speech rights, certain conditions that service providers must comply with in order to be eligible for the limitations on liability, the scope of injunctive relief available to copyright owners and the conditions under which injunctive relief can be granted, and special provisions that address the protection of user privacy.

## The Definitions of Service Providers

To start with, there are actually two different definitions of service providers. The broadest limitation on liability for material that is simply online applies only to service providers that are transmitting or routing digital online communications or are providing access to such communications, without modifying the content of the material sent or received. The modification provision relates only to material modifications, not to conversions from one form to another or to other automated forms of alteration that may be required by different protocols or systems. The second definition applies to all of the other limitations on liability and defines a service provider as "a provider of online services or network access, or the operator of facilities therefor," including an entity meeting the other definition. Admittedly, there isn't much difference between these two definitions, but the content companies were concerned that the second definition could be interpreted to include just about anyone (and perhaps it could), so they insisted on the distinction.

The remainder of this section will describe the legal rules established by the DMCA, as paraphrased and explained. Chapter 5, *What Is an ISP to Do (or Not)? Content and Activity Regulations to Live By*, will then explain in even more practical terms how you are supposed to comply with these rules and the other rules described in this chapter.

## The Mere Conduit Exemption

As already mentioned, if you are a service provider meeting the first definition (meaning you are basically operating as just a conduit), you can avoid monetary liability for copyright infringement as a result of transmitting, routing, or providing connections for material through your equipment, even if that equipment was operated for you by someone else. This rule applies for the provision of intermediate and transient storage of the same materials in the course of transmitting, routing, or providing such connections. These definitions cover what are generally referred to as "mere conduit operations," including the basic operation of a network or router, the provision of access services, or the operation of a network exchange, such as MAE East. Note that the only type of storage covered is intermediate and transient storage, not temporary.

Generally this means that the storage must be quite fleeting, such as the storage of packets in a router for queueing, forwarding, and flow-control purposes, but that could also include other equipment that requires a longer period of time to properly process packets that are merely being transmitted or routed, such as some of the quality-of-service (QoS) equipment being planned for use in the future. Also note that this is only a limit on the service provider's monetary liability. This means you can still be found liable for copyright infringement and therefore subject to an injunction. Offhand, injunctions sound pretty bad, but the DMCA includes very strict provisions governing the conditions under which injunctions can be ordered and limiting the scope of any injunction that a court decides to order, so keep that in mind when you see injunctions mentioned in the following text.

### Conditions for Applicability

The service provider's limitation on liability under the DMCA for mere conduit operations is subject to the following conditions, which you should readily meet, assuming you fall within the first definition of service provider:

- The transmission of the infringing material must be initiated by or at the direction of someone else, that is, the infringer, and not you.
- The mere conduit operations must be carried out through automatic technical processes without selection of the infringing material by you, that is, actual programmed equipment versus little elves in boxes.
- You must not select the recipients of the infringing material except as an automatic response to the request of another person, such as when operating an automated mail or list server.
- No copy of the stored infringing material can be kept in a manner ordinarily accessible to anyone other than the anticipated recipients, or for longer than is reasonably necessary for the mere conduit operations.
- The infringing material must be transmitted without substantive modification of its content, but the repackaging of data and analog conversions of data are okay.

## Other Limitations on Liability

To take advantage of the DMCA's protections covering caching, hosting, and information location tools, you must likewise meet the first definition or the second definition of a service provider. I will deal with caching and information location tools first and then move on to hosting. Since all three areas are subject to notice and take down, I will describe each area before explaining how notice and take down actually works. As with the mere conduit, and subject to certain conditions, you can completely avoid only monetary liability, but not injunctions, for providing system caching. Likewise, the same basic conditions and limits on injunctive relief previously mentioned with respect to mere conduit operators apply to system cache operators.

### Caching

*System caching* is defined in the DMCA as the intermediate and temporary (not transient) storage of material on your equipment, even if someone else operates that equipment for you. *Temporary storage* is not defined, but both the DMCA and similar legislation introduced in Australia in 1999 make it clear that system or network caching and browser caching were meant to be included within the definition. It is interesting to note that the Australian bill does not permit caching for the purpose of listening to music on a computer. I suppose the lobbyists for the music industry in

Australia are even more unrealistic than those in the United States. For the limitations on liability for system caching to apply under the DMCA:

- The stored material must be put online by a first person, other than you.

- That material must be transmitted from the first person through your equipment to a second person at the direction of the second person.

- The storage must be carried out through an automatic technical process for the purpose of making the material available to users of the equipment, who, after the material was transmitted as previously described, requested access to the material from the first person.

The best way to understand this language, of course, is to take it out of the context of legislative mumbo jumbo and tie it back to the world we know.

With reference to cache configuration, illustrated in Figure 3.1, assume you use a system cache as a proxy server, and an originating site operated by a copyright owner such as Disney has put copyrighted material on a page accessible through the following URL: www.disney.com/goodstuff.html. When your customer requests that URL, the stored material corresponding to that URL will be transmitted to a cache server in your network or one operated for you by another company, and then forwarded to your customer. Since the cache server's storage operation is automatic and exists for the purpose of returning the same stored page to the next customer requesting the same URL, the entire operation comes under the definition of system caching under the DMCA.

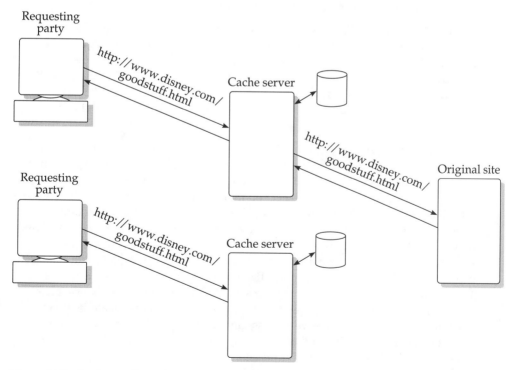

**Figure 3.1**  Cache configuration.

In addition to these conditions, there are additional conditions that must be met in order to fully take advantage of the DMCA's protections for system caching:

- The cached material must be transmitted to the requesting user without modification of its substantive content as originally transmitted to the cache server.

- You must comply with all refresh, reload, or other updating rules specified by the originating site, provided these rules are in accordance with generally accepted industry standard data communications protocols and the rules are not used to prevent or unreasonably impair the caching of the material.

- You cannot interfere with technology that returns information to the original site as though the cached site was the original site, provided that the technology does not significantly interfere with the performance of your equipment or the caching of the material, is consistent with generally accepted industry-standard data communications protocols, and does not extract any more information from the cached site than would have been extracted from the original site.

- The cached site must follow the same conditional access requirements, that is, payment of a fee or provision of a password, as were in place at the original site for the same information.

- If the material at the original site is infringing, you must respond appropriately—in other words, by taking down the material or blocking access to it—to a compliant notice, but only if the material has been taken down or blocked at the original site, and the compliant notice further includes a statement that the material has been taken down or blocked at the original site.

These last two requirements exist because it obviously does little good to have the cached site take any action that hasn't first been performed at the original site, lest the cached site simply cache the infringing material again and the whole process start over. Of course, once the material is removed from the original site, it will shortly thereafter disappear from the cached site, so it is highly unlikely that you will ever have to respond to a compliant notice regarding material at a cached site.

Hopefully, the language describing the system cache is general enough to cover a wide variety of network caching functions and equipment, such as quality-of-service equipment. Just in case, keep in mind that the adoption of new technologies using different methodologies could subject you to new liability, so always recheck this section before adopting different technology. For example, a mirror cache is often used as an example of a type of cache technology that does not fit the system cache definition. I do not think this is true, however, because the statute does not say that the service provider cannot be the person who requests the URL. Thus, you could request a copy of the entire site in order to make the material available to your customers. There is also no requirement that anyone actually request the material once it has been cached, so it would be immaterial that a mirror cache stored material that was never requested by anyone. Nevertheless, since service providers typically cooperatively operate mirror caches at the originating site's request, it is unlikely that this question will be tested in court anytime soon.

## Information Location Tools

You can likewise avoid monetary liability, but not all injunctions, for using information location tools to refer or link users to an online location that contains infringing material or activity. Information location tools are defined as directories, indexes, references, pointers, or hypertext links. As with the other sections of the DMCA, there are strict conditions limiting your coverage. These conditions are as follows:

■ You cannot know the material or activity to be infringing, or in the absence of actual knowledge be aware of facts or circumstances that make the infringing material or activity apparent, or fail to expeditiously remove or disable access to the material or activity upon obtaining such knowledge or awareness.

■ You cannot receive a financial benefit directly attributable to the infringing activity when you have the right and ability to control that activity, such as if you were to receive a fee each time a customer clicked on a *banner advertisement* that then took that customer to an infringing site.

■ You cannot fail to respond expeditiously to a compliant notice regarding the reference or link, that is, by taking down the material or blocking access to it.

## Hosting

Despite all of the rules established to deal with the provision of mere conduit operations, caching, and linking, the single most common source of copyright infringement involves hosting. When you host a customer's web site you are storing any material that customer decided to post to that site and because the computer hosting that site is operated by you, any infringing material on that site can be traced back to you. Sometimes, however, the material can be traced back only to your upstream service provider; that is, you operate the computers, but you actually buy Internet access from a wholesale provider. In such cases, a copyright owner's notice is likely to go to your wholesale provider, who might then decide to pass that notice on to you. Either way, you need to be cognizant of the rules that apply to hosting by virtue of the DMCA.

As with the other sections of the DMCA, you can avoid only monetary liability, but not all injunctions, when you host material. *Hosting* is defined as storing infringing material at the direction of a user on equipment controlled or operated by or for you. The conditions controlling application of the DMCA's protections are almost identical to those relating to information location tools:

■ You cannot know the material or an activity using the material on your equipment to be infringing, or in the absence of actual knowledge be aware of facts or circumstances that make the infringing material or activity apparent, or fail to expeditiously remove or disable access to the material or activity upon obtaining such knowledge or awareness.

■ You cannot receive a financial benefit directly attributable to the infringing material or activity when you have the right and ability to control that material or activity, such as if you were to receive per-hit fees for third-party access to the site rather than some form of metered service tied directly to the infringement. This does not mean that all forms of metered service will meet this financial benefit test, either. But, if you establish a metered service that is designed to specifically take advantage of an increase in traffic to a site with infringing material, and you have the right and ability to control the material or activity on that site, you have problems.

- You cannot fail to respond expeditiously to a compliant notice claiming the material to be infringing or the subject of infringing activity, that is, by taking down the material or blocking access to it.

## The Knowledge Standards

In reality, the actual knowledge requirement set forth here is relatively weak, which is why the apparent knowledge, or red-flag, standard was developed. You can actually know that material or activity is infringing only when you actually know that the material is infringing *and* that the true owner has not authorized its use. For example, if you find a copy of a song stored on a hosted site, you would first need to know the song was copyrighted, which you might assume but not actually know. Then you would have to know that the owner or someone authorized by the owner could not have put the song there, which you might also assume but likewise not actually know. The content companies figured out fairly early on during the negotiations of the terms of the DMCA that an actual knowledge standard provided them with little protection, so the real fight was over the language of the red-flag standard.

The content companies wanted the red flag to be the incredibly easy-to-prove "could have known" or "should have known" standard. Under this standard, as long as you could have known or should have known that the material or activity was infringing, then you should be liable. Obviously, you could have known that there was infringing material on a hosted page if you went through every single page stored on every single computer you hosted. Likewise, a large content company could easily convince a judge that you should have known that the infringing material was on your hosted computers. The content companies also wanted service providers to be liable when they failed to investigate anything they considered suspicious. For example, the content companies assumed a web site would have a sudden increase in traffic only when it offered infringing material, rather than any of the thousands of legitimate reasons for such traffic, such as a free car contest. While this was an outrageous position to take, the content companies did make the legitimate point that service providers should not be allowed to come across material they suspected of being infringing and do nothing about it. I eventually came up with the wording for the compromise language, during one of the congressionally sponsored negotiation sessions. This language states that, in the absence of actual knowledge, a service provider cannot be "aware of facts or circumstances from which infringing activity is apparent."

There are many different facts or circumstances that have perfectly legitimate origins. I intended for this language to help draw a distinction between those facts and circumstances that make you wonder (such as a sudden increase in traffic) but don't really make you aware of anything, and those that make it apparent that something illegal is going on. For example, you might run across a customer's site called the Red Hot Warez Site. If you realized that *warez* is a term that is often used to describe stolen software, then the name of the site might make you suspicious, but it would not on its own make illegal activity apparent. The customer might have thought the name would get attention, although the site has nothing to do with software, or the Red Hot Warez might be the name of a new garage band. Since you don't have an obligation to further investigate, you might want to stop right there. But if you also know that the site uses a lot of storage space, has experienced heavy download traffic, and is offering to sell copies of Microsoft Windows 98 for $5, then it should be apparent to you that illegal activity is afoot.

Although there is no obligation to investigate each and every site hosted on your network, as previously noted, obviously illegal sites can't be ignored. If you become aware of a customer's site that has copies of hundreds of popular songs that couldn't possibly be legal, you should at least contact your customer to ask whether they own the songs or are authorized to make copies available on the site. Since the answer to that question is probably obvious, you might wish to take the more prudent step of telling the customer to immediately remove the questionable material before you are forced to take down the site. In reality, however, ISPs usually do not engage in activities that cause them to become aware of the specific content of their customers' sites, so it is unlikely that you will have to deal with an actual or apparent knowledge situation. So, although it is important that you know about these standards, it is more likely that you will have to deal with receipt of a notice under the DMCA, which is becoming quite common.

## Notice and Take Down

If you receive a notice, regardless of whether it is compliant as explained in the following, you will probably have to respond to it in some way. A compliant notice must be in writing and meet the following specific requirements of the DMCA:

1. The notice must be signed, physically or electronically, by someone authorized to act on behalf of the owner of the exclusive right, such as the distribution right, that is allegedly infringed.

2. The notice must identify the copyrighted work allegedly infringed. A single notice can cover multiple works at a single online site if the notice includes a representative, but not exhaustive, list.

3. The notice must identify the allegedly infringing material or activity and provide enough information to enable you to find the material.

4. The notice must provide information that is reasonably sufficient to permit you to contact the complaining party, such as a mailing address, telephone number, and/or e-mail address.

5. The notice must include a statement that the complaining party has a good-faith belief that use of the allegedly infringing material is not authorized by the copyright owner, its agent, or the law.

6. The notice must include a statement that the information in the notice is accurate and, under penalty of perjury, that the complaining party is authorized to act on behalf of the owner of the copyright allegedly infringed.

If a notice does not *substantially* comply with these requirements, the notice is not considered compliant. In this context, *substantially* means that there can be no fatal flaw in the necessary information, such as the location of the allegedly infringing material or the good-faith statement. If the telephone number has a typographical error, however, and it is still possible to contact the complaining party in another way, the notice would be considered compliant. If you receive a noncompliant notice, but that notice includes the information set forth in requirements 2, 3, and 4, then you must promptly attempt to contact the complaining party or take other reasonable steps to assist the complaining party in fixing the notice. Until you have received a compliant notice, the fact that the complaining party has sent you a noncompliant one, talked to you on the phone, or sent you e-mail cannot be used against you to show that you had either actual or apparent knowledge of the infringement. This last point is a very important protection for ISPs.

### The Noncompliant Notice

During negotiations, some content companies stated that they wanted to be able to send an ISP a long list of copyrighted works and make that ISP responsible for making sure none of the listed works were transmitted or stored on the ISP's network. The content companies did not get their way in this regard, but that hasn't stopped some content companies and their attorneys from trying anyway. See Side Law: *Star Wars, Episode I*. As it turns out, if a complaining party cannot identify the allegedly infringing material, or won't identify its allegedly infringed copyright, or doesn't provide you with sufficient contact information, you can completely ignore the notice, which is what most ISPs did in response to the Lucasfilm letter.

## Special Rules for Colleges and Universities

Many colleges and universities function as ISPs for students and faculty, and sometimes for alumni. Since the faculty members and graduate students of such institutions are often considered employees and aren't always so careful, these institutions were concerned that they might be more at risk than traditional ISPs. The DMCA therefore establishes special rules for nonprofit educational institutions. For the purposes of the mere conduit and system caching provisions, faculty members and graduate students are not considered to be part of the institution. As a result, their infringing activities cannot destroy the institution's protections. Likewise, for the purposes of the information location tools and hosting provisions, the faculty member's and graduate student's knowledge or awareness of infringing activities cannot be attributed to the institution. In both cases, however, there are more special conditions. For a preceding three-year period, the infringing activities of the member or student cannot have involved the provision of online access to instructional materials that were required or recommended for a course taught at the institution by such person.

## Side Law: *Star Wars, Episode I*

A law firm representing Lucasfilm sent a letter to a large number of ISPs just before *Star Wars, Episode I* was released. The letter stated that the "information set out below provides you with the notice required under the DMCA with regard to unauthorized electronic files relating to the upcoming film." The letter goes on to identify a list of copyrighted materials and Lucasfilm trademarks (which are not covered by the DMCA), and a photocopy of a copyrighted article from *CNN Interactive* about movie piracy. Since the letter did not identify the allegedly infringing material, however, it was not a compliant notice, regardless of what it said, and it could not be used as evidence of an ISP's knowledge. This type of letter was exactly what the DMCA sought to prevent.

Within the same period, that institution cannot have received more than two other DMCA notices relating to that member or student. The institution must also provide all users of its equipment with informational materials that accurately describe and promote compliance with U.S. copyright laws. In exchange for these special rules, the institutions agreed to be subject to broader injunctive relief.

## Protections for ISPs against Abuse and Mistake

To protect ISPs from misrepresentations by copyright owners and customers, the DMCA includes additional safety provisions. If someone knowingly materially misrepresents that certain material or activity is infringing, then that person shall be liable for any damages, costs, and attorneys' fees that result. This was intended not only to punish overzealous copyright owners, but to prevent non–copyright owners from trying to use the notice-and-take-down provisions of the DMCA to unfairly hurt a competitor or someone they didn't like. Since the DMCA also allows for removed or disabled materials to be put back under certain circumstances, the DMCA includes matching provisions that punish customers who lie to have material put back. In either case, a service provider will not be liable for removing or disabling material or activity in good faith, regardless of whether the material or activity is ultimately determined to be infringing.

This good-faith exception does not apply, however, if you remove material or disable access in response to a notice and fail to take reasonable steps to promptly notify your customer of your action. In the event that your customer provides you with a counternotice, you must then promptly provide a copy of the counternotice to the complaining party and inform them that you intend to replace the removed material or cease disabling access to that material within 10 business days. Unless the complaining party informs you that it has filed an action seeking a restraining order to prevent the customer from engaging in further infringing activity on your equipment or network, you are obligated to replace the removed material or cease disabling access to it in not less than 10 or more than 14 business days following receipt of the counternotice.

# Counternotice and Protecting Customers

The counternotice provisions were developed to reasonably protect the constitutional rights of your customers. In the absence of the DMCA, a copyright owner would have to go to court to get an injunction against an ISP in order to force that ISP to take down or disable access to infringing material. The judicial process requires a copyright owner to show that it would likely succeed on the merits of an infringement action and that an injunction would be justified under the circumstances. This process typically ensures that the alleged infringer's rights are not overtly abused and provides an avenue for punishing copyright owners that misuse the courts. This process creates a real dilemma for copyright owners, however, because injunctions take a significant amount of time to obtain and can be very costly, and while they are waiting for the court to act, the damage from the infringement continues at a rapid pace. Notice and take down, on the other hand, provides fast and cheap relief.

While I might like to pretend that I thought of the idea for notice and take down entirely on my own, I did not. I got the idea from a news report regarding a 1995 legal settlement between the Church of Scientology and Netcom (now part of Mindspring Enterprises). Although the settlement has never been published, the news article said that the parties had settled a copyright dispute involving material posted by a Netcom customer by agreeing to a process for more quickly resolving future disputes involving church copyrights. If the church notified Netcom that material infringing on a church copyright was on the Netcom network, Netcom would block access to the material. This seemed like a very logical solution, so I incorporated it into one of the proposed amendments I offered to Congressman Rick Boucher later that year. At that time, and for years later, I argued that the notice-and-take-down process was the perfect solution to the copyright owner's dilemma. It was also a very good solution to a problem plaguing ISPs. Before the DMCA, ISPs commonly received complaints from people—called in to operators or sent as poorly worded or cryptic e-mail and letters—alleging copyright infringement by the ISP's customers. Conscientious ISPs investigated these complaints to determine whether they were true, but, as a result, often found themselves in an unwanted position between the interested parties.

Under the DMCA, the content companies gave up their right to seek monetary damages against ISPs and agreed to limits on their rights to injunctive relief in return for the swift justice made possible through the notice-and-take-down provisions of the DMCA. ISPs agreed to abide by the terms of the DMCA in exchange for much greater business certainty and to remove themselves from disputes between content companies and customers. However, since the courts were taken out of the basic notice-and-take-down process, the counternotice was created to provide customers with some of the protections previously provided by the courts. If a customer is notified by an ISP that material or activity posted by the customer has been or will soon be removed or disabled, the customer has a right to respond via a counternotice and have the ISP's action reversed. To be effective, a counternotice must be in writing and must meet the following requirements:

- The customer must sign the counternotice, physically or electronically.
- The counternotice must identify the material removed or disabled and the location at which it appeared prior to such action.

- The counternotice must include a statement, under penalty of perjury, that the customer has a good-faith belief that the material was removed or disabled by mistake or misidentification.

- The counternotice must include the customer's name, address, and telephone number, as well as a statement consenting to federal jurisdiction and agreeing to service of process, thereby making it easier for a content company to get injunctive relief if the counternotice is defective.

## DMCA Identification Subpoenas

Even though a content company has sent a notice to an ISP and been able to get allegedly infringing material removed or blocked, the content company may still want to pursue the alleged infringer. This can be difficult, however, because many web sites, especially illegal ones, do not identify the person(s) operating the site. Content companies cannot trace the IP address back beyond the ISP holding the IP address, and ISPs typically cannot disclose the names of their customers without breaching contracts with such customers or otherwise violating the customers' privacy rights. In consideration of this problem, the DMCA enables a copyright owner to get a subpoena forcing the service provider to identify the alleged infringer. The request to a court for a subpoena must include a copy of the notice provided to the ISP, the proposed subpoena, and a sworn declaration stating the purpose for seeking the subpoena and stating that the information will be used only to protect the copyright owner's copyrights.

If you receive a subpoena, you are obligated to expeditiously disclose the requested information, usually by a specified date, unless the subpoena violates federal law in some way. There is no obligation to appear in court to defend the subpoena on the customer's behalf or to notify your customer that you have been served with such a subpoena. This has not stopped people whose identity was revealed through the subpoena process from publicly accusing their ISP of failing to protect them. Over Memorial Day weekend in 1999, AT&T was served and promptly complied with a DMCA subpoena to reveal to Bridge Publications, a corporation owned by the Church of Scientology, the name of a WorldNet customer. The WorldNet customer, known online as "Safe," claimed that AT&T had failed to give him reasonable time to respond to the subpoena. As already noted, while the DMCA does not require you to provide your customer with any notice or a reasonable time to respond, your terms of service with your customer may include different obligations, so don't forget to check your contract in your rush to comply with the subpoena. For his part, Safe claims he is switching Internet and long-distance service to MCI WorldCom—an excellent choice!

## No Monitoring Required

Aside from the subpoena provisions, the DMCA does a decent job of protecting the privacy of your customers. The DMCA includes language that specifically states that nothing in the DMCA can be construed to condition its protections on monitoring your service or affirmatively seeking facts indicating infringing activity, unless pursuant to a standard technical measure, which I will describe subsequently. The DMCA states that you are not required to gain access to, remove, or disable access to material in cases where doing so would be prohibited by law.

# Technical Compliance

The technical measures mentioned in the preceding paragraph are part of the conditions for eligibility under the DMCA. Although I and representatives of other ISPs provided convincing arguments for why it was technically infeasible and economically unreasonable to expect ISPs to do many of the things proposed in the NII legislation, the content companies never did trust us. As a result, the limitations on liability established by the DMCA apply only if you:

■ Adopt and reasonably implement, and inform customers of, a policy that provides for the termination of customers who are repeat infringers.

■ Accommodate and do not interfere with standard technical measures.

Negotiations over the definition of a repeat infringer were long and hard and netted nothing. In the end, we agreed not to provide a definition, so a repeat infringer could be whatever you decided it should be. I was satisfied with the decision not to define *repeat infringer* because every proposed definition included legitimate parties. A company can get into copyright infringement trouble because of, for example, the content of an advertisement, an errant employee's use of some desktop software, or improper photocopying. It is probably safe to assume that large, diverse companies such as IBM have been repeatedly accused of copyright infringement. Historical artifacts such as this, however, should not influence any decision to terminate service to a company like IBM just because it may be a repeat infringer. Although the content companies were never willing to completely let go of the repeat infringer concept, they did eventually concede that the lack of a definition was better than no reference to repeat infringers.

We did agree on a definition of standard technical measures, although this definition means little and illustrates an equal lack of trust on the part of service providers with respect to the content companies. This term is defined to mean technical measures that are used by copyright owners to identify or protect copyrighted works that:

■ Have been developed pursuant to a broad consensus of copyright owners and service providers in an open, fair, voluntary, multi-industry standards process

■ Are available to any person on reasonable and nondiscriminatory terms

■ Do not impose substantial costs on service providers or substantial burdens on their systems or networks

Having spent a considerable amount of time working on standards development, it is safe to say that the first part of this definition will be difficult to meet, especially in combination with the second and third parts. This is why I was willing to agree to this definition. To give you an idea about why the content companies were not trusted, one prominent content company representative actually stated that ISPs should be able to adopt technology that would enable a bell to ring inside a router each time a packet of infringing information went through that router. This type of "constantly ringing" comment actually helped to maintain our resolve through the dog days of the negotiations.

## Injunctive Relief

In the unlikely event that a copyright owner is not satisfied with notice and take down, the owner can seek injunctive relief, but the copyright holder will have to be able to make a strong showing regarding its likelihood of success on the merit of its infringement action. The injunctive relief will also be limited in scope and subject to a number of protective considerations. For example, a court can order a mere conduit operator only to stop providing access services to a customer engaged in infringing activity or to block access to a specific, identified, online location outside the United States. But before the court can order even these types of injunctions, the court must consider:

- Whether the injunction would significantly burden the ISP's network or operations

- The magnitude of the harm to the copyright holder if steps were not taken to prevent or restrain the infringement

- Whether implementation of the injunction would be technically feasible and effective and would not interfere with access to noninfringing material at other online locations

- Whether a less burdensome and comparably effective means of preventing or restraining access to the infringing material was available

Given that it is not possible to pull a transatlantic cable up out of the water, cut it open, and reach your hand inside to thereby block access to a specific online location outside the United States without falling all over these considerations, the scope of such injunctive relief is reasonable.

Assuming these considerations can be satisfied, copyright owners can get injunctive relief with respect to system caching, hosting, and even information location tools, but again, the scope of any such injunction will be limited. For example, the court can order you to stop providing access to an infringer's materials or access services to that infringer. The court can also order any other relief the court considers necessary to prevent or restrain infringement, provided such relief is the least burdensome to you among the forms of relief comparably effective for that purpose.

## What If You Don't Like the DMCA?

You can also elect not to comply with the terms of the DMCA to limit your liability without affecting your right to rely on any other defenses that would otherwise be available to you. Thus, if you think the DMCA is a bad law, you can opt out from its protection and take your chances under traditional copyright law. Keep in mind, however, that traditional copyright law is long on liability and short on defenses. Whether you like the DMCA or not, failure to comply with its terms is probably more trouble than it is worth, which is also true with respect to most of the other laws and regulations that are being passed in relation to the Internet. Many of these other rules are discussed in the Chapter 4, *Other Internet-Specific Laws*.

# CHAPTER 4

# Other Internet-Specific Laws

Although intellectual property laws have had and will continue to have a significant impact on the Internet, intellectual property was not the first Internet-related legal area to be regulated. The first Internet-specific law of any significant consequence was probably the Communications Decency Act (CDA), which went into effect on February 8, 1996. The CDA was followed fairly closely by the German multimedia law, called the Federal Act Establishing the General Conditions for Information and Communications Services, which went into effect on August 1, 1997. I will talk about the CDA in this chapter and about the Germans' foray into cyberspace in Chapter 5, *What Is an ISP to Do (or Not)? Content and Activity Regulations to Live By.*

Many other Internet-specific laws now exist or are being created on a wide variety of subjects that will impact ISPs. For example, in some countries it is illegal to compare your product or service to that of a competitor. Some countries, such as the United States, have constitutions that protect citizens' rights up to certain limits, while other countries are dictatorships whose citizens have few individual rights. Correspondingly, some countries encourage communication on almost any subject, while others impose tight restrictions on almost anything said. Although many countries restrict pornographic material, especially child pornography, others let almost anything go.

At least 18 countries have legislation that restricts speech that is considered excessively violent or likely to incite crimes of violence. Materials that will promote hatred or vilify people on the basis of race, gender, sexual preference, or disability are also banned. Private information of others cannot be used, and defamatory, false, misleading, or fraudulent materials are regulated. Even materials that reflect cultural attributes that are contrary to other people's cultural interests are controlled. All of these laws, and many others, are now being turned in the direction of the Internet, and at some point in time, virtually any law that exists in the physical world will be applied to the cyberworld in some way or another. It is impossible to identify, explain, and apply every one of these laws in the context of the Internet. However, I can at least identify some of the major ones that have already been applied to the Net, identify some of what is coming, and help prepare you for what hasn't even been thought up yet.

At the very least, you can be assured that more laws are on the way. For example, in April 1999, the European Commission (EC) released the Action Plan on Promoting Safer Use of the Internet. The objective of this plan, which extends to 2002, is to restrict the circulation on the Internet of illegal or harmful content and the illegal use of the Internet. In particular, the EC hopes to promote services, such as a European network of hot lines, that address "content on the Internet that is contrary to human dignity, for example, child pornography, extreme forms of violence, incitement to racial hatred and xenophobia." By establishing and promoting a hot-line network, the EC hopes to provide a mechanism for removing illegal content from host servers. The EC also hopes to encourage the application of filtering and rating systems for Internet content. To achieve this objective, the EC anticipates that technologies similar to *meta-data content labels* will be established to allow Internet users to control the type of content to which they may be exposed. It is contemplated that the classification of such content will be performed by content providers, third-party experts, local Internet administrators (ISPs), or even automated tools, and that the filters will not only be located in a user's computer, but also in *local area networks* (LANs), *proxy servers*, search engines, and hosted web sites.

As I write this, I am attending the International Conference on Electronic Commerce and Intellectual Property, sponsored by the World Intellectual Property Organization (WIPO) in Geneva, Switzerland. More than 700 participants, mainly lawyers and politicians, from all over the world are attending this conference to discuss and learn how to apply intellectual property laws to the Internet and the Information Society, as the Internet and e-commerce are collectively referred to in much of the world. I am speaking at the conference about service provider liability issues, of course, but service provider concerns take a backseat to the intellectual property issues that are driving this conference. The representatives of each of the governments participating in this conference will return to their countries not only to work on applying intellectual property laws to the Information Society, as practiced in their countries, but also to begin or continue the process of applying additional laws to the Internet, which brings us to the subject matter of this chapter. Some of the more significant laws being applied to the Internet are set forth in the following sections.

## Privacy, Publicity, and Defamation

From a legal perspective, your right to privacy can be defined in four distinct ways:

1. The right not to have your physical solitude intruded upon, such as could occur if someone eavesdropped on your private discussions or took pictures of you from an adjacent property.

2. The right not to have embarrassing private facts disclosed in public.

3. The right not to be placed in a false light in public.

4. The right not to have your name or likeness appropriated for commercial benefit.

As you can see, the right to privacy includes elements of what you probably thought were separate rights: privacy and publicity. The difference between privacy and publicity has to do primarily with the nature of the resulting injury. If your pocketbook is injured, then your right to publicity has probably been injured. If your psyche has been injured, then your right to privacy has probably been injured. Since most people have a hard time following this distinction, however, I will just stick with what most people think of as privacy and publicity.

The concept of privacy is usually equated with the privacy of personal information and activities. Since people are quite different the world over, privacy means something different to almost every person within every culture in the world. The right of privacy is intended to protect against intrusion upon an individual's private dignity and self-esteem. Privacy also depends on who you are. If you are famous, especially if you have purposely sought the public's attention, you can generally expect a lesser degree of privacy than can people who are not famous. Whether you are famous or not, however, everyone has a certain right to publicity, that is, the commercialization of your name, image, or persona. Hence, the right of publicity is intended to protect against commercial loss caused by appropriation of an individual's personality or likeness for commercial exploitation. Everyone also has a right not to have false things said about themselves by others, which is generally referred to as *defamation*. Given the interrelationship between each of these concepts—privacy, publicity, and defamation—they are dealt with together, starting with privacy.

## Privacy

The privacy issue rears its rather ugly head in a number of different ways with respect to the Internet. The most common way is through the direct collection of personal information from web sites. Many web sites, including ISP customer service sites, have been set up to collect such information from people accessing the site. This information ranges from someone's name and contact information, to complete demographic data, to very personal questions about that person's lifestyle. People have freely provided this information because they thought they had to do so in order to get service, or simply out of ignorance or misplaced trust in the operators of the web site. Before you laugh, how many of you have answered all of the questions on a warranty form because you thought your warranty would not be honored if you did not? Better yet, how many of you have purchased a magazine subscription or some similar item from a sweepstakes company because you thought your winning number would not be drawn if you did not? When web site operators began to trade or sell this data to other people, who then used it for marketing purposes or worse, the people from which the data was collected began to express grave concerns.

Many users have since figured out that data was being collected about them and their Internet usage habits in a number of more subtle approaches. *Cookies* are computer records of information that are sent from one web site to a user's computer that enable that web site or another, by accessing the cookie from a PC's hard drive, to identify certain types of activities that were engaged in by that user. Java programs, applets, ActiveX programs, and other client-based scripting technologies can also be used to collect vast amounts of data about users or their habits. This data can be collected for legitimate purposes, to which most users would not object, but it can also be used to target-market goods and services to users, which can be quite annoying. For example, in 1999, Nissan accidentally sent the e-mail addresses of over 24,000 potential automotive customers to the others. Shortly thereafter, AT&T emailed 1,800 customers of a long-distance program and likewise included the e-mail address of each of the other customers.

The manner in which different societies are dealing with this issue of the privacy of personal information is very interesting. Tribal-based cultures have almost no expectation of privacy within their cultures, but they expect significant privacy outside of their cultures. More than 40 countries have enacted, or are in the process of passing, privacy laws, including much of Europe, but not the United States—yet. While Americans have historically had a relatively low expectation of privacy, Europeans have generally expected a significantly greater degree of privacy regarding their personal information. To deal with European privacy expectations, the European Union has passed a privacy directive that is in the process of being adopted, in different ways, by each of the member countries in the EU. This directive requires ISPs, e-commerce businesses, and others within the European Community to disclose how they intend to use any personal information they collect. While companies within the United States and in other countries are adopting similar efforts on a voluntary basis, these efforts may never guarantee the same level of privacy expected in Europe, and this may be a problem. The EU Privacy Directive also requires countries trading with its member countries to adopt measures that *adequately* protect personal information and threatens to cut off data transfers to countries that do not.

The definition of *adequate protection* is the subject of great debate, but basically the Europeans appear to feel that self-regulation is insufficient, and the United States disagrees. While legislation has been introduced in Congress to address this issue, it is far from certain whether any such legislation will become law in the near future. In the meantime, the U.S. administration has taken the position that self-regulation is the best solution within the United States, supplemented by the implementation of privacy policies on federal web sites and relying on enforcement actions by the Federal Trade Commission (FTC) when consumer protection issues are at hand. For example, the FTC does not require companies to adopt online privacy policies, but if a company does publish a policy, the FTC will prosecute any complaint alleging a failure to comply with that policy under consumer protection laws. While the FTC is contemplating seeking legislation on privacy and antifraud regulations, other legislation has been proposed to require web site operators in the U.S. to publish privacy guidelines. These latter provisions have been included in controversial—and failed—legislation having to do with broadband access issues, however, so they are unlikely to pass anytime soon.

In the Netherlands and the United Kingdom, legislation has already been passed establishing independent privacy agencies, with more than 50 and more than 100 employees, respectively, to take complaints, proactively investigate, and take legal action against privacy violators. While the United States has appointed a privacy counselor, this position merely provides advice to the administration and will not directly handle consumer privacy issues. The EU finds this effort to be wholly inadequate. As with all things politic, whether the United States' efforts are sufficient is a matter of governmental philosophy. In general, the U.S. government tries to avoid regulating the activities of its citizens because its citizens don't want the government telling them what to do, while many Europeans want their governments to tell them what to do, so the governments are more than happy to do so. A good reason for regulating yourself and asking the government to stay out is that you may not like what you get when the government does get involved. For example, a bill was introduced in the United States in 1999 that would have required ISPs to keep track of which subscribers didn't mind receiving unsolicited e-mail. The problem with this proposal, however, was that it also required the list to be made public, so that all those listed could be guaranteed of quickly being deluged with spam until they asked that their names be taken off the list. ISPs don't need this kind of burden, nor do they need half-baked legislation.

## A Self-Regulated Approach

A self-regulatory approach, including codes of conduct and trademarks, can provide a viable tool in enhancing consumer trust in electronic commerce and ISPs. In the United States, the Better Business Bureau's BBB Online program and the TRUSTe program sponsored by a company called TRUSTe provide codes of conduct, trademark certification, and a limited amount of policing—to members for a fee. An alternative approach to self-regulation, of course, is to simply establish a reasonable privacy policy and stick by it, but far too few companies stick with any policy they establish. When the FTC studied 1,400 web sites in 1998, it found that only 14 percent of those sites actually had privacy policies that informed visitors of their data collection practices. By 1999, a similar study showed that the number of sites with privacy policies had increased to over 65 percent, but only 9.5 percent of those sites actually met what were considered to be the basic elements of an appropriate policy.

In the United Kingdom, the Netherlands, and a growing number of other countries, many companies are adopting the Which? Web Trader scheme, although it may have different names in different countries. Which? Web Trader members (membership is free) must agree to follow a Code of Practice and must supply certain details and contact information to Which? Web Trader in order to receive permission to display the Which? Web Trader trademark. The Code of Practice aims to ensure that consumers are treated fairly, that consumer complaints are heard, and that member companies are expected to make things right in response to a complaint. The Code of Practice for Which? Web Trader is as follows:

- A member company needs to be governed by the law of the country in which it is a member of Which? Web Trader.
- Consumer complaints need to be dealt with effectively.

- Member companies need to provide details about their procedures for solving disputes.
- Prices should be clear to consumers, with no hidden charges such as for taxes, packaging, or delivery.
- Member companies should clearly tell consumers how to pay for offered goods or services.
- Member companies must provide full contact details.
- Member companies must give consumers the possibility to opt out and refuse direct marketing material.
- Member companies must provide a customer service phone number, say when this service is available, and state clearly the cost of the calls.
- The terms and conditions in consumer contracts should be in English or in the official language of the appropriate country.
- Member companies must make it clear whether they are providing a guarantee.

If a consumer wants to buy goods from electronic commerce merchants outside of a particular country, they can find a list on a specified web site of international partners who manage similar, affiliated schemes in other countries. In the United Kingdom, Which? Web Trader can be found at www.which.net/webtrader/.

## Technical Solutions

Speaking of standard approaches, there is another approach: the development of privacy-enabling technology standards. One such proposed standard is the Platform for Privacy Preferences (P3P), which was developed by the World Wide Web Consortium, a web-based standards group, and which aims to automate the sharing of personal information between a consumer and a web site. Lobbying organizations, such as the Direct Marketing Association, have pointed to P3P as an example of how technology might stave off privacy laws, such as Senator Leahy's Electronic Rights for the 21st Century Act, which was first introduced in 1999. This bill would make it harder to disclose information about customers for commercial purposes, increase privacy protection against governmental surveillance, and subject booksellers and libraries to civil liability for the unauthorized disclosures of personal information collected from library and book sale records. While such legislation might give consumers more control over how their personal information is used by online businesses, industry groups maintain that such regulations would be unduly cumbersome and expensive.

## Electronic Communications Privacy Act

No discussion of privacy on the Internet would be complete without some discussion of the U.S. Electronic Communications Privacy Act (ECPA). The ECPA was intended to protect Internet-based communications as telephonic communications are currently protected. Thus, the ECPA requires legal due process standards to be met before Internet-based communications may be handed over to law enforcement officials. In addition, the ECPA prohibits individuals and service providers from monitoring the content of communications over the Internet. A number of people have told me that they are capable of intercepting traffic from the Internet. In response to my assertion that intercepting traffic sounded like an incredible waste of time because of all of the junk they would also receive, they have insisted that they can be extremely selective. I have turned down offers to have this selectivity demonstrated because I did not want to be a witness to the commission of a crime—if their claims turned out to be true. Generally, since ISPs are not in the business of intercepting traffic, the ECPA would not seem to apply, but as it turns out, there are many circumstances where you will either want to intercept traffic or someone else will demand that you do so.

Law enforcement officials might want you to intercept traffic transmitted by users of your network who are suspected of committing crimes. A customer may want you to intercept traffic over your network involving messages to or from an employee or contractor of the customer. Your human resources department or security department might want you to intercept traffic from employees or contractors who are suspected of doing something wrong, such as stealing things from the company. Since the ECPA generally states that it is unlawful to *intercept* such traffic, it is very important to determine whether you come under any exemptions that would make taking such action okay.

Anytime you are asked to do anything by law enforcement officials, contact a lawyer and make sure the law enforcement officials provide you with the necessary legal documents to compel you to take such action. The intent here is not to make law enforcement's job any harder, but you could be liable for the consequences of any action taken without sufficient legal justification, and there have been plenty of cases where law enforcement officials were just a little too quick to jump the gun. When it comes to monitoring your own employees or the employees of a customer, an initial reading of the ECPA statutes would lead one to believe that these people are subject to broad protection, but other statutory exceptions and subsequent judicial decisions have significantly narrowed any protection. For example, 18 U.S.C. 2512(2)(a), in combination with the definition provided at 18 U.S.C. 2510(5)(a), permits the utilization of devices that intercept e-mail so long as (1) the intercepting device is part of the communication service provider's network, and (2) the device is used in the ordinary course of business.

The Fifth Circuit Court of Appeals interprets the *intercept* language in the ECPA to mean only the acquisition of an electronic message during the actual transmission of the message from one party to another. The court also noted that *interception* does not cover the retrieval of stored messages from network memory. This decision was based in part on 18 U.S.C. 2701(c)(1), which permits the person or entity providing the electronic communication service, or someone authorized by such person or entity or authorized by a user of the service with respect to a communication of or intended for that user, to access stored communications. In *Bohach v. Reno*, 932 F. Supp. 1232, 1236 (1996), a federal district court held that the ECPA "allows service providers to do as they wish when it comes to accessing communications in electronic storage."

When it comes to taking action on behalf of a customer, however, you need to make sure you have the customer's written authorization to act on its behalf. Note that 18 U.S.C. 2511(2)(a)(2) provides an exemption from liability for employers who provide electronic communications services to employees for intercepting, disclosing, or using the content of an employee's e-mail message where such actions are necessary to protect the rights or property of the company. In particular, this section includes in its exemption any "operator of a switchboard, or an officer, employee, or agent of a provider of wire or electronic communication service, where facilities are used in the transmission of a wire or electronic communication." Thus, this section protects you only as long as you are acting as the employer's agent.

According to 18 U.S.C. 2511(d), someone can intercept a communication when they have previously received consent to do so from one of the parties to the communication. Since many employers now include consents of this type in agreements signed by employees and contractors, the employer can pass on the interception right to the ISP.

## Children's Privacy

The collection of personal data from children is one area where the United States has already enacted legislation. The Child Online Privacy Protection Act (COPPA) was signed into law in 1998. It provides that web sites cannot collect information from children under the age of 13 without first obtaining parental consent. The difficulty has been that no one is quite sure how a web site should go about collecting such consent. Children's advocates want the FTC to require web sites to get written permission on paper before collecting data from children 12 and under. Other groups want schools to become digital signature certificate authorities that can verify children's and guardians' identities online. The signature would include preclearance on what information can be collected from a child, what cannot, and how to contact a guardian. Other groups fear that either of these solutions would be too burdensome and costly and urge that a type of notice and opt-out system be adopted.

In any case, in October 1999, the FTC issued rules to take effect on April 21, 2000, that implement the requirements of the COPPA. While observers generally lauded the rules, several issues remain unsettled. For example, it is not always clear what type of parental consent must be obtained for different date collection activities. For now, the rules adopt a *sliding scale* of consent (e.g., unauthenticated parental e-mail at the low end, or hard-copy written permission at the high end). These rules will be reassessed in two years to take account of users' experiences and developing technology.

Personally, I don't think people should even attempt to collect any information from children at all—children often have no sense of privacy, of the risks involved, and of what is appropriate. The parents are the ones who are going to have to buy whatever it is that the web site is trying to sell, so why not just stick with the parents? I don't like child-oriented television advertisements, either, but that is another subject.

Legislation has also been introduced to further modify the COPPA to require special parental consent before any primary or secondary student could obtain school-based Internet service from an ISP or other Internet-based service provider who collects information from students in personally identifiable or aggregate form. Although this legislation did not go anywhere in 1999, which is why I am not even providing a title or number for the bill, it is likely that similar legislation will be reintroduced in 2000 or in later years. This type of proposed legislation would extend the COPPA's coverage to any student as old as 18 years of age, and would cover aggregate information. At the very least, such legislation would require written consents from the parents of all students participating in existing school-based Internet access programs and expand the notice obligations for ISPs. It could also establish a dangerous precedent that the collection of aggregate information from minors, including for network management purposes, requires parental consent.

## Publicity

While there is no federal right to control your publicity, a number of states—such as New York, California, and Florida, where lots of celebrities live—have enacted right of publicity laws in their states. Typically, these laws are designed to protect a famous person's name, voice, likeness, or persona from being impersonated or otherwise used for commercial purposes without their consent. Actress Hedy Lamarr, for example, filed a suit against Corel Corporation in Florida for use of her image in a photograph that appeared on a CD-ROM. But even ordinary citizens have learned to take advantage of these laws. A California woman, who is not famous, filed a similar suit against Corel for use of her photograph on a CD-ROM and on its Internet site in violation of the state's right of publicity statute. It isn't likely that a right of publicity claim against a customer for whom you provide access or web hosting services will get you in trouble. You may nonetheless be subject to a subpoena seeking facts about your service provision or you may be subject to injunctive orders requiring you to remove offending material.

On the other hand, if we are talking about your own web site, you need to be very careful about posting pictures of anyone who has not provided you with a release or a license—and don't rely on a photographer's assurances. Unless the photographer is willing to sign a contract agreeing to indemnify you in case you get sued (make sure the photographer can actually make good on any such promise) or you get insurance to cover your use, as will be discussed subsequently, you need to take care of this matter yourself. Stick with cute pictures of dogs, cats, and inanimate objects.

## Defamation

False statements about somebody that are spoken are considered to be slanderous. When those same statements are written down, such as on a web site, in a chat room, or in e-mail, they are called *libelous*. When a libelous statement hurts the reputation or image of a person or company, it is considered to be defamatory. Related actions in unfair competition, trade disparagement, and a variety of other claims can likewise spring from such matters. Back in 1995, a lawsuit was brought by Stratton Oakmont, Inc., against someone who accused the company of fraud stemming from one of its initial public offerings. This accusation was published on an electronic bulletin board operated by Prodigy. In this case, the court ultimately ruled that Prodigy acted as the publisher of the information posted on its bulletin board and that, as a publisher,

Prodigy should be liable for any resulting libel or defamation. Prodigy was found to be the publisher because it exercised editorial control, like the editor of a newspaper, over the posting to its site to make its service family friendly. This decision led to the rapid disappearance of most moderated boards, chat rooms, and message services.

Section 230 of the Communications Decency Act, which was partially ruled to be unconstitutional (but only partially), and which I will discuss in some detail, solves this problem in the United States. Section 230 says that information service providers are immune from liability as a publisher, where the ISP has only published the information from a third-party information content provider. AOL has successfully used this provision of the CDA in its defense in a number of defamation and libel suits brought against it, resulting from acts by its customers. A very different rule appears to exist in England. Under the Defamation Act, exercising editorial control of posted information may subject an ISP to liability as a publisher or editor, thereby depriving the ISP of a defense. While there is a defense known as the *innocent dissemination defense,* that defense is available only to parties that have acted reasonably and have no reason to believe that they have done anything to cause or contribute to the publication of a defamatory statement. In a U.K. suit brought against Demon Internet Limited, an English ISP, an unknown U.S. member of a Usenet newsgroup carried by Demon had posted an allegedly defamatory message, which Demon refused to remove when so requested. The court ruled that Demon had published the information, and since it acted unreasonably in refusing to remove the material, especially once it knew something about it, it could not avail itself of the defense. Demon has decided to appeal this case.

The plaintiff in the Demon case has apparently also won defamation suits in Australia and New Zealand, but I don't know if ISPs were involved in such decisions. Perhaps they responded in a faster manner than did Demon. In Singapore, the National Kidney Foundation has sought a court order requiring ISPs in Singapore to disclose the names of those who circulated a defamatory e-mail. The e-mail was originally sent to 48 people, and although the party that originally posted it apologized and agreed to pay damages, the foundation wants to track down all copies of the message and is going after those 48 people and the ISPs to do it. Similarly, U.S. courts have been issuing subpoenas requiring ISPs to reveal the names of customers who posted allegedly defaming and disparaging messages on message boards. Since a number of Internet services such as AOL and Yahoo! allow people to post anonymously, and the IP addresses of their messages cannot be traced back past the ISP hosting the service, the defamed parties are finding that they have to try to get the names from the ISPs. Most ISPs, however, refuse such requests because of customer confidentiality concerns. But most ISPs have provisions in their acceptable use policies that allow them to reveal such information in response to court orders, and that is exactly what has been happening.

## Indecency versus Obscenity

In response to reports of "dirty" pictures and books being mailed to troops in the field during the later part of the American Civil War, Congress passed a law making it illegal to send any "obscene book, pamphlet, picture, print, or other publication of vulgar and indecent character" through the U.S. mail. An expanded version of this law, known as the Comstock Law, also made it a crime to distribute lewd or lascivious publications or pictures. Words such as *obscene, vulgar, indecent,* and *lewd* have always been difficult to define because their definitions largely depend on each individual's subjective interpretation. Although some adults might claim to know such material when they see it, others are not so sure, and certainly what is obscene to some is not to others. Nevertheless, politicians and courts have struggled to define such words as best they could, often on the basis of the perceived need to protect children. Early tests for obscenity centered on whether the material in question tended to corrupt the morals of a young or immature mind. In this context, neither the intended audience nor the overall artistic merit of the material mattered.

This began to change, however, in 1922 after the publication of James Joyce's *Ulysses*. When copies of the book were seized, the publisher, Random House, successfully sued the U.S. government in a decision that created a new standard: Publications must be considered in their entirety. If such publications have artistic or literary merit when taken as a whole, they cannot be entirely banned on the basis of isolated pictures or passages that might be offensive to some. Thus, the test moved away from being based on the sensitivities of the most vulnerable to those of the average. This basic principle has been expanded over time, at least in the United States under the protections of the First Amendment to the Constitution, to include all ideas that have even the slightest redeeming social importance, whether they are unorthodox, controversial, or perhaps even hateful to the prevailing climate of opinion. With respect to certain types of pornographic material, however, the measure of prevailing opinion has to be determined by applying the standards of the community in which such material is distributed. Under this test, it is possible for the same material to be considered unacceptable in a conservative town and acceptable in a larger, more diverse community such as New York City.

## The Basic Test for Obscenity

So how do you determine whether something really is illegal? First off, most people remember the *community standard* language and generally recognize it as the test for obscenity, but there is more. You must also remember to apply the aforementioned socially redeeming importance test and view the work as a whole, and analyze the wording of the laws of the state in which the alleged crime was committed. While the Supreme Court did attempt to establish a general definition that could be used in this regard in a case called *Miller v. California* in 1973, you will see that it didn't really help that much. In *Miller,* the Court stated that material is *obscene,* and therefore unprotected by the Constitution, if:

1. The average person, applying contemporary community standards, would find the materials, taken as a whole, to arouse immoral lustful desire, that is, *prurient interest.*

2. The materials depict or describe, in a patently offensive way, sexual conduct specifically prohibited by applicable state law.

3. The work, taken as a whole, lacks serious literary, artistic, political, or social value.

Since this is a rather complicated definition, it is best to try to parse it by asking a number of questions regarding the material:

1. Is it designed to be sexually arousing?

2. Is it arousing in a way that one's local community would consider unhealthy or immoral?

3. Does it depict acts whose descriptions are specifically prohibited by state law?

4. Does the work, when taken as a whole, lack significant literary, artistic, scientific, or social value?

## Application of the Obscenity Test to the Internet

Since 1973, this has been the prevailing standard in the United States, and still is, but the introduction of the Internet and its widespread use for the distribution of pornographic material have served to further complicate matters. For example, in 1994 federal prosecutors succeeded in obtaining a conviction against a California couple on 11 counts of transmitting obscenity through interstate phone lines because a computer bulletin board they operated made sexually explicit pictures available to subscribers in Tennessee. Despite the fact that similar material was freely available in California and was not considered obscene in that state, the court ruled that the community in which the material was made available should be used to determine the standard that should be applied. Prosecutors picked Tennessee, of course, because Tennessee had a generally conservative populace and therefore had correspondingly rigid community standards. In the context of the Internet, which inherently recognizes no geographic boundaries, this meant that the lowest common denominator—that is, the most conservative standard—had to be applied to everything, thereby making almost any pornographic material on the Net illegal.

## The Communications Decency Act

Against this backdrop, in 1996 the United States decided to see what it could do to further define obscene material and to take it a step further and attempt to define what Congress viewed as indecent communications. Since Congress was moving toward the adoption of an overhaul of the Communications Act of 1934, it decided to include a number of additional laws as part of the Telecommunications Act of 1996 to deal with this issue. One of these laws was the Communications Decency Act (CDA), which has quite a few sections, only some of which are relevant to this discussion.

The Telecommunications Act of 1996 was not the best vehicle for this endeavor. Due to political desires and intense lobbying by a vast array of interested parties, it is extremely ambiguous in parts and generally poorly drafted. In addition to doing a less than adequate job of breaking open the local phone markets in the United States to competition and failing to provide any definition for the term *telecommunications device*, the CDA included two particularly controversial provisions that illustrate the poor drafting. One provision made it a crime to use a *telecommunications device* to make an *obscene or indecent* communication to a minor, knowing that person to be a minor. The other provision made it a crime to use an *interactive computer service* to "knowingly . . . display in a manner available" to anyone under 18 a communication that "in context, depicts or describes, in terms patently offensive as measured by contemporary community standards, sexual or excretory activities or organs, regardless of whether the user placed the call or initiated the communication." As soon as the CDA was signed into law, it was attacked on constitutional grounds.

The first provision of the CDA, dealing with obscene or indecent communications, was struck down because, even though obscene material is not protected, indecent material is, in most cases. This means that the CDA was struck down only with respect to indecency, not obscenity. Many people believe that the CDA was struck down as a whole, but it was not—just the parts that dealt with indecency or did a bad job of defining obscenity. So what is indecent? One definition, provided by the FCC and generally described by comedian George Carlin as the "seven dirty words," can be interpreted to include just about anything that offends someone's sensibilities without rising to the level of obscenity. The only kind of indecent material or speech that can be controlled by the government (again, only with respect to the United States) is indecent speech that is included in certain types of pervasive broadcasts. And this is only the case because of the possible exposure of the material to children. Hence, private cable channels fall under different rules, as do certain types of late-night broadcast. Keep in mind, children are a special case in all regards, as well they should be, and I will discuss the unique rules that apply to them shortly.

The second provision also got into trouble, as I suggested, for doing a bad job of defining obscenity or, rather, attempting to redefine obscenity. As already described, the second provision leaves out a number of the components of the obscenity test constructed by the Supreme Court and attempts to add in an odd mixture of what can best be described as indecency language. Civil liberty groups pointed out that the language, "display in a manner available," was too vague and that the community standards analysis, such as applied in the aforementioned Tennessee case, should not be applied to the Internet. ISPs joined in condemning this portion of the CDA because the breadth of the language implicated every party, including ISPs and browser makers, involved in the *display* of something illegal. While the statute did say "knowingly . . . displays" to a minor, it only specified the intent to display the material, not the intent to make it available to a minor. Hence, whether someone intended a minor to see it or not, it was illegal if you intended for it to be displayed and a minor happened to see it. Since ISPs and browser makers intend for almost everything they transmit or enable to be displayed in some way or another, they were potentially liable for everything. The Supreme Court agreed and struck down this provision of the CDA as unconstitutional because it was overly broad (violating the First Amendment) and vague (violating the due process requirements of the Fifth Amendment). Because the provision was struck down in whole, the Court did not address the issue of whether community standards apply to the Net, but the general belief is that at least that portion of the obscenity test will eventually be restructured.

Finally, the CDA also included an additional provision directed to obscene communications, such as e-mail and bulletin board postings, that are made with the intent to annoy. The Supreme Court has upheld this provision, so such communications can be repressed without violating the Constitution. This law can actually come in handy for ISPs in the fight against spammers (which I will discuss in the next section)—especially those that send spam with embedded links to pornographic sites that might also include obscene materials.

## Special Laws Relating to Children

Although disappointed with the Supreme Court's quick repudiation of major portions of the CDA, Congress was not deterred by the CDA's self-destruction and quickly passed the Child Online Protection Act (COPA). The COPA is generally referred to as CDA II because it was Congress's second attempt at regulating the decency of communications. The COPA sought to make it a crime for commercial web sites to give minors access to *harmful material,* which is defined as any sexually explicit communication that lacks "serious literary, artistic, political, or scientific value." Violators of this law would face fines of up to $50,000 and prison terms of up to six months, per offense. This law was narrower than the CDA in a number of respects. First, it applied only to the World Wide Web (not e-mail and not newsgroups) and it applied only to "commercial" web sites. Second, after ISPs had been scared into action by the CDA, they made sure that it included provisions that exempted ISPs for simply transmitting or hosting material. Third, the knowledge standard was reconstructed to make it more specific—that is, less broad—and therefore, hopefully, more likely to pass constitutional muster. The new phrasing used the language "knowingly and with knowledge of the character" of the communication. Finally, the standard was limited only to material that was "harmful to minors."

The COPA was immediately attacked as unconstitutional and, like the CDA before it, a federal district court issued a preliminary injunction against enactment of part of the law. The injunction was based on a finding that the language of the act was still too vague and too broad because it could be interpreted to include indecent, rather than just obscene, material. This decision was promptly appealed to the Third Circuit Court of Appeals and, although the court has not yet issued its opinion on the matter, it appears pretty clear that the injunction will be upheld. In particular, during oral argument, one judge asked, "Isn't the answer here to empower parents [with filtering technology] to protect their children from [Internet smut]?" As with the CDA, only a portion of the COPA was attacked and therefore ruled on. This decision did not enjoin the provision in the COPA that requires ISPs to inform their subscribers about the availability of screening software to help subscribers filter out material that offends them in some way. I will remind you of this requirement in Chapter 5, but keep in mind that this is where it comes from.

## Obscenity Rules Need Not Apply

I previously stated that when it comes to child pornography, the rules that apply to obscenity tend to go out the window. Although this statement would not be readily apparent within the context of the COPA, keep in mind that the COPA did not deal with child pornography; rather, it attempted to address the issue of communicating "harmful material" to minors. The sexual exploitation of minors is addressed in a variety of federal child-porn statutes, such as 18 U.S.C. 2252. This statute outlaws knowingly transporting, shipping, receiving, or distributing via interstate or foreign commerce by any means, including by computer or mail, any visual depiction involving the use of a minor engaging in sexually explicit conduct and any visual depiction of such conduct. Violators can be fined up to $250,000 and imprisoned for up to 15 years. Such statutes do not address the issue of whether the material in question is "obscene," whether a community standard applies, or whether "serious" artistic value is a consideration. These statutes are not concerned with issues of "expression." Child pornography is constitutionally *un*protected speech, so these laws are designed to promote the protection of children by attempting to destroy any potential market that could exist for the child pornography materials.

It is important, however, to recognize what is considered to be child pornography and what is not. First, the federal statutes are limited to visual depictions, not text, although this is not the case in some states. Second, material that depicts child sex, but does not use a child, does not qualify as child pornography. Hence, textual depictions of such activity, such as may be found in the most disgustingly offensive newsgroups on Usenet, are not considered to be child pornography and are therefore subject to the normal protections of the First Amendment. If a newsgroup posting or any other textual depiction, such as Nabokov's novel *Lolita*, included a visual depiction, however, the harsher standard applies, regardless of the textual content.

# Child Porn Is Child Porn, Animated or Not

So what is a visual depiction? So far, courts have found that computer-generated or computer-altered material that appears to be child pornography, but did not actually involve the sexual use of a real child, is not considered to be child pornography. Whether this makes any sense depends on your perspective. Technically, the statutes were intended to prevent children from being harmed, so if no child was used, then no child was harmed. I disagree with this perspective. It is almost impossible to distinguish between certain types of computer-generated or altered images and real images. If computer-aided child pornographic material is readily made available to the depraved souls who are attracted to such material, that is only likely to lead to further depravation, which can eventually lead to harm to real children. It is generally accepted that children who have been sexually abused often end up as emotionally troubled adults, which can lead to many other problems for the abuse victims as well as for the society within which they live. We should be doing what we reasonably can do to prevent even one child from being subjected to abuse (not just sexually oriented abuse), and if that means not protecting computer-generated child pornography, then so be it.

I say that we should do what we *reasonably can do* because there is a limit to how much responsibility should lie on the shoulders of the various entities participating in utilization of the Internet. For example, a residential Internet access customer recently asked her ISP to prevent pornographic messages from being delivered to her child's Hotmail account. Since Hotmail is a web site–based e-mail service, all e-mail messages delivered to a Hotmail account are first delivered to the Hotmail server and then transferred to the Hotmail account as standard data packets. Even though the ISP may provide access to the customer, the ISP is not providing an e-mail server and isn't even delivering mail that conforms to e-mail protocols. As such, there is nothing the ISP can do, other than recommend that the customer set up an e-mail account with the ISP and employ filtering software to filter out potentially offensive messages. Whether Microsoft's Hotmail service should have some obligation in this regard is a different matter.

## Protection of Children from Sexual Predators Act

The Protection of Children from Sexual Predators Act of 1998 (PCSPA) requires ISPs to report incidents of child pornography to the appropriate federal agency. In this case, ISPs are defined as providers of an electronic communication service or a remote computing service to the public, through a facility or means of interstate or foreign commerce. These terms are taken from other laws and include pretty much anything any type of ISP does. Also, for the purpose of the PCSPA, child pornography is defined by sections 2251, 2251A, 2252, 2252A, and 2260 of title 18 of the U.S. Code.

For the most part, child pornography is any actual nude photo or image of a child that is not clearly innocent (such as a baby's bath picture) or clearly artistic. No image that depicts a nude child in a seductive way or engaged in a sexual act will be considered to be innocent or artistic—no matter how famous the artist. Generally, you recognize most child pornography when you see it, but some situations can be difficult to judge. I discuss the specific requirements of complying with the PCSPA in Chapter 5.

Under the PCSPA, electronic communication service and remote computer service providers who "obtain knowledge of facts or circumstances from which a violation of child pornography laws is apparent" (this is the same knowledge standard used in the DMCA) are required to report it to federal authorities. Monitoring is specifically not required, but a failure to report any child pornography that is found can result in fines from $50,000 (first time) to $100,000 (subsequent times).

Child pornography laws previously tried to hedge against the possibility of destroying someone's life as the result of a single incident of the inadvertent possession of child pornography. These laws made reference to "3 or more" images. The PCSPA modified existing child porn laws to add a so-called zero tolerance provision. Now, the possession of one or more pieces of child pornography can result in a fine or a prison sentence. The PCSPA did, however, add a new affirmative defense for possession of one or more images if you tried promptly and in good faith to destroy the images or report the pornography to law enforcement. Although the zero tolerance program may be well intentioned, I am concerned that it goes too far—even though I am a strongly opposed to child pornography.

Most residential Internet users have little knowledge of how browser software operates and how downloaded images are stored in their computers. Many users who accidentally access child pornographic images on the Internet do not realize that many of those images are automatically stored in their computers, for example, in the

Cache file used by Netscape Navigator or the Temporary Internet file use by Microsoft Explorer. If law enforcement officials thereafter had some reason to look at their computers, they could find these images and the users would have no choice but to attempt to rely on the aforementioned affirmative defense. Granted, law enforcement officers aren't running around with subpoenas demanding access to most people's computers, so this scenario may not be played out very often, but it would be wrong to see a single innocent person wrongly charged with this type of crime.

## Other Action around the World

The federal government in the United States, of course, is not the only government attempting to regulate visual or textual pornography. A number of states, including New Mexico, Virginia, and Michigan, have passed laws that prohibit exposing minors to *harmful* material via the Net or providing minors access to *indecent* online material. The New Mexico law has been judged to be unconstitutional. Legislation has been passed or is in the process of being approved in the United States and within the European Union to require ISPs to notify authorities if they encounter child pornography on the Internet. A French court recently ordered Altern, a French company that provides free web hosting services, to pay an 80,000 Eurodollar penalty for not controlling the publication of illegal material stored on its servers. A Bavarian judge convicted Felix Somm, former manager of CompuServe Germany, for allowing pornographic material to be stored on CompuServe's computers in Germany. While Somm never did go to jail and, to the best of my knowledge, the verdict was never made final after significant international protest, this case was an early illustration of one danger involved in operating an Internet business. As it turns out, the legal position in Germany is not so bad. Germany has passed a number of laws that make it clear that server hosting does not oblige the ISP to control the content hosted unless the ISP has positive knowledge of illegal content (such as child pornography), in which case the ISP is obliged to act. In the Somm case, even though the prosecutor acknowledged to the judge once the case had started that Somm did not actually know of the illegal content, the judge simply couldn't understand how that was possible and found him guilty anyway.

In 1998, the Swedish parliament passed a new act to regulate electronic bulletin boards. The act not only applies to BBSs but also to most services providing information on the Internet, such as Web servers and Usenet news servers. This act is basically the Swedish version of the CDA in the United States. In accordance with the law, an ISP is responsible for illegal content, even if the illegal content was submitted by users of the ISP's service. This responsibility is limited to what is obviously illegal according to certain other acts, for example, racial agitation, child pornography, or copyright infringement. To fulfill the requirements of the law, the supplier must supervise the contents of the service. If checking every single message transmitted through the service proves to be too cumbersome, however, the ISP can handle the supervision through an abuse board, to which users can complain about illegal messages. An English translation of the act is available at the following URL: www.dsv .su.se/~jpalme/society/swedish-bbs-act.html.

Likewise, Singapore and Australia have recently adopted legislation that restricts pornography and other offensive content on the Internet. The complaint-based laws require ISPs to either offer filtered services with filtering software to customers or block illegal sites on unfiltered services when provided with a notice. Under the Australian law, for example, complaints filed with the Australian Broadcasting Authority (ABA) would be reviewed in accordance with a national classification system for online content, similar to that developed for television and magazines. The ABA would then issue take-down orders or warnings to ISPs that fail to take down illegal material and fail to take reasonable steps to prevent access, if technically feasible, to foreign sites hosting illegal content. The ABA would be able to levy a graduated series of fines against ISPs that ignore the ABA. The Australian law, which took effect on January 1, 2000, has been deeply criticized around the world. The president of the American Civil Liberties Union (ACLU) went so far as to portray the Australian government as the "global village idiot" for its adoption of this law. The ACLU doesn't need to travel far to find village idiots.

In the United States, a number of bureaucrats have been pushing for a bill that would require ISPs to provide computer software or other filtering or blocking systems that allow customers to prevent minors from accessing material on the Internet. Of course, *material* is not defined, although it is presumed to only include *bad content,* whatever that is. Since filtering software and other blocking systems are hardly foolproof, this type of legislation could cause ISPs to be liable for failing to prevent a minor from accessing material, notwithstanding the ISP's use of filtering technology. To make matters worse, this legislation might require the ISPs to offer filtering at cost or for free and might even require the ISPs to renegotiate the terms of service with each and every one of its existing customers.

# Spamming, Cramming, Spoofing, and Trespassing

Other than the fact that some of the topics in this section rhyme with each other, you might be wondering how they relate. The first three—spamming, cramming, and spoofing—all have to do with unauthorized acts by a third party. As I will subsequently more fully describe, spamming is an unauthorized form of messaging, cramming is an unauthorized form of billing, and spoofing is an unauthorized form of identifying (actually, misidentifying) oneself. Trespassing sneaks into this group because this age-old form of property protection has emerged as one of the primary weapons against any unauthorized use of an ISP's network resources.

## Spamming

I will spare you the agony of reading another joke involving the word *spam.* While different parties define electronic spam in different ways, a fairly common definition includes "the unsolicited transmission of bulk e-mail and/or the posting of off-topic messages to Usenet newsgroups or other Internet lists." One common spamming practice is to flood the Internet with messages to numerous Internet users who have

---

## Side Law: The Scourge of the Internet

MCI was actually the first ISP to announce a policy to ban spam on its network and to bar users of its Internet network services from sending spam. At the time, MCI's senior vice president for Internet architecture and engineering, Vint Cerf, stated that "[s]pamming is the scourge of electronic-mail and newsgroups on the Internet. It can seriously interfere with the operation of public services, to say nothing of the effect it may have on any individual's e-mail system. Spammers are, in effect, taking resources away from users and service suppliers without authorization."

---

not consented to receive such messages, regardless of whether the users actually dislike or complain about receiving such messages. The term *spam* was coined to analogously describe the spread of these less-than-desirable messages across the Internet. While many spam messages deal with themes such as pornography or get-rich-quick schemes, a message may be defined as spam regardless of its content. There is no such thing as benign or ethical spam just because the spam promotes a worthy cause.

Little has changed in terms of the impact and undesirability of spam, so most ISPs have adopted Acceptable Use Policies (AUPs). Among other things, AUPs typically ban spam from the ISP's network and give the ISP the ability to terminate a user's account when that user has been responsible for sending spam.

When ISPs have done a bad job of controlling spam on their networks, an anonymous group that tracks the flow of spam through public interconnection points will issue a *death threat* to the slack ISP. In the past, the death threat would warn the ISP to clean up its act or face a *denial-of-service* or *black-holing* attack by the members of this group. A denial-of-service attack can take many forms, but a common technique is to send massive numbers of messages to an ISP that require the ISP to take some action in response to these messages. The processing of these messages, which are sent over and over again for a period of hours and even days, prevents the ISP from being able to process any other traffic, thereby denying the ISP the ability to provide any other service. A black-holing attack involves the blocking of e-mail or net news contributions from the ISP that fails to police spam. While I do not wish to condone vigilante justice such as this, these death threats have proven to be extremely effective deterrents to ISPs that thought they could make a quick buck by taking business from known spammers.

On the legislative front, a number of states have passed spam-related laws, but only with respect to activities occurring within those states. A number of spam bills have been introduced by the U.S. House and Senate, but each bill takes such a different approach to dealing with spam that no single bill has received much attention. The most recent bill to be introduced, by Representative Heather Wilson, is called the Unsolicited Electronic Mail Act of 1999. This bill would have the FCC create and maintain an opt-out list for anyone who does not want to be sent spam. The FCC would then be empowered to penalize those that send spam to anyone who has added their name to the list. The Direct Marketing Association (DMA) has already introduced an automated version of the same thing that allows anyone to access a web site and add their name to a do-not-spam list. Unfortunately, the DMA solution relies on reputable companies to sign up for the service and abide by its system. The worst spammers are not going to join the DMA.

Wilson's bill would also let ISPs opt out of transmitting spam, either on the sending or on the receiving end, and would let ISPs charge spammers to cover the cost of transmitting their spam. The bill would also criminalize the misidentification of a return address on a spam message (otherwise known as *spoofing*). In general, opt-out systems have drawn criticism by antispam groups, which favor an outright ban on spam. Others prefer an *opt-in* system, in which senders of spam cannot send a message to anyone not on the list.

## Cramming

*Cramming,* as a concept, has been known in the telecommunications business for a number of years. Phone cramming occurs when an unscrupulous third-party company causes an unwanted service to be added to your phone bill. Phone companies introduced the concept of permitting third-party charges to be added to phone bills a number of years ago, to permit customers to consolidate charges from various interrelated providers such as psychic hot lines. This also permitted customers to hide certain types of charges that they didn't necessarily want someone else in their household to see on a regular charge card bill. Some fraudulent operators figured out that this enabled them to slip other charges onto phone bills without the phone company's knowing anything about the nature of the charge (and therefore without their being able to challenge it), and with the customer's being afraid to call the charge into question. As one would expect, this practice has made its way to the Internet as well.

The FTC has brought enforcement actions against a number of individuals and businesses for billing or debiting consumers' credit card accounts for unordered or fictitious Internet-related services. Charges of $19.95, a typical Internet service charge, from companies with names like Online Billing and Netfill would show up on individuals' cards and, unless these individuals looked closely, they might not recognize that the charges were not for their Internet service. When the individuals would call their credit card companies to investigate the charges, they would be told that the charges were for Internet services, adult services, or electronic bulletin board services. Some of these false charges were exposed, however, because the individuals so charged did not have Internet access and didn't even own computers. I have not seen an ISP actually pulled into one of these disputes yet, but I figure the likelihood of that occurring is not too far away.

## Spoofing

*Spoofing* occurs when someone alters the header of a packet or e-mail message in such a way that the packet or message appears to have been sent by someone other than the actual sender. This is a particularly popular trick among spammers, who use this technique to redirect response traffic to someone else, thereby avoiding detection and the task of having to sort through all of the angry replies they get in return. I can imagine why a political dissident might want to remain untraceable and therefore may need the ability to put a false identifier on a packet or message without violating the law, but anonymity and spoofing are two very different things. At the same time, I know a number of innocent bystanders who have been hurt from having had their addresses used as spoofed addressed on many different types of messages. A student's address at Stanford University was spoofed on a violent, racist message distributed to users of the Stanford network. While the student was eventually cleared of any wrongdoing, he was nevertheless subject to detention and questioning, and probably still suffers from being wrongly accused of authoring the message. In another case, a legitimate business's address was used as the return address on some widely distributed spam. People responding to the spam flooded the business with so much e-mail, some of which threatened violence against the business and its owners, that it was forced to close down its operations for a period of time. Although it eventually brought suit against the spammer to attempt to recover its damages, it will never be made whole. Hence, the number of people who might need to spoof is greatly outweighed by the number of people who are being hurt by spoofing.

Typically, if an ISP's customer is performing one of these unauthorized acts, the ISP can terminate the customer's service for breach of contract, assuming the ISP's terms-of-service agreement or acceptable use policy states that spamming, cramming, spoofing, and many other acts are forbidden. Even where the ISP does not have appropriate terms of service in place, the ISP may still be able to terminate its service if the customer fails to follow common industry practices, i.e. *netiquette.* This latter situation arose in Canada, where an ISP did not specifically forbid spamming, but did require its customers to follow generally accepted rules of the Internet. When the ISP terminated a customer's service for distributing spam, the customer sued for breach of contract, but a Canadian court agreed with the ISP's argument that the customer had violated the netiquette of the Internet and denied the customer's claim.

## The Reemergence of Trespassing Laws

The situation is different, however, where the spammers are not the ISP's actual customers and are just sending messages to the ISP's network end users. Although a healthy spread (oops—sorry, I did say no jokes!) of antispam legislation either has been passed into law or is being considered, the most successful weapon against spam so far has been the good old trespassing laws. Trespassing laws have been used for years to seek damages and to obtain injunctions to prevent any reoccurrence, where one party has entered another party's property without authorization. Real property trespassing cases have been successful even where there has been no physical damage, on the theory that the trespass denied the owners of their undisturbed enjoyment of their land. Likewise, trespassing laws have been extended to the Internet because an ISP's network is like its real property and should be protected from unauthorized use by other parties even where there has been no physical damage. To strengthen their cases, however, ISPs generally allege that the actions of spammers have caused physical damages by overburdening the ISP's network or denying access to services by other parties.

The state of California is a good example of a local government's adoption of anti-spam legislation. If an ISP adopts an antispam policy (adoption is not required) and the ISP's network is located in California or is used to send spam to California residents, then the ISP can seek to recover damages. The ISP can seek the greater of its actual damages or civil damages of up to $50 per spam message, with a maximum of $25,000 per day. Similar legislation, the Can Spam Act of 1999 (seriously!), H.R. 2162, was introduced in the U.S. House of Representatives. This bill would permit ISPs to enforce their antispam rules by giving them the power to sue spammers who violate their spam policies. In Virginia, a new state law was passed that provides for prosecution of "fraudulent, unauthorized, or otherwise illegal" spam and that updates trespassing laws to include the use of an ISP's facilities without permission. The state of Washington has both antispam laws and antispoofing laws. Federal legislation was introduced that would prohibit the transmission of spam and spoofing, as well as the sale or distribution of a computer program that conceals routing information (with civil damages only). This measure was tied to a bill, the Internet Freedom Act of 1999, H.R. 1686, that attempted to introduce controversial changes to the cable access and broadband access laws, so it is not likely to be passed anytime soon. The politicians are onto spam, and since it is an act for the perpetrators of which few people have sympathy, you can expect to see many additional legislative efforts in the future.

# Hyperlinking, Portals, and Framing

Try to imagine how the World Wide Web would operate without hyperlinking. Internet portal sites would probably not exist. Directory services would be extremely cumbersome to use. You would have to write down every URL that you wanted to use or cut and paste all of them into your browser. Even browsers would not operate the same way. Now imagine that hyperlinking existed, but providing a hyperlink made you potentially liable for any violation of the law that occurred at the linked web page. What if the web page to which you originally linked was legal, but subsequently became illegal? Would you then have an obligation to constantly recheck a linked page just to make sure it stayed legal? What if you could link to another site only if you first obtained the permission of the owner of that site, despite the fact that the site was otherwise open to the public?

## Hyperlinking and Deep Linking

As far as I know, the hyperlinking issue first arose during the early stages of the DMCA negotiations. At that time, copyright holders still thought it was appropriate to hold ISPs liable for every copyright violation on the Net; they wanted to outlaw hyperlinking to an infringing site as well. The ISPs attacked this concept and argued that hyperlinking was so fundamental to the use of the World Wide Web that any attempt to regulate it would cause irreparable damage to the Internet. A compromise was eventually worked out, as described in Chapter 3, *A Special Law for ISPs: The DMCA*, which protects ISPs as long as they don't knowingly provide a link to infringing material and attempt to profit from doing so, but it was a long, hard-fought battle. Unfortunately, this was just the beginning of the hyperlinking issue. Hyperlinking issues appear in almost every piece of Internet-related legislation being considered around the world. For certain types of content, such as child pornography, the free-wheeling days of the past, which allowed Internet users to provide links to anything, are over.

A number of suits have also now been filed to prevent deep linking. A *deep link* is a hyperlink that takes a user to a specific web page deep within a web site, rather than to the home page for that site. Deep linking is an issue because certain web sites have been constructed to prevent users from getting to certain lower-level pages within their sites without first going through higher-level pages. If a lower-level page is access protected, this type of preventive measure can be enforced. Many web site operators, however, do not protect lower-level pages, thereby allowing anyone with a URL for a specific page (identified by directories, subdirectories, and a file name) not only to bypass the higher-level pages, but to bypass the access protection itself. Bypassing protection and pages in this fashion cuts down on traffic for advertisements on higher-level pages.

Other web site operators have worked out deep linking license agreements that permit licensees to provide such links and to advertise their ability to do so. For example, Ticketmaster Online allows sites like Yahoo! and Knight-Ridder to maintain deep links into the ticketmaster.com site, enabling them to link directly to a page selling tickets to a particular event. When Microsoft used the same deep links in its Sidewalk sites (which Microsoft has since sold to Citysearch) without an agreement with Ticketmaster, Microsoft was sued. This suit eventually settled without any legal decision (Microsoft agreed to stop deep linking to ticketmaster.com), so we don't know how the court would have ruled on the issue, but Ticketmaster has now filed a similar suit against Tickets.com. Since this issue is more fundamental to Tickets.com's business than it was to Microsoft's, this suit might actually go to trial and result in a decision. Keep your eyes peeled!

## Portals

*Portal* sites, like Yahoo! or Excite, of course, have to be concerned about all of these issues because hyperlinking and especially deep linking are fundamental to their businesses. When the portal business was relatively new, there was general acknowledgment that it wasn't a good idea to develop rules that would affect these sites, but the fabulous success of these sites may be their single biggest problem. People have caught on to the fact that there is money to be made by controlling someone else's ability to link to a site, so as portal company stocks go up, the trepidation that initially existed about creating rules that negatively impacted portal sites will go down.

## Framing

A frame is a small window, which may include text, pictures, links, and so on, within a larger browser window. Obviously, you can construct frames of your own information without consequence, and you can display other people's publicly available web sites (by creating a link to that site) on your screen in any size you desire. Constructing a web page with linked frames to other people's information can be a big problem. Since most web sites are copyrighted and a copyright includes the exclusive right to create derivative works, the linked framing of anything less than an entire page from another site (and possibly the entire site) could be considered the creation of a derivative work. When you frame someone else's information in such a way as to create confusion or to present their information as your information, you are probably going to get sued for copyright and trademark infringement, as well as for unfair trade practice violations.

# Digital Signatures

A *digital signature* is a piece of data that is sent with an encoded message to uniquely identify the originator of that message and to verify that the message was not altered after it was sent. In November 1999, the U.S. House of Representatives passed H.R. 1714, the Electronic Signatures in Global and National Commerce Act (E-SIGN), followed by the passage of a similar bill in the Senate (S. 761). The differences between the two bills are to be worked out in a House-Senate conference, which will result in congressional passage (and likely presidential signature) and enactment sometime in 2000. The E-SIGN legislation will allow consumers and businesses to use electronic signatures, in the same way they use handwritten signatures, when engaged in online business transactions. This removes the legal uncertainties that have surrounded the status of electronic signatures and records.

To date, many states have enacted similar but somewhat differing laws. To resolve the confusion, all 50 states have been working on a Uniform Electronic Transactions Act (UETA), which is expected to be completed soon and offered to the 50 state legislatures for adoption. Until then, E-SIGN would preempt current state laws. At the urging of states and the Department of Commerce, an initial two-year deadline for states to enact their standard law was increased to four years. E-SIGN also directs the secretary of commerce to promote the principles of the legislation overseas (see the following discussion about a similar measure moving through the European Union). E-SIGN requires that the technologies used for signature authentication be technologically neutral; in other words, functionality requirements do not discriminate in favor of or against any particular technology or company. The primary difference between the House and Senate versions is that the Senate version confers legal validity on electronic signatures only for commercial transactions affecting interstate commerce.

The EU is also getting close to adopting the proposed Directive on a Common Framework for Electronic Signatures. This proposal was first made by the European Commission in 1998. It lays down minimum rules concerning security and liability, and ensures that digital signatures are legally recognized throughout the EU. It also provides minimum requirements on certification services, which can be offered without prior authorization, although member states are free to set up voluntary accreditation schemes for certification service providers. As will likely be the case in the United States, the EU Directive will probably adopt technical neutrality as a key principle.

Such legislation will also likely adopt the principle that the legal recognition of signatures be based on mutual recognition, rather than requiring a new, burdensome administrative procedure for some type of *certification authority*. In other words, the requirements for accreditation of a certificate authority should maintain appropriate levels of security, but should not set the standards so high as to require extensive governmental oversight or create artificial barriers to entry.

# Importing/Exporting of Software, Technology, and Content

Almost all countries have laws regulating what can be imported to and exported from each country. The United States, for example, attempts to regulate the import of certain types of products from other countries to prevent crop infection and domestic price erosion, or simply to economically repress other countries (for example, Cuban cigars and Iraqi oil). Likewise, the United States also attempts to regulate the export of certain types of products or information from the United States to other countries for national security reasons. The technology that can be imported or exported is specified in detailed regulations, but the rules are totally open when it comes to Canada and fairly loose when it comes to any NATO member country or another country with which the United States has close political ties. The rules are extremely strict when it comes to countries with which the United States has recently been at war (Iraq) or with which diplomatic relations are strained (China). Under these rules, some things simply cannot be exported, such as nuclear technology and certain levels of supercomputer technology. Most other things can be exported upon grant of an export license, depending on where they are going and why.

One of the most important things to keep in mind under these rules is that failure to get an appropriate export license could result in significant fines and prevent you from exporting anything to anybody for some period of time. One of my former employers failed to get an export license for some computers it shipped to a company that was a front for the government of a highly restricted country. Not only was this extremely costly, it was also embarrassing because the company was subjected to a congressional investigation and a lot of bad press. It is also important to realize what constitutes exporting. In the industrial age, exporting focused primarily on the shipment of physical products and maybe the exporting of manufacturing technology, so people still think of exporting as physically shipping something out of the country. Permitting a foreign national from a restricted country to tour your facility or work at your company is also considered to be an export.

## Cryptography

Although the development of computers and the Internet has changed many things, these rules (in increasingly watered-down form) still exist. Hence, because virtually anyone in the world can tour your publicly available web site, it is not a good idea to put export-restricted information on that site or to otherwise export restricted technology or content from that site. This sounds fine, in general, until you consider the technology incorporated into Internet-related software or how certain types of Internet sites operate. For example, many different forms of software incorporate encryption technology that has long been on the list of highly restricted technologies. Since encryption technology can be used to protect the content of an electronic message, governments have been concerned that terrorists, criminals, and unfriendly government agents would use the technology to hide their activities from espionage agencies. Since the quality of the encryption is highly dependent on the bit length of the key used by the encryption software to encrypt a message, export regulations have largely focused on the bit length of the key.

Based on a study released by the Electronic Privacy Information Center, called *Cryptography and Liberty 1999,* relatively few countries have supported domestic or export controls on encryption. The United States was one of the few exceptions, and it has taken a huge effort to get the United States to back away from its position. Initial U.S. export regulations on key length were completely ineffective. First, the encryption technology they prevented U.S. citizens from exporting out of the United States was already freely available around the world. Second, exportable key lengths were so short that the underlying encryption software was not secure. Readily available computers, operating on their own or in a network, could easily decrypt messages encrypted with short keys. It obviously did little good to allow people to use and export insecure security software. While the battle raged over increasing the length of the key, alternative suggestions arose, such as key escrow and key recovery schemes. Typically, you could export encryption technology that used a key equal to or less than a certain bit length without restriction. If you wanted to export encryption technology with a longer key, you had to either escrow the keys with a trusted third party or government agency, or enable the government to extract the key when it deemed it necessary. ISPs, software companies, and civil libertarians have fought to reasonably loosen the export restrictions on encryption technology for many years.

Along with many other people, I have testified before Congress in response to a number of these schemes. In 1998, in response to yet another key recovery proposal, I started my testimony on behalf of MCI Communications by stating:

> MCI believes that controls on the use of strong encryption, including key recovery systems, are contrary to the best interests of the American people for at least three reasons. Such controls could: (1) harm the ability of American businesses to compete with foreign companies for foreign and domestic customers; (2) undermine the enormous potential of the Internet, including global electronic commerce, to improve the lives of all Americans; and (3) violate the constitutional right to privacy and abrogate the protections of the 4th and 5th Amendments. In addition to these important considerations, there are a number of practical problems associated with key recovery systems that render them futile or even counterproductive.

Later in 1998 the United States became a signatory to the Wassenaar Agreement, a 33-nation pact on munitions that includes cryptography export controls. Although the Wassenaar Agreement was not binding on any nation that signed it (it is only a pact, not a treaty), it did influence the U.S. government to adopt a policy that permitted the export of 56-bit-length keys after a one-time review, without a key recovery requirement. While this was considered progress in the United States, the Wassenaar Agreement actually tightened restrictions on browsers, e-mail applications, and electronic commerce hardware and software in other countries. U.S. legislation then sought to have this policy extended to cover 64-bit-length keys, but anything less than 128 bits long was generally considered to be insecure by the industry. At the same time, Daniel Bernstein, who developed an encryption method while he was a doctoral candidate at the University of California, Berkeley, decided to challenge an export regulation that prevented him from posting his work on a web site so other scientists could review and comment on his work. This resulted in a 1999 decision by the Ninth Circuit Court of Appeals that export regulations on encryption source code were unconstitutional because they amounted to prior restraints on speech rights (source code is a form of speech) that violate the First Amendment.

## Change Is in the Wind

As a result of all of this and the political importance of making the high-technology industry happy before the 2000 elections, the United States finally relaxed its controls on the export of encryption technology in late 1999 and further in 2000. The new policies allow U.S. firms, after a one-time review of their products, to sell encryption products without bit-length restrictions to customers in all but a handful of countries and certain foreign governments and military establishments. Although there is still considerable criticism of the policy and its one-time review requirement, especially by academics, the new policy could be a monumental step forward. The final rules can be found at www.eff.org/pub/Privacy/ITAR_export/1999_export_policy/ 19990916_wh_cryptopolicy_pr.html.

## Importing Banned Material

The latest import/export controversy has nothing to do with cryptography and everything to do with a more fundamental aspect of Internet commerce. Through the use of a search engine, people around the world can locate information on almost anything they want, including many things I wish they couldn't find, such as hate literature and bomb-making instructions. And, just as the Internet allows farmers in poor countries to find drought-resistant grains, it also allows Germans to buy copies of *Mein Kampf* and other banned books from online book sellers such as Amazon.com and Barnesandnoble.com. The e-commerce merchants defend their actions by stating that their policy is to sell any book in print to any customer who wants to buy it and that it is up to the customer to figure out whether they are allowed to have such a book imported into their country. Plenty of precedents exist, however, for the principle that merchants shipping products into other jurisdictions are obligated to uphold the laws of the jurisdiction to which those products are being sent. As long as you don't operate a business or own any assets in the country into which you are shipping illegal goods, then these laws probably won't have a practical effect on you— unless you just so happen to respect other people's cultures.

# Gambling, Guns, Alcohol, and Money on the Internet

At long last, we reach the end of this chapter on the current laws that impact ISPs, but let me remind you that I have covered only the beginning of the regulated Internet. Assuredly, I have already failed to cover a number of the different laws that apply to ISPs, but I have tried to make up for this by stating on numerous occasions that almost any illegal act that can somehow be perpetrated on the Net will one day be regulated. However, many new laws, covering acts that are not presently illegal or regulated, will be regulated on the Net, and I have briefly outlined them here.

## Gambling

Gambling is legal in some communities such as Las Vegas (although regulated), but illegal in others such as Minnesota. Arguably, someone in Las Vegas should be able to gamble at an online casino operated in Nevada without violating any laws, and a Nevada casino should be able to advertise on its web site to attract such gamblers to that site. But what happens when the Minnesota resident sees the advertisement and places a bet on the web site?

Without a single bet being placed, this question is being tested in a lawsuit between the state of Minnesota and Wager Net, a private company that advertised its future gambling web site as a legal way to bet on sports from anywhere in the country. To further complicate matters, Wager Net advertises only from a web site based in Las Vegas, the gambling services are actually run by an operation based in Belize, where sports gambling operations are legal with the proper license. While this matter is pending, many other Internet-based casinos are up and running (more than 500 according to *Interactive Gaming News*) and taking money from anyone foolish enough to place a bet. In response, a number of states and countries have done nothing, others are considering regulating and licensing them, and a few have successfully prosecuted violators of existing or newly enacted antigambling laws. The state of Missouri obtained a guilty plea on a misdemeanor charge against a Pennsylvania resident for running an Internet gambling site that was available in Missouri. The state of New York even won a conviction against a company that tried to prevent New York residents from gambling on its site.

In the New York case, the company had built-in safeguards to prevent residents from states where gambling was illegal from placing bets on its system. An investigator in the New York Attorney General's office was able to bypass the safeguard by entering a valid Nevada address and checking a box that stated that the investigator was a resident of a state where gambling was legal. Hence, despite the company's efforts to not violate the law, the judge ruled that the efforts were insufficient because they could be readily bypassed and the provided information was not verified. This, of course, raises questions about how an Internet gambling site could ever take enough steps to prevent someone from gambling who was set on lying in order to get access to the cybercasino. Suggestions for how to verify customer-supplied information include checking credit card records, performing credit history reports, and running tracking software while the customer is online in an attempt to locate the server address the customer is using to access the Internet. This last suggestion isn't believed to be workable because many ISPs' operations prevent traces back to the actual server providing access.

All of this becomes meaningful to ISPs, even if they don't also operate gambling sites, because of recent legislative attempts to hold ISPs liable for allowing customers to operate gambling sites and because of a suit by a woman who lost a lot of money. I will deal with this woman's suit first. After losing more than $70,000 by placing bets at more the 50 different cybercasinos and being sued by her credit issuer for unpaid bills, the woman sued the bank and Visa and MasterCard for engaging in unfair business practices and aiding and abetting a crime by giving the cybercasinos merchant accounts to process bets. In early 1999, a California court refused to dismiss the suit on the grounds that doing so would deprive the woman of her right to address alleged violations of the law. Although she didn't sue her ISP or the ISP for the cybercasinos, a number of people have speculated that such possibilities were not too farfetched.

## The Internet Gambling Prohibition Act

Given the variance in state laws and enforcement efforts, especially with regard to New York, it is probably a good thing that the federal government is considering the passage of federal legislation regulating Internet gambling. In late 1999, the U.S. Senate passed the Internet Gambling Prohibition Act of 1999 (IGPA). The U.S. House of Representatives is working on an almost identical bill, so it is highly likely that legislation substantially similar to the IGPA will be passed by Congress and signed by the president. I will therefore treat the IGPA as though it is the current law of the land. Even if the House passes a different bill and a compromise between the two is required, you can be guaranteed that the difference will not be that significant—there is a lot of political momentum behind such legislation.

Although the IGPA broadly prohibits online gambling and restricts online advertising, it also provides ISPs with limited immunities from both federal and state antigambling laws. The IGPA will not protect ISPs from unfair business practice suits or similar suits based on tort laws, such as in the aforementioned case from California.

As initially proposed, this legislation would have provided no protection for ISPs whose systems or services were used to operate or advertise any non-Internet gaming operations, even though such operations or advertisements might otherwise be entirely lawful in the state in which the gambling took place. This meant that an ISP could have been liable for violation of this law simply for hosting a state lottery web site or hosting a web site for the Las Vegas or Atlantic City Chamber of Commerce that contained hyperlinks to hotels with regular casino gambling. Luckily, as passed, the IGPA took a less aggressive approach.

The IGPA starts with a broad prohibition and then provides ISPs with protection from liability under certain circumstances. Thus, the IGPA makes it illegal to knowingly use the Internet or any interactive computer service to place, receive, or otherwise make a bet, or to send, receive, or invite information that would assist in the placement of a bet or wager. Violations of this law can result in fines of up to $20,000 and/or up to four years in prison. Criminal proceedings under the IGPA can be initiated by state or federal law enforcement, or by the authority specified in accordance with a tribal-state compact negotiated under the Indian Gaming Regulatory Act, in cases that involve violations occurring on Indian land. A professional sports organization or amateur sports organization whose games, or the performances of whose athletes in such games, were alleged to have been the basis of a violation of IGPA may seek to enjoin violations of the IGPA through civil proceedings, but not against ISPs.

## Conditional Immunity under the IGPA

Consistent with the basic model established by the DMCA, ISPs are not liable under the IGPA or any other provision of federal or state law prohibiting or regulating gambling or gambling-related activities when the ISPs are acting as mere conduits. In other words, an ISP is not liable if its facilities or services are used to transmit, route, or provide connections for gambling-related material or activity (including intermediate and temporary storage in the course of transmitting, routing, or providing connections), if:

- The material or activity was initiated by or at the direction of another person.
- The transmitting, routing, or provision of connections is carried out through an automatic process without selection of the material or activity by the ISP.
- The ISP does not select the recipients of the material or activity, except as an automatic response to the request of another person.
- The material or activity is transmitted through the system or network of the ISP without substantive modification of its content.

Likewise, an ISP is not liable for illegal gambling-related material or activity at an online site hosted by the ISP, or arising out of referring or linking users to such a site, if the material or activity was initiated by or at the direction of another person, unless the provider failed to expeditiously respond to an appropriate notice.

To be eligible under either immunity provision, the ISP must maintain and implement a written policy that requires the ISP to terminate the account of subscribers after receipt of an appropriate notice. Furthermore, the ISP cannot knowingly permit its servers to be used to engage in illegal gambling activities, with the specific intent that such servers be used for such purpose.

A notice can be sent by either state or federal law enforcement agencies acting within their authority and jurisdiction. (If you have any question about either of these two issues, seek legal advice.) An appropriate notice must:

- Be in writing (paper or electronic)
- Identify the material or activity that allegedly violates the IGPA, and allege that such material or activity violates the IGPA
- Provide information reasonably sufficient to permit the ISP to locate and possibly block the material or activity

- Be supplied to an agent of the ISP (as designated in accordance with the designation of agent provisions in the DMCA), if available

- Provide information reasonably sufficient to permit the ISP to contact the agency that issued the notice, including the name of the agency and the name and telephone number of an individual to contact at the agency

- Declare under penalty of perjury that the person submitting the notice is an official of the agency

Upon receipt of such a notice:

- The ISP is obligated to expeditiously remove or disable access to the allegedly illegal material or activity residing at that online site.

- If the ISP is not in control of the site in question, it must notify the agency that provided the notice that it was not the proper recipient of such notice, and upon receipt of a subpoena, cooperate with the agency to identify the person controlling the site.

Within 24 hours of issuing a notice to an ISP, the law enforcement agency can seek injunctive relief to prevent further use of the ISP's facilities or services by the alleged violator of the IGPA. Although this does not mean that an ISP's immunity is subject to a 24-hour response time, when the IGPA says *expeditiously,* it does mean fast. Hence, if you are not currently capable of responding to a notice within 24 hours, you need to be prepared to be subjected to injunctive actions by law enforcement agencies and possible liability for failure to respond quickly enough.

The two types of injunctive relief available to agencies for mere conduit activities are:

1. Restraining the ISP from providing access to an identified subscriber (by termination of the subscriber's account), if the court determines that there is probable cause to believe the subscriber has used such access to violate the IGPA.

2. Restraining the ISP from providing access by taking *reasonable steps* specified in the order to block access to a *specific, identified, foreign online location.*

Nobody is really sure what the term *reasonable steps* is supposed to mean. When this legislation was first introduced by Senator Kyl in 1998, a number of ISP representatives, including myself, met with him to explain that it wasn't possible for ISPs to block foreign sites. While Senator Kyl acknowledged this fact, he was unwilling to completely remove the language, so after a long series of exchanges, *reasonable steps* ended up being the agreed-upon text. In conjunction with the considerations that a court must take into account when structuring an order of injunctive relief (discussed in detail subsequently), this presumably means that a court will not order an ISP to shut down a circuit to a particular country just to block a particular site in that country. Of course, if there were other circuits into that country or other forms of access, the traffic would simply be routed around the blockage. This also presumably means that a court will not order an ISP to block all traffic from a *specific, identified, foreign online location,* by requiring the ISP to monitor for and block all Internet Protocol (IP) packets bearing a certain IP address. Not only would such a requirement have a severe impact on the performance of all affected routers or gateways, it would probably be an exercise in futility because the foreign site would only have to employ a stable and legal web site with hyperlinks that employ *dynamic IP addressing* to send users to the illegal site—thereby avoiding the block.

The three types of injunctive relief available to agencies for hosting and linking activities are:

1. The same orders available for mere conduit activities.
2. Restraining the ISP from providing access to the material or activity at a particular site residing on a server operated or controlled by the ISP.
3. Such other injunctive relief as a court considers necessary to prevent or restrain access to specified material or activity prohibited by the IGPA and residing on a server operated or controlled by the ISP, that is least burdensome to the ISP among the forms of relief that are comparably effective for that purpose.

When considering any form of injunctive relief under the IGPA, as is also the case with injunctions under the DMCA, the court is required to consider:

- Whether such an injunction, either alone or in combination with other such injunctions issued and currently operative, against the same ISP would significantly or unreasonably (taking into account the conduct of the ISP) burden either the ISP or the operation of the ISP's systems or networks
- Whether implementation of such an injunction would be technically feasible and effective and would not materially interfere with access to lawful material at other online locations
- Whether other less burdensome and comparably effective means of preventing or restraining access to the illegal material or activity are available
- The magnitude of the harm likely to be suffered by the community if the injunction is not granted

To make sure that the court takes these considerations into account and does not order an ISP to take action in total ignorance of how Internet technologies work, an injunction cannot be ordered unless the ISP is first served with a notice of the intended action and is given an opportunity to appear before the court.

## Advertising and Promotion of Non-Internet Gambling

Because, among other things, the IGPA prohibits the use of the Internet to invite information assisting in the placing of a bet or wager, the IGPA is considered to outlaw the advertising and promotion of illegal Internet gambling activities as well. But what about non-Internet gambling? Are banner advertisements linked to otherwise legal casino web sites legal? Is it okay to host the Las Vegas chamber of commerce?

The IGPA addresses the advertising and promotion of non-Internet gambling, which would include various physical casinos, because of the proliferation of gambling-related advertisements on the Internet and the possible liability of ISPs under other, preexisting, federal and state laws. Accordingly, the IGPA provides that ISPs are immune from liability under federal or state law prohibiting or regulating gambling or gambling-related activities or under any state law prohibiting or regulating advertising and promotional activities for:

- Content provided by another that advertises or promotes non-Internet gambling activity that violates one of the aforementioned laws (unless the ISP is engaged in such a business), arising out of any mere conduit, hosting, or linking-related activities

- Content provided by another that advertises or promotes non-Internet gambling activity that is lawful under federal law and the law of the state in which such gambling activity is conducted

This means that all of the linked banner advertisements by the Las Vegas casinos on your web site probably aren't going to subject you to immediate liability. Before you get too comfortable with that, though, there are some eligibility requirements that have to be met to qualify for such an immunity. To be eligible under the immunity provision, the ISP:

- Must maintain and implement a written policy that requires the ISP to terminate the account of subscribers after receipt of an appropriate notice

- Cannot knowingly permit its servers to be used to engage in illegal advertising or promotion of non-Internet gambling activities, with the specific intent that such servers be used for such purpose

- Must offer residential access customers, at a reasonable cost, computer filtering or block software or another service that would enable customers to filter or block access by minors to online Internet gambling sites that violate the IGPA

The notice provisions and injunctive relief provisions applicable to non-Internet gambling advertising and promotion are basically the same as those already described. The filtering/blocking provision is completely unrealistic (it is not technically feasible or economically reasonable) and probably will not withstand Constitutional scrutiny (i.e., it is too vague).

## General Provisions of the IGPA

As long as an ISP takes an action in good faith to comply with a notice or a court order under the IGPA, the ISP is immune to claims for damages and penalties, forfeitures, and civil or criminal liability resulting from such actions.

ISPs are not obligated to monitor for material or uses of its service, so even if a court does order you to monitor for and block certain IP addresses, you might want to remind the court of this disclaimed obligation. ISPs are also not obligated to gain access to, remove, or disable access to material except in response to a notice or court order.

Subscribers who have had their accounts terminated are permitted to challenge the agency responsible for the termination action.

## Exceptions of the IGPA

The broad provisions of the IGPA do not apply to certain types of gambling-related activities. These activities include:

- Otherwise lawful bets related to lawful state and multistate lotteries, placed on a private network, at a terminal physically located within a open public facility
- Otherwise lawful bets related to a legal live horse or dog race, placed on a closed-loop subscriber-based service, initiated from within a state that permits such activity
- Otherwise lawful bets related to certain types of gaming activities at casinos operated on Indian lands

## Guns

It is already illegal under federal law for either a dealer or an individual to simply ship a gun to a buyer after the receipt of payment. The weapon must first be shipped to a licensed gun dealer in the state where it is being purchased and then physically picked up by the buyer after a security check. So, although it is already technically illegal to purchase a firearm strictly over the Internet, this has not stopped people from buying and selling guns through message boards, web sites, and chat rooms. One Internet auction site (eBay) has already stopped the auctioning and sale of guns on its web site. Thus, the Internet Gun Trafficking Act was introduced in 1999 to tighten the regulations regarding the transfer of firearms over the Net. This act would require any seller of a firearm to get a federal license to sell firearms and for web site operators that host firearm sales to register their sites with the secretary of the treasury, which runs the Bureau of Alcohol, Tobacco and Firearms (ATF). Finally, the bill would require sites that resell guns to prohibit prospective buyers and sellers from contacting one another directly. All sales contacts would have to be made through a licensed broker.

This may seem to be a fairly extreme measure, but because I think private gun ownership should be highly regulated, it doesn't bother me. Moreover, since it is my understanding that the youths responsible for the Colorado Columbine High School slayings directly contacted an independent gun dealer through the Internet, who then illegally sold them at least one gun, a forced broker might have at least prevented them from obtaining more deadly weapons. It probably wouldn't have prevented their demented actions, but anything that would have made it harder for them to get the guns in the first place couldn't be that bad. As with other Internet activity–based legislation, ISPs should be prepared to deal with legislation that would require them to help law enforcement and not knowingly assist in the violation of any laws.

## Drugs

While there are a number of legitimate online pharmacies that sell only those prescriptions sent to them by licensed physicians and do not directly prescribe medications, regulators are actively targeting other sites and doctors that are prescribing medication without proper precautions. Since the prescription drug industry is already heavily regulated (and, yes, I know, it doesn't prevent people from getting illegal drugs), there is still a great deal of uncertainty about how to regulate Internet-based operations—if at all. The state of Illinois has at least enacted legislation that permits state regulators to establish rules and regulations for Internet-based pharmacies doing business in Illinois, but it remains unclear whether this legislation was even necessary. Nevertheless, since interstate and foreign commerce are involved in most Internet-based operations, it is highly likely that federal legislation will be introduced on this issue as well in the near future.

In the meantime, at least one Internet-related drug law has already been passed by the U.S. Senate. A similar bill will be considered by the House in 2000. The Methamphetamine Anti-Proliferation Act of 1999 (MAA) includes a section on the advertising of drug paraphernalia and Schedule I controlled substances, such as methamphetamine. The MAA amended the Controlled Substances Act to include a provision making it illegal to directly or indirectly advertise for sale drug paraphernalia and certain controlled substances. Since this amendment potentially implicated ISPs for violations of the MAA and other antidrug laws by other persons, a provision was also added to give ISPs immunity under certain circumstances.

Under the MAA, an ISP is not liable, if it satisfies the conditions for eligibility, when its facilities or services are used by another to locate illegal online material, provided the ISP does not control or modify the material to which such a location tool refers or links. One condition is to comply with the notice-and-take-down procedures of the MAA. An ISP must remove or disable access to matter that violates the MAA within 48 hours (not including weekends and holidays) of receipt of an appropriate notice that describes a particular online site residing on a server controlled or operated by the ISP. The ISP must designate an agent for service of notices in accordance with the DMCA's designation of agent requirements. An appropriate notice must identify the matter, allege that such matter violates the MAA, and provide reasonably sufficient information to permit the ISP to locate the matter and sufficient information to permit the ISP to contact the federal official providing the notice. ISPs that fail to take down the material within the prescribed time period are deemed to have knowingly permitted their servers to be used to engage in illegal activity.

While the MAA generally does not apply to browser software, it does apply to the provision of browser software that provides matter consisting primarily of illegal material or that holds itself out to others as a source of, or directory for, or means of searching for illegal matter. I have never seen browser software that performs such a primary function, but then I've never searched for controlled substances using my browser. Maybe I'm missing something. The immunity provisions for ISPs in the MAA include similar limitations. An ISP that knowingly permits an online site on its server to be used to engage in activity that the ISP actually knows to be prohibited by the MAA will not be protected. Sites that hold themselves out as a source of or means of searching for matter prohibited by the MAA fall outside of the immunity provisions as well.

# Alcohol

Alcohol sales, advertising, and use are other areas for which the regulations vary greatly from state to state, and country to country. A number of states, including California, have recently enacted legislation to require anyone selling alcoholic beverages online to verify the age and identity of any buyers when products are delivered.

Florida, Georgia, Kentucky, Tennessee, and North Carolina have gone one step further and made it a felony to ship alcoholic beverages directly to residents in their states. It has long been a misdemeanor (that carried only a small fine) to ship alcoholic beverages into these and other states. Upgrading this law to a felony puts the federal production permits of any brewer or vintner that breaks the law at risk. While the Twenty-first Amendment gives states the right to regulate the distribution of alcohol within their borders, federal legislation has also been introduced to give states access to federal courts to prosecute out-of-state alcohol shippers who break the laws. Hence, you won't even be able to hide behind your lack of personal jurisdiction in a state to avoid liability.

On the federal side, legislation will soon be enacted (different versions were passed by the House and Senate) that will prohibit Internet sales and interstate shipments of alcohol products in *violation of state law* (as previously noted). This legislation will provide state attorneys general with the authority to seek injunctions in federal courts to stop alcohol shipments that violate state laws. Injunctive relief will be available only against the entity shipping the alcohol in violation of applicable laws, not against communications companies used by third parties for advertising and other communications purposes. Since the Senate version did not contain clarifying language with respect to ISP liability, this is one of the differences that will have to be worked out in conference. Given the Senate's understanding of the need for ISP liability limitations, at this point, it is unlikely that this issue will present a significant hurdle in the way of resolution.

## Money Laundering

Money laundering has been practiced through electronically controlled accounts for many years, so the introduction of money laundering to the Internet isn't much of a surprise. What is different about using the Internet for money laundering is that some Internet transmissions can be more readily traced after the fact than was possible with older technologies. Of course, money launderers are probably pretty savvy, so I wouldn't be surprised if they deployed many different types of tricks to fool anyone attempting to trace them.

Where things will get interesting is in the area of securities fraud on the Internet. Apparently, fraud artists are using the Internet for traditional investment frauds, such as stock price manipulation schemes. Again, it isn't clear that any new legislation will be required to deal with these issues solely with respect to the Internet, but as with everything else the temptation to do something is likely to be so high that some form of legislation should be expected.

## And On and On

Aside from the fact that you might need to deal with each of the regulated areas discussed here, the broad range of subjects should illustrate an important point: that regulation of the Internet, in some way or another, is here to stay. Assuming that you have accepted this principle, it is now time to learn what you need to do—or not, as the case may be—to comply with many of these laws and regulations. Chapter 5 provides many answers.

# What Is an ISP to Do (or Not)? Content and Activity Regulations to Live By

What would you do if the U.S. Postal Service suddenly adopted a new law, without any explanation about why it was doing so, that required all return addresses to be written on the back flaps of all letter envelopes? Like most people, you would probably begrudgingly comply with this law, even though you didn't understand it, because you would want to make sure your letters were delivered. Conversely, if the Postal Service first engaged in a public awareness campaign to explain that it was implementing new mail processing equipment that required the return addresses to be written in that location, you might still resent the change. Nevertheless, you would probably feel more comfortable about complying with the law because at least you would understand the history and reasoning behind it.

In this chapter, I harvest the wheat from Chapter 2 (*Intellectual Property and Other Laws Made Simple*), Chapter 3 (*A Special Law for ISPs: The DMCA*), and Chapter 4 (*Other Internet-Specific Laws*), leave all of the chaff behind, and add some extra topics to bind it altogether. I also explain some laws for the first time and add extra detail to others that I could not fully address without first detailing laws like the DMCA. In other words, I have already provided you with the history and reasoning behind many of the laws and regulations that existed at the time this book was published, so now I'll just fill in the blanks and tell you what you can and cannot do as an ISP. I'll also make some suggestions about complying with laws that do not yet exist, but that are likely to be passed. If you do not understand why it is necessary for you to do or not do something stated in this chapter, go back to the appropriate prior chapter and refamiliarize yourself with the laws and their backgrounds. In some cases, the requirements may still not make sense, but that may be unavoidable. For example, letter envelopes come in all sorts of different sizes and shapes, and the flaps are oriented in different locations on different envelopes, so the example at the beginning of the chapter doesn't make any sense even with an explanation about the processing equipment. No amount of explanation will clarify some laws, but even when they don't make sense, as long as they are constitutional (and constitutionality is not something you should try to determine on your own), you will still have to comply.

# The DMCA Dos and Don'ts

Chapter 3 did a pretty thorough job of explaining the DMCA, so here I'll just boil it down even more. Because the DMCA was a compromise of multiple competing interests, the resulting requirements of the Act are not always easy to follow or understand, but ISPs are finding themselves complying with these requirements on an ever increasing basis.

Side Law: Scientology Comes Full Circle illustrates a few recent examples of what ISPs in the United States have faced since implementation of the DMCA. There are many more such examples. In each case, the facts are different, and that will assuredly continue in the future, but you need not be concerned with the facts unless you want to be. Because the DMCA applies only in the United States, you are not subject to the law if you operate entirely outside its borders. On the other hand, if you operate inside the United States, but the content in question is located outside its borders, the DMCA may still apply, though technically you are not required to comply with the "safe harbor" provisions of the DMCA. This means you don't have to comply with a notice under the DMCA, and you can even choose to fight a DMCA subpoena from a court, provided you are willing to accept the copyright infringement liability risk along with your customers. If you aren't willing to take such risks, then

---

## Side Law: Scientology Comes Full Circle

On July 19, 1999, salon.com published an article entitled "Copyright—or wrong?" (at www.salon.com/tech/feature/1999/07/22/scientology) that described the Church of Scientology's discovery and use of the DMCA to support what many describe as the church's *repressive activities.* Recall that the idea of *notice and take down* arose from another dispute involving the Church of Scientology. The article described how ISPs, such as Frontier GlobalCenter, Best, and AT&T Corporation, have had to respond to DMCA notices and subpoenas. In one case, the ISP partially blocked a customer's hosted site in response to a DMCA notice. After receipt of a counternotice from the customer and passage of the 10-day deadline for the church to initiate private litigation with the customer, the ISP stopped its partial block of the site. AT&T promptly complied with a subpoena requiring it to reveal the identity of a WorldNet subscriber who had allegedly posted excerpts for a Scientology publication on the Usenet group alt.religion.scientology under a pseudonym. Although the subscriber subsequently complained that AT&T failed to notify him of the subpoena before its compliance, the DMCA does not require ISPs to do so.

you need only to comply, when you aren't otherwise immune, regardless of the facts involved. No matter what you decide to do, keep in mind that I am not providing you with legal advice, and you should not rely exclusively on what I say in this book. My goal is to teach you enough about the laws to help you avoid the big problems and to provide you with enough education to enable you to know when to ask for help or more information from your own lawyer.

## Designating an Agent for Receipt of a DMCA Notice

The DMCA provides only limited forms of immunity to ISPs who comply with its terms. One such term is that you comply with the notice-and-take-down rules. So that copyright holders do not have to track you down, the DMCA requires you to designate an agent for receiving DMCA notices of claimed infringement if you wish to take advantage of the DMCA protections. The U.S. Copyright Office, which is a part of the Library of Congress, maintains the list of designated agents at www.loc .gov/copyright/onlinesp/list. This is also a great place to go if you want to get a fairly extensive list of ISPs. Although there is no required procedure for designating an agent with the Copyright Office (you could simply send it a letter), the Copyright Office does suggest that you use its form, which can be found at www.loc.gov/copyright/onlinesp/.

## When Is an ISP Immune?

Only ISPs that are transmitting or routing digital online communications or are providing access to such communications (a "mere conduit") are subject to the immunity provisions under most circumstances. If you are immune, you cannot be sued and subject to monetary liability for copyright infringement. You can still be subject to an injunction in accordance with the terms of the Act. To qualify as a mere conduit you cannot have any substantive control over the content you carry. This means that the following conditions apply:

- You cannot initiate the content (be the first to put it online).
- The transmission/routing of that content has to be automatic (not subject to your discretion).
- You cannot select the particular recipients of that content except in response to automatic requests (mail lists are okay).
- Temporary copies you make in your network during transmission and routing cannot be "ordinarily accessible" to anyone but the recipient and cannot be maintained for a longer period than "reasonably necessary" for transmission.

Under these conditions, you can provide access, run a backbone network, run an e-mail server, and run quality-of-service applications that may require some packets to be stored in the network for an indeterminate period of time while other packets are passed through the network.

You must also comply with the eligibility requirements set forth later in this chapter under the heading Eligibility.

There are no filtering or monitoring requirements in the DMCA. During negotiations, ISPs successfully argued that network-level filtering would be prohibitively expensive and would slow down the operation of critical components of the network. In this context, I mean only *payload* (the actual content of any Internet transmission) monitoring and filtering. I do not mean to include the monitoring or filtering of any protocol-related information associated with that payload as may be necessary to monitor network performance, combat spam, or maintain network security. Nevertheless, a number of public advocacy groups have recently figured out that QoS software employed in some of the latest Cisco Systems broadband routing equipment could make it possible for ISPs to block or restrict consumers from reaching certain sites. For example, the wide-scale deployment of such technology, coupled with the Internet Content Rating Association's efforts to rate and tag content, would enable ISPs to essentially inhibit the flow of certain types of content by significantly lowering its priority in comparison to most other traffic. While this may sound acceptable in some regards, keep in mind that no matter how well intentioned payload monitoring or filtering might be, either activity presents a slippery slope for ISPs. Once it can be demonstrated that an ISP could perform network-level monitoring or filtering for any kind of content payload without significantly impacting network operations, the laws will probably be modified to require such acts.

## Hosting Content and Complying with Notice and Take Down

If you host content, even though you may also provide access, and many smaller ISPs do, the hosting activity is considered to be outside of the immunity provisions for mere conduit operations because you are considered to have the ability to control the stored content. An ISP "controls" content only when that content is stored on the provider's host servers and the service provider is permitted to access that content. If the server hosting the troublesome content is merely colocated at your facilitates, and you do not have the contractual right to access and control the content therein, you are not considered to be in control of the content. For example, you may be obligated to perform maintenance and backup operations for a customer's server and therefore have system administrative access to the server, but your contract may forbid you from actually accessing any of the specific content stored therein. If you do have the right to access and manipulate that content, you will probably have to comply with the DMCA on behalf of the customer.

In either case, to avoid monetary liability and to be able to take advantage on the notice-and-take-down (NTD) safe harbor provisions, the following conditions must apply:

- You must designate an agent to receive a DMCA notice and file that contact information with the U.S. Copyright Office.

- You must establish a procedure for processing DMCA notices and publish that information on your web site.

- You cannot have actual knowledge of the infringing content (this can occur only when you know the content is protected by copyright and the person originating that content has no right to use it).

- You cannot be aware of facts or circumstances from which infringement is apparent (i.e., your customer probably does not have the right to sell copies of popular personal computer software for 90 percent off list price).

- If you somehow get knowledge, you must act on that knowledge expeditiously (as though you had received a notice—see following).

- You cannot receive any "direct financial benefit" from the infringing activity.

- Once you receive a compliant DMCA notice, you must respond expeditiously to that notice (although no specific time limit is set forth in the Act, I would venture to say that it means something in between "immediately" and "as soon as you get around to it").

You are not obligated to perform any substantive analysis of the underlying copyright claim presented in a compliant notice. If you do perform an analysis, you do so at your own risk because doing so might cause you to respond nonexpeditiously.

Do check the notice carefully, because many notices received by ISPs are not compliant. A notice must *substantially* comply with these requirements of the Act to be considered compliant. In this context, *substantially* means that there can be no fatal flaw in the necessary information, such as the location of the allegedly infringing material or the good-faith statement. Even if a notice is not compliant, if it fulfills any of the following conditions, then you must promptly attempt to contact the complaining party or take other reasonable steps to assist the complaining party in fixing the notice:

- Identify the copyrighted work allegedly infringed.

- Identify and provide you with enough information to enable you to find the allegedly infringing material.

- Provide you with contact information, such as a mailing address, telephone number, and/or e-mail address, for the complaining party.

If a notice does not substantially comply, you are obligated only to inform the person who sent you the notice that the notice is not compliant.

When you receive a compliant notice, you must either remove the content specified in the notice or block outside access to that content. Some ISPs attempt to notify their customers first and hope the customers will take care of the problem. Although this is a nice customer service, and certainly something to consider with respect to your large customers, a significant time lag could also subject you to liability, so be careful. Once you have blocked or removed the content, you must notify your customer that you have done so.

You are not obligated to inform customers whose information was blocked or removed that they have the right to submit a counternotice, but you may choose to do so. Keep in mind, however, that certain content may be so controversial that you would be better off if particular customers were unaware of this right.

If you do receive a counternotice, the blocked or removed content must be restored in not less than 10 or more than 14 days after receipt. If you receive an injunction from a U.S. court requiring you not to restore the material or a copy of a complaint filed against your customer in U.S. court by the copyright holder seeking to have its rights in the content upheld, then you must continue to block the material.

You must also comply with the eligibility requirements subsequently set forth under the heading Eligibility.

## Information Location Tools

An *information location tool* is a fancy way of saying *search engine, hypertext link,* or *directory*. These latter terms were not used in the DMCA because nobody wanted to define one type of technology in the legislation only to have it quickly replaced by a different type of technology. The term *information location tool* should encompass a large range of different technologies that can be used to locate information now and into the future. Once information is located, it will obviously have to be conveyed to the person or agent looking for it, and because that process probably requires the information to be reproduced, distributed, and possibly made available to the public, the copyright laws will be implicated.

The Act's definition of an ISP (aside from the limited definition that applies only to mere conduits) is obviously broad enough to cover web cache operators, web hosting operators, portal operators, and anyone else offering an information location service. Information location tool or service providers were considered to be so much like web hosting providers that the same basic rules apply. Rather than restate them here, simply refer to the dos and don'ts set forth in the immediately prior section.

The only difference between web hosting providers and information location tool providers relates to NTD. A DMCA notice to an information location tool provider has to identify the link or reference, rather than the location of the infringing material, associated with the infringement. Although the Act does not specify that an information location tool provider must specify an agent for receiving DMCA notices, the Copyright Office has indicated that this was an oversight that it intends to correct. It is best to otherwise treat information location tools the same as web hosting. You should designate an agent.

## Caching and Other Forms of Storage

The temporary storage of content, as might occur in a router or mail server, is considered to be an "intermediate" or "transient" form of storage under the DMCA and therefore comes under the mere conduit provisions stated previously. The storage of content on a hosted server comes under the hosting provisions noted earlier.

The storage of content in a web or system cache is subject to a third set of rules. Although an ISP is in control of the cache servers that it uses, it is not in control of the content on such servers. ISPs typically use programmed rules running on the server to determine which content to cache and for how long. Thus, the software makes these decisions, not the ISP (even though the ISP may have programmed the general instructions). Because a caching service provider is both blind to the specific content being selected to be stored in its cache servers and highly motivated to adopt programmed rules that frequently refresh or update content, the type of copying that goes on inside a cache server does not hurt the content provider and should not be a concern.

Furthermore, the web or system cache discussed in Chapter 3 and illustrated in Figure 3.1 allows an ISP to distribute content geographically around the world, thus permitting easier access to that content (which benefits the content provider) and reducing the communications costs associated with repeatedly accessing the same content (which benefits the ISP). According to a Global Internet Project (GIP) paper entitled *Preventing Internet Bottlenecks: The Role of Caching* (www.gip.org/caching .htm), users of Inktomi Corporation's caching software have experienced hit rates of up to 80 percent from the web cache. This means that up to 80 percent of user requests are served from the web cache rather than from the original source. Hence, web caching significantly reduces redundant traffic on the Internet and substantially improves the efficiency of the Internet.

There are other forms of cache, of course, such as the type of caching that takes place in an individual's personal computer under the operation of browser software, the computer's operating system, or the computer's microprocessor. Although internal computer caching operations may technically infringe copyrights when copyrighted materials are reproduced within the computer, the DMCA did not address this type of cache activity. *Mirroring* or *mirror caching* refers to the practice of setting up separate but identical sites on different servers so that if one server is unavailable or experiencing more traffic than it can handle, the traffic can be automatically diverted to a mirrored site. Because mirroring is usually based on contractual arrangements between the original source and the provider of the mirror cache, it is unlikely that a true mirror cache would be subject to notice under the DMCA.

If you web-cache, you must comply with certain requirements under the DMCA in order to avoid monetary liability for infringing copyrights in the cached content:

- You must be only caching the content and not also putting that content online (i.e., infringers can't use the cache provisions to hide from liability).
- Your cache must operate by passively transmitting the content at someone else's direction (this requirement is similar to the immediately preceding one).
- Your cache must operate through an "automatic technical process," which means that it cannot select specific content.
- You cannot modify the cached content.
- Your cache must conform to programmed refreshing rules established by the original source (this assures content owners that the cached material is fresh).
- Your cache cannot interfere with technology that would have returned certain information to the content owner if the content had been accessed from the original source (unless that technology would interfere with your network operations, is not consistent with standard practices, or extracts additional information from the network).
- You have to duplicate any copyright protection mechanisms from the original source to the cache, such as password protection or copyright notices.

- You have to comply with a slightly modified DMCA notice. The modification requires that the notice must state that the material has been taken down or blocked at the original source. This means you need not comply with a notice when doing so will do little good (the infringing material will just be reached the next time a user requests it).

If an original site permits caching but employs a ridiculous refresh rate or employs technology that interferes with your cache, you do not need to comply with the applicable provisions. Of course, this doesn't necessarily mean much because you probably can't or wouldn't want to cache that site anyway. In short, you don't have an absolute right to cache anything you want to cache, but if a site allows itself to be cached, then the owner of that site can complain only if you fail to comply with the DMCA.

You must also comply with the eligibility requirements set forth momentarily under the heading Eligibility.

# Conditions for Eligibility, Injunctive Relief, and User Privacy

None of the limitations on liability (including the mere conduit provisions) established by the DMCA apply to ISPs who fail to comply with some very basic eligibility requirements.

## Eligibility

Only two general eligibility requirements under the DMCA apply to all ISPs regardless of the function they perform:

1. You must adopt, reasonably implement, and inform customers of a policy that provides for the termination of customers who are repeat infringers.
2. You must accommodate and not interfere with standard technical measures.

A *standard technical measure* is something that relates to a technology employed by copyright owners to identify or protect copyrighted works and that is subject to the following conditions:

- It has been developed pursuant to a broad consensus of copyright owners and service providers in an open, fair, voluntary, multi-industry standards process.
- It is available to any person on reasonable and nondiscriminatory terms.
- It does not impose a substantial cost on service providers or a substantial burden on their systems or networks.

## Injunctions

Even if you are eligible under the DMCA and have complied with the particular requirements of the relevant section to limit your monetary liability, you can still be enjoined in certain situations:

1. *Mere conduits* can be required by a court to

   ■ Terminate access to an infringing subscriber.

   ■ Block access to a specific site outside of the United States "by taking reasonable steps" to block that site. No one has sought an injunction seeking to have an ISP block a specific foreign site, so I really don't know how "reasonable steps" is going to be defined, but I don't think it includes scanning every packet header looking for a particular IP address to block.

2. *Other types of ISPs* can be required by a court to

   ■ Terminate an account.

   ■ Block access to a specific infringing site.

   ■ Take any other action the court deems appropriate as long as it's the least burdensome of alternative actions available to the ISP.

The limitations on injunctive relief do not apply to "nonprofit educational institutions" acting as ISPs. Accordingly, it appears that as long as the court "gives the service provider notice and an opportunity to appear" (to challenge the injunction) and takes into consideration the burden on the network and technical feasibility, the court can enjoin this type of ISP in any way the court deems fit. Don't feel too sorry for the universities and colleges, however; their representatives specifically requested this language because they wanted to show up in court to fight copyright battles on behalf of their customers (students and teachers) when other ISPs were loath to do so. The DMCA also contains very fact-specific protections for such service providers when an employee engages in or facilitates an infringement. If you are a "nonprofit educational institution" ISP and this type of situation arises, have your attorney carefully review the DMCA to determine how the limitations on liability apply to your organization.

## User Privacy

You are not required to monitor your network for infringing activity in order to qualify for the limitations on liability. You also do not have to "affirmatively seek facts indicating infringing activity." And you are not obligated to "gain access to, remove, or disable access to material" when doing so would be illegal. This means that you do not have to go looking for trouble, you do not have to pay money or try to hack into a protected user site, you do not have to establish a regular practice for tracking down infringing customers, and you do not have to take any action in response to a noncompliant notice. You never have to invade a user's privacy for the purpose of complying with the DMCA, unless required to do so in accordance with a compliant DMCA notice or a court order. Even if the copyright holders are able to develop technology, such as embedded watermarks, that enable ISPs to identify copyrighted packets that are watermarked, that technology will not enable ISPs to detect infringing packets, because the ratio of watermarked packets to nonwatermarked packets will be too small and it is not technically feasible to even attempt to check each packet for a watermark.

# The EU Copyright Directive Proposal and E-Commerce Directive Proposal

The European Union's (EU's) Copyright Directive proposal, otherwise known as a Proposal for a European Parliament and Council Directive on the Harmonization of Certain Aspects of Copyright and Related Rights in the Information Society, has been in the process of working its way through the EU's legislative process for a number of years. It is still a proposal, however, so it does not yet exist as an official directive in Europe. If you need a refresher on how laws are created in Europe, now is a good time to review Chapter 1, *WWW: The Wild, Wild West?* When the Copyright Directive was first proposed by the EC in 1997, it was intended to implement the WIPO copyright treaties and modernize copyright law in Europe in view of the digital age. There were many aspects to the initial proposal that ISPs did not like, such as the fact that it went much further in creating copyright protection in the EU than was required by the WIPO copyright treaties.

At this time, the proposed Copyright Directive has received an opinion from the European Parliament (EP), which included amendments that would make the directive even more favorable for copyright holders. The EC thereafter modified the proposed directive, but did not accept all of the EP's amendments. Because there is a conflict between the EC and EP, the Council of Ministers established a number of working groups to produce additional amendments to resolve the conflicts. Government officials from the copyright and cultural affairs offices of the respective governments largely staff these working groups. Hence, most of these people are unfamiliar with this entire issue, are very pro-copyright, and don't really care what happens to ISPs. As a result, the scope and coverage of the rights to be granted to copyright holders by the proposed Copyright Directive are much broader than the rights granted by the DMCA.

In addition, the proposed directive does very little to limit those rights when it comes to ISPs. In anticipation of strong opposition by ISPs, libraries, and educational institutes (the latter two entities being traditional opponents to broad copyright laws), the EC included language that deferred all liability issues to the proposed E-Commerce Directive. The E-Commerce Directive is known as the Proposal for a European Parliament and Council Directive on Certain Legal Aspects of Electronic Commerce in the Internal Market. Although it was generally appreciated that the proposed E-Commerce Directive would deal with liability, ISPs were still concerned that the Copyright Directive might go into force long before the E-Commerce Directive (the former was proposed a year before the latter). ISPs have therefore sought to have the proposed Copyright Directive amended to link its passage directly to the E-Commerce Directive. So far, the EP has only agreed to language that states that the two directives will largely come into force at the same time. At this time, the two directives are expected to go into force sometime in late 2000 or early 2001, and they will not be implemented within the member states until one or two years later.

# What's Similar to the DMCA and What's Different?

A combination of the Copyright Directive and the E-Commerce Directive (at least with respect to the liability of ISPs) in the EU would be roughly equivalent to the DMCA in the United States. In contrast to the DMCA, which deals solely with copyright issues, the proposed E-Commerce Directive also includes provisions relating to the following:

- The laws applicable to the establishment of e-commerce businesses
- The enforceability of electronic contracts
- Commercial communications with online users of e-commerce businesses
- The liability of ISPs in a horizontal context
- Out-of-court settlement of e-commerce disputes

I will discuss the various additional aspects of the proposed E-Commerce Directive shortly, under the heading The E-Commerce Directive Proposal, but first let's look at the proposed Copyright Directive.

## The Copyright Directive Proposal

One of the biggest controversies surrounding the proposed Copyright Directive is that it presently includes language that would make temporary copies subject to copyright protection in Europe. Although temporary copies have been subject to some degree of copyright protection in the United States for some time, this is a new concept in Europe. Temporary copy protection has not been an issue in the United States because U.S. law also included exceptions to the protection where the temporary copies didn't really hurt the copyright holders. Because European law never included temporary copy protection, it didn't include any exceptions either, so ISPs have been concerned about what the copyright holders intended to do with such rights once they got them.

The EU, at least, recognized that the copyright holders were not entirely to be trusted in this regard, either, so an exception was included in the draft for the types of temporary copies that are made in computers and networks. Unfortunately, the language that has been proposed so far isn't very good. For example, the EC's amended proposal in May 1999 stated that the exception would only "allow certain acts of temporary reproduction, such as transient and incidental reproductions, forming an integral part of and essential to a technological process carried out for the sole purpose of enabling the use of a work or other protected subject matter and which have no separate economic value on their own; whereas under these conditions this exception should include acts of caching or browsing." The copyright holders hated this language because they didn't think the proposed Copyright Directive should include any exceptions (see the discussion about "authorized" that follows). The ISPs didn't like this proposed language because it says only that caching and browsing "should" be included, it didn't address mere conduit, it had too many limitations, and was it subject to interpretations of economic value. As I mentioned earlier, although caching benefits the content holders, it also monetarily benefits the ISP, and many ISPs could imagine copyright holders demanding a piece of the cost savings. Anyway, this whole provision is still subject to negotiation and will probably not be completely resolved until sometime in 2000.

Although the WIPO copyright treaties included language stating that certain copyright laws should not apply to the mere provision of physical facilities for enabling or making available communications, the initially proposed Copyright Directive did not include similar language. Although the EC has corrected this mistake, the EP has sought to change the word *facilities* to *equipment*, which would necessarily exclude the provision of a service itself. This is another conflict that will hopefully be favorably resolved by the Council of Ministers.

The biggest controversy relating to the proposed Copyright Directive relates to an amendment by the EP to include language stating that any transient or incidental act of reproduction had to be "authorized by the right holders or permitted by law and must have no economic significance for the right holders." The EC rejected the EP's language, especially the "authorized" requirement, because a prior authorization requirement is completely impractical. There is no way an ISP could possibly attempt to get a preauthorization to make a copy of every packet transmitted across its network. Although the "permitted by law" language appears to provide an out, this language was intended to include only certain exceptions that are not normally included in the business activities of ISPs.

## The E-Commerce Directive Proposal

Before the EC officially proposed the E-Commerce Directive, it had suggested that the proposal would be very similar to the DMCA. At the representatives' request, I met with representatives responsible for drafting the proposal to discuss the history, language, and specifics of the DMCA. Based on such statements and discussions, I thought the proposal would be similar to the DMCA, but it was really quite different. I was therefore initially quite disappointed with this outcome. I have since realized that European laws are created and structured in a completely different way from those in the United States. Although the proposed directive would have been inappropriate legislation in the United States, it was quite appropriate for Europe.

Most of the differences between the DMCA and the proposed E-Commerce Directive relate to the level of detail included in the proposal. The DMCA is very specific in almost every regard, including the definitions of ISPs, conditions for eligibility, notice provisions, injunctive relief considerations, and so forth. The proposed E-Commerce Directive, at least initially (it has had some detail added to it by the EP and the EC), was general and vague. As it turns out, I did not realize that directives were historically drafted in this fashion because the EU long ago recognized that it was too difficult to implement an overly specific directive within the extremely varied legal systems of each of the member states. Some European countries, for example, do not have a form of injunctive relief that is equivalent to what exists in many other countries. This fact makes it difficult to draft injunctive relief provisions that can be implemented in each country.

I also thought the proposed E-Commerce Directive would be limited to ISP liability issues. In the United States, legislation is typically limited in scope, except before the end of the session, when many separate bills will be included in larger bills (e.g., federal spending bills) that have to be passed. The other issues addressed by the proposed directive include the designation of laws applicable to e-commerce (the so-called Internal Market Clause), commercial communications, electronic contracts, and alternative dispute resolution. Let's look at each area.

## ISP Liability

The proposed E-Commerce Directive addresses most of the same liability issues addressed by the DMCA (mere conduit, hosting, and caching), but does not specifically deal with *notice and take down* (NTD) and does not presently include language dealing with information location tools. Although the EC has indicated that it might reconsider its decision not to include language regarding information location tools, its implementation of NTD will likely remain quite different from that of the DMCA. The proposal is not limited to copyright liability. It deals with all other liability issues in a horizontal fashion, including copyright infringement, trademark infringement, defamation, and infringement of a member state's other laws, such as those dealing with pornography. While the proposal does not state so explicitly, the limitations on liability appear to apply to both civil and criminal liability. In contrast to the DMCA, however, copyright holders are not prevented from obtaining injunctive relief against ISPs, where available.

To benefit from the limitations on liability for specific types of activities (e.g., hosting), a number of conditions, which are basically identical to similar conditions in the DMCA, must be met. The EP proposed a great number of amendments in this area that were not accepted by the EC, so the ministers are once again being called forth to resolve the dispute. For example, the EP modified the knowledge standard from a DMCA-like "actual knowledge" and "not aware of facts or circumstances" standard to a "does not know or was not in a position to know" standard. The "position to know" standard is much too close to the dreaded "should have/could have known" standard that was ultimately rejected during negotiation of the DMCA. The EP also proposed requiring ISPs to remove infringing material "immediately," as opposed to "expeditiously." It would be very difficult for a smaller ISP, especially one that does not provide 24-hour-a-day, 7-day-a-week customer service, to comply with this type of requirement.

## Internal Market Clause

The proposed directive was intended to cover all information society (electronic commerce) services between businesses and between businesses and consumers, even if those services were provided free of charge to the recipient. This would include online newspapers, databases, financial services, professional services (lawyers, doctors, estate agents, etc.), entertainment services, marketing, advertising, and so on. As originally proposed, all service providers (ISPs, lawyers, doctors, etc.) would be subject to the laws of the country of their establishment. The place of establishment of a service provider is considered to be the place where that service provider is effectively located. In other words, the placement of servers in one country is not sufficient to establish a presence in that country. E-commerce businesses are enamored with this aspect of the proposal because it frees them from having to comply with all of the laws of each member state. As a result, a Spanish consumer purchasing a book from a web site in England would be subject to the laws of England with regard to that sale, not to Spanish consumer protection laws.

While the proposed directive was making its way through the EP, the EC prepared a number of seemingly unrelated regulations addressing applicable law and jurisdictional issues related to updates of the 1968 Brussels Convention on jurisdiction and enforcement and the 1980 Rome Convention on the laws applicable to contractual obligations. When conventions are adopted as regulations, they become law rather than general agreements in principle. The draft Brussels Regulation (to legalize the convention) would establish that consumers may always *sue at home* (i.e., in their country of residence). Although the Rome Convention will not be reviewed until next year, there is significant concern that it will establish the country of destination as the default provision when contracts do not stipulate what law shall apply. As you can see, in contrast to the proposed directive's country-of-origin principles, the proposed or possible regulations would heavily favor consumer interests, not ISPs'. With respect to the EC, this is a prime example of the right hand of the EC not knowing what the left hand is doing. Anyway, the entire matter has become extremely contentious, and I have no idea how it will be resolved. You must at least consider it possible that the proposed E-Commerce Directive will be further amended to remove or further limit the Internal Market Clause.

## Commercial Communications

The proposed directive requires ISPs to render accessible information relating to the name of the ISP, the address at which the ISP is established, and contact information for the ISP, such as an e-mail address, value added tax (VAT) number, or corporate registration number. In an effort of cut down on spam and spoofing (which will be discussed in further detail), all commercial communications by an ISP (remember the proposed directive includes any service provider in this definition) must clearly identify their source of origin, and all promotional offers, competitions, or games (where permitted) must be presented accurately and unequivocally. Spam must be identified as such as soon as the recipient receives it. ISPs are required to observe opt-out registries (discussed later).

## Electronic Contracts

The proposal would establish the validity of electronic contracts in all member states, provided the ISP explained in clear terms how such contracts were to be formed and followed other formalities, unless the contracts required notarization, required registration with a government authority, or related to family law or estate law. The proposal will therefore require member states to change many existing laws applicable to electronic contracts that would otherwise prevent electronic contracts from being effective or that would diminish their legal effect.

## Alternative Dispute Resolution

The proposed directive also includes requirements that service providers draft self-regulating codes of conduct and use alternative dispute resolution in disputes between ISPs and their customers. Traditional forms of alternative dispute resolution include mediation and arbitration.

## Immunity and Indirect Notice

Despite all of the problems with the proposed E-Commerce Directive at this time, things are looking up, and there is a good possibility that many of the preceding problems will be corrected, at least with respect to ISP liability. In the end, there is a good chance that the proposed directive will look very similar to the DMCA, although still not quite as detailed, and applied on a horizontal basis. Thus, while it will not include exactly the same provisions as the DMCA, they will be similar enough that whatever you are doing in the United States will largely work in Europe (check with local counsel to be sure, however). The notice provisions, however, are unlikely to look like the direct notice provisions adopted in the United States.

The U.S. notice system is called *direct notice* because copyright holders send their notice directly to the ISP. The favored system in Europe, already adopted in England for dealing with child pornography complaints, is an indirect notice system whereby notices are sent to a third party. The third party then verifies the notice, does any investigation that is required, and informs the ISP only if the ISP has to comply with the notice. The indirect notice system was considered, but rejected, in the United States because nobody wanted to have to pay for the third party. The United Kingdom's Internet Watch Foundation is funded by British ISPs. There are some advantages to an indirect notice system, especially if you have to pay only when you use the service. The idea of not having to dedicate staff for the purposes of complying with notices (especially if NTD gets adopted in other areas) and having a third party evaluate notices for defects is particularly attractive.

## Domain Names and Related Names

The current U.S. administration has said that it doesn't think domain name piracy legislation is needed in view of ICANN's recent adoption of a policy addressing cybersquatting issues and corresponding uniform dispute resolution rules to be enforced by ICANN's registrars. Nevertheless, Congress will not be able to keep itself out of this juicy issue. Hence, unless the president threatens to veto the legislation, the Domain Name Piracy Prevention Act, or something very similar to it, is likely to become law. This law will probably include a limitation on the liability of registrars and registries that suspend, cancel, or transfer domain names pursuant to a court order or in accordance with the registrars'/registries' own policies prohibiting cybersquatting. This limitation is designed to encourage registrars and registries to work with trademark owners to prevent cybersquatting. At the same time, registrants are protected from overreaching trademark owners who knowingly and materially misrepresent information to the registrars and registries. ICANN's rules really are much better than this legislation, however, because in accordance with this law, the registrant will be required to go to court to get an injunction to have its domain name reinstated as a result of a trademark owner's bad act. The ICANN rules provide registrants much more effective protection without forcing them to bear such a heavy burden to right a wrong. Under either the likely law or the ICANN rules, however, as long as a registrar or registry is not acting in bad faith, that registrar or registry should be able to avoid any kind of direct or indirect liability for trademark infringement relating to domain names they have registered.

The creation of user names is another area of concern for ISPs with regard to trademarks and right-to-publicity laws. After years of complaints and lawsuits, a number of ISPs are beginning to restrict their customers' right to pick any user name they choose (e.g., "generalmotors" or the name of a celebrity). AOL has already implemented a policy to restrict customers from creating user names that include trademarks and celebrity names (e.g., cindycrawford@aol.com). If a customer uses this type of user name to impersonate the celebrity or to cause some other kind of trouble, you could find yourself in court along with your customer, trying to explain why you let that customer use that name. Even if you don't want to monitor the adoption of user names up front, you may want to adopt a policy that allows you to cancel names if you discover a trademark or right-of-publicity infringement or some other violation of the law.

If you operate as a domain name registrar, a domain name registry, or other domain name registration authority (registrar/registry/other), you now have to be aware of the Anticybersquatting Consumer Protection Act of 1999 (ACPA), which is discussed in greater detail in Chapter 2. Under the ACPA, trademark holders and celebrities can bypass ICANN's recently adopted Uniform Dispute Resolution Policy (UDRP) and go directly to court to force the forfeiture, cancellation, or transfer of a domain name containing a trademark or celebrity's name that was registered in bad faith with the specific intent to profit by selling that domain name. If you have acted in concert with the party seeking to register such domain names, you might find yourself similarly liable.

The ACPA says that a registrar/registry/other may be liable for injunctive relief if the registrar/registry/other:

- Fails to expeditiously provide certain documentation to a court hearing a domain name dispute under the ACPA. These documents must be sufficient for the court to establish the court's control and authority regarding the disposition of the registration and use of the domain name—meaning evidence of the court's jurisdiction over the matter and the parties involved and evidence regarding the identity and activities of the party that obtained the registration.

- Transfers, suspends, or otherwise modifies the domain name (except upon court order) during pendency of the ACPA action (i.e., don't spoil their fun!).

- Willfully fails to comply with any court order regarding the previous items.

A registrar/registry/other will not be liable under the ACPA if it refuses to register, removes from registration, transfers, temporarily disables, or permanently cancels a domain name:

- In compliance with a court's order under the Trademark Act

- In the implementation of a reasonable policy by such registrar/registry/other prohibiting the registration of a domain name that is identical to, confusingly similar to, or dilutive of another's mark

If a registrar/registry/other takes an action based on a knowing and material misrepresentation by another person that the domain name in question is identical to, confusingly similar to, or dilutive of a mark, then that person shall be liable to the registrar/registry/other for any damages, including costs and attorney's fees, incurred by the registrar/registry/other as a result of such action.

Finally, a registrar/registry/other will not be liable under the ACPA if it registers or maintains a domain name for another absent a showing of bad-faith intent to profit from such registration or maintenance of that domain name. Obviously, if you have knowledge of such bad-faith intent, you will stand in the shoes of the so-called pirate.

# Gambling, Drugs, Alcohol

Given the existence of anti-Internet gambling laws in New York, Missouri, Minnesota, and other states, the federal government wasn't likely to be far behind, and so was born the Internet Gambling Prohibition Act of 1999 (IGPA). Given the likely passage of legislation substantially similar to the IGPA and similar state laws, I would strongly advise against operating an online casino or knowingly providing services to one. In the New York cases discussed in Chapter 4, the court said that it was "irrelevant that Internet gambling is legal in Antigua. The act of entering the bet and transmitting the information from New York via the Internet is adequate to constitute gambling activity within New York State." Setting up computer operations in gambling safe havens will be insufficient protection from the law. Providing services to someone whom you know to be violating the law could be considered aiding and abetting, so just because you aren't the one running the casino doesn't mean it is okay. You better keep a close eye on your salespeople.

## The Internet Gambling Prohibition Act

For the most part, the IGPA (see Chapter 4 for details) is just like the DMCA, except that it is applied to Internet gambling and the advertising and promotion of the non-Internet gambling–related matters and activities instead of copyright infringement. As noted in Chapter 4, the IGPA is not yet law, but the differences between the bill reported here and the eventual law are likely to be so inconsequential that you might as well follow the IGPA. The IGPA broadly prohibits knowingly using the Internet or any interactive computer service to place, receive, or otherwise make a bet, or to send, receive, or invite information that would assist in the placement of a bet or wager. Under appropriate circumstances, however, ISPs operating as mere conduits or providing hosting or linking services or activities are immune from liability.

An ISP is not liable if its facilities or services are used to transmit, route, or provide connections for gambling-related material or activity (including intermediate and temporary storage in the course of transmitting, routing, or providing connections), if the following conditions apply:

- The material or activity was initiated by or at the direction of another person.
- The transmitting, routing, or provision of connections is carried out through an automatic process without selection of the material or activity by the ISP.
- The ISP does not select the recipients of the material or activity, except as an automatic response to the request of another person.
- The material or activity is transmitted through the system or network of the ISP without substantive modification of its content.

Likewise, an ISP is not liable for illegal gambling-related material or activity at an online site hosted by the ISP or arising out of referring or linking users to such a site if the material or activity was initiated by or at the direction of another person, unless the provider failed to expeditiously respond to an appropriate notice.

To be eligible under either immunity provision, the ISP must maintain and implement a written policy that requires the ISP to terminate the account of subscribers after receipt of an appropriate notice. ISPs are required to follow the same designation of agent-for-receipt-of-notice rules established in the DMCA and set forth earlier in this chapter under the heading Designating an Agent for Receipt of a DMCA Notice. In addition, the ISP cannot knowingly permit its servers to be used to engage in illegal gambling activities with the specific intent that such servers be used for such purpose.

Upon receipt of a notice from either state or federal law enforcement agencies, an ISP is obligated to expeditiously do one of the following:

- Remove or disable access to the allegedly illegal material or activity residing at that online site.

- If the ISP is not in control of the site in question, the ISP must notify the agency that provided the notice that it was not the proper recipient of such notice; on receipt of a subpoena, the ISP must cooperate with the agency to identify the person controlling the site.

Unlike under the DMCA, however, you must comply with an IGPA notice *within 24 hours* to avoid being subject to an injunction. As previously stated, if you are not currently capable of responding to a notice with 24 hours, you need to become capable, or be prepared to be subjected to injunctive actions by law enforcement agencies and possible liability for failure to respond quickly enough.

If you are subject to an injunction, as a mere conduit or for hosting or linking activities, the court can order you to cut off access to a subscriber or block access to a foreign site. Furthermore, as a hosting or linking provider, the court can order you to cut off access to certain material or activities at a site you control or can order any other relief the court considers appropriate. A court is required to consider the following:

- Whether such an injunction, either alone or in combination with other such injunctions issued and currently operative against the same ISP, would significantly or unreasonably (taking into account the conduct of the ISP) burden either the ISP or the operation of the ISP's systems or networks

- Whether implementation of such an injunction would be technically feasible and effective and would not materially interfere with access to lawful material at other online locations

- Whether other less burdensome and comparably effective means of preventing or restraining access to the illegal material or activity are available

- The magnitude of the harm likely to be suffered by the community if the injunction is not granted

However, there is no guarantee that a court will actually consider these things unless you appear in court during the hearing on the injunction. The court is required to make sure you get notice of the proceeding and to let you appear, but doing so will cost you a considerable amount of money, so if you think it is even likely that you will ever be subject to an IGPA notice, I encourage you to look hard and *fast* at your response procedures and capabilities.

The IGPA also provides ISPs with immunity (subject to similar notice-and-take-down requirements) from liability (under and federal or state law prohibiting or regulating gambling or gambling-related activities or under any state law prohibiting or regulating advertising and promotional activities) for the following:

- Content provided by another that advertises or promotes non-Internet gambling activity that violates one of the aforementioned laws (unless the ISP is engaged in such a business) arising out of any mere conduit, hosting, or linking-related activities

- Content provided by another that advertises or promotes non-Internet gambling activity that is lawful under federal law and the law of the state in which such gambling activity is conducted

This immunity, however, is subject to numerous conditions, including the following:

- An obligation to maintain and implement a written policy that requires the ISP to terminate the account of subscribers after receipt of an appropriate notice

- A prohibition from knowingly permitting your servers to be used to engage in illegal advertising or promotion of non-Internet gambling activities with the specific intent that such servers be used for such purpose

- A requirement to offer filtering software or services to your residential access customers at a reasonable cost

ISPs that take any action in good faith to comply with a notice or a court order under the IGPA are immune from third-party damage claims or other criminal penalties.

ISPs are not obligated to monitor for material or uses of its service under the IGPA. I interpret the no-monitoring obligation to mean that an ISP cannot be ordered to monitor for and block IP addresses at the router or switch level. An ISP is also not obligated to gain access to, to remove, or to disable access to material except in response to a notice or court order.

## Prohibitions against Drug Paraphernalia and Controlled Substances

Although it is already illegal to sell controlled substances, it is highly likely that legislation will be passed in 2000 banning the offer for sale and advertising of drug paraphernalia and controlled substances (without a prescription). The likely passage of this law will surprise no one, because almost anything can be found on the World Wide Web, and almost anything can be offered for sale at an online auction. In one case, eBay permitted an auction for 500 pounds of marijuana to continue for over 24 hours, with bids reaching as high as $10 million, before the auction was stopped. A number of ISPs have also received requests from customers to filter out and ban sites that provide psychedelic drug recipes or allow individuals to more readily locate their local neighborhood pushers.

The ultimate law may not be identical to The Methamphetamine Anti-Proliferation Act of 1999 (MAA), but it probably won't be too different, either, especially given the popularity of antidrug legislation in an election year (2000). The MAA includes a provision making it illegal to advertise, directly or indirectly, drug paraphernalia and certain controlled substances. As an ISP, you are not liable under the MAA when someone uses your facilities or services to locate illegal online material, provided you do not control or modify the material to which such location tool refers or links. Also, you must comply with the notice-and-take-down procedures of the MAA. You must remove or disable access to matter that violates the MAA within 48 hours (not including weekends and holidays) of receipt of an appropriate notice that describes a particular online site residing on a server controlled or operated by you. I remain hopeful that the final version of such legislation will be more lenient about the required response time. You are required to follow the same designation of agent-for-receipt-of-notice rules established in the DMCA and set forth earlier in this chapter under the heading Designating an Agent for Receipt of a DMCA Notice. An appropriate notice must identify the matter, allege that such matter violates the MAA, provide reasonably sufficient information to permit you to locate the matter, and offer sufficient information to permit you to contact the federal official providing the notice. If you fail to take down the material within the prescribed time period, you will be deemed to have knowingly permitted your facilities or services to be used to engage in illegal activity.

## Alcohol and International Actions

A prohibition on the online sale of alcohol is also expected to be enacted by the federal government. Although most states already ban or restrict the direct shipment of alcohol, those states have a difficult time bringing actions against out-of-state shippers. The new federal law will enable states to bring their actions under state law in federal court so they can have broader jurisdiction. As with previously discussed laws, this law is also likely to include a limitation on the liability of ISPs for the acts of their customers.

While some countries, such as Belize and Antigua, have sought to encourage Internet gambling and similar acts, many other countries in addition to the United States are seeking to ban such activities. Bermuda recently proposed the outright ban on the sale of pornography and gambling. Australia has also announced a senate inquiry into online gambling, which is something that ISPs in Australia should watch pretty closely, given Australia's propensity for regulating the Internet.

## ISP Liability Gone Amok

The United States has hardly been the lone country attempting to rein in what it considers to be illegal practices on the Internet. The situation involving criminal charges against CompuServe and its former president for nothing more than failing to respond promptly, which will be discussed later in this chapter, is a good example (not *good* actually, but worth noting) of how out of control the liability situation can get with respect to ISPs if legislation isn't drafted carefully. I have mentioned Australia a few times, so let's look at what it has done and how it affects ISPs "down under."

## Horror Stories from Down Under and Other Nice Places to Visit

On 21 April 1999, the Australian minister for Communications, Information Technology, and the Arts proposed a new regulatory framework for ISPs in Australia. This proposal was designed "to meet the legitimate needs and interests of the community, while ensuring that industry development and competitiveness would not be stifled by overzealous laws, or inconsistent or unpredictable regimes." On its face, this statement sounds appropriate and encouraging. Unfortunately, there is little evidence that the proposal actually complies with the minister's design.

In accordance with this proposal, the Australian Broadcasting Authority (ABA) would investigate complaints from the public about "offensive" material online. The ABA would then take action with respect to any material that was rated X or R (and that was not protected by adult-verification procedures). The ratings would be determined by current National Classification Board guidelines. How all of this material was supposed to get rated wasn't actually discussed. A community advisory body would also be established to monitor for illegal material and receive complaints to be passed on to the ABA.

ABA actions would include the issuance of notices to ISPs requiring the ISPs to prevent access to any prohibited material hosted in Australia. If the material was sourced overseas, the ABA would direct the ISP to either comply with an industry code of practice or an ABA standard (i.e., reasonable steps that are technically and commercially feasible) to prevent access. Industry codes of practice would be expected to cover e-mails that direct one's attention to highly offensive or illegal material. Upon receipt of notice, an ISP would have one working day (not 24 hours) to take down the material.

However, if the ISP provided a service that prevented user access to certain material, such as through use of a filtered site, the ISP would be exempt from the ABA notices. ISPs would be subjected to a graduated scale of sanctions for failure to comply with ABA notices. ISPs that did comply would be indemnified from litigation instituted by customers affected by the ISP's compliance.

Shortly thereafter, the minister published a FAQ regarding the reasoning behind his proposal. This document can be found at www.dcita.gov.au/nsapi-text/?MIval=dca_dispdoc&ID=3871. How's that for a simple-to-use URL? I don't think the minister and his staff quite get it. Anyway, in the FAQ, the minister states that his proposal is practical because, despite all of the regulations associated with it, it will ensure "the supply of internet carriage services at performance standards that reasonably meet the social, industrial and commercial needs of the Australian community," while not imposing unnecessary financial and administrative burdens on industry. At this time, very few Australian ISPs can quite imagine how this will be possible.

To make matters worse, the decision regarding what constitutes an "unnecessary financial and administrative burden" seems to rest solely with the government. The minister also stated that "[t]he Government takes the view that it is unacceptable to make no attempt at controlling illegal or highly objectionable material on the basis that it may be difficult," and "it may be feasible technically and commercially, for big ISPs to filter (and many already do), but not so for small/backyard ISPs." This means that Australia anticipates the application of different compliance standards for different-size ISPs. How an ISP's size is to be determined, and in accordance with what system of measure, remains to be seen and will undoubtedly be at the sole discretion of the Australian government.

Personally, I find many of the minister's statements troubling. While the minister at least acknowledged that "there could be compliance costs and possible adverse effects on network performance" if the government were to mandate the use of certain technologies, the minister did not exclude that possibility. In fact, the minister even recommended that the government do so if ISPs were "unable or unwilling to develop" appropriate industry procedures. The most troubling aspect of this law, and the minister's statements about it, relates to the basic attempt to treat the Internet like a broadcast medium. In fact, the government even says that "[t]he [proposal] does not impose more onerous regulation than that applying to conventional media." This is idiotic. If you read through the proposed bill and all of the commentary about it, there is a dangerous mix of a misunderstanding of the Internet and how it works and a complete indifference to the impact of the proposal if the government didn't get what it wanted. This is not the model of freedom and democracy followed in most industrialized countries. Nevertheless, the proposal was passed by the Australian legislature by a two-vote margin in May 1999 and became law on January 1, 2000. ISPs must have developed and be operating under a code of practice by March 1, 2000 or the ABA will establish its own standards.

ISPs immediately protested the passage of the law. One ISP, Connect.com, claimed that the new law would require it to spend $1.5 million on new filters and content controls. Other ISPs claimed they might go broke if they were forced to face daily fines for content they did not originate and did not control. Opponents also said that the new law was moving Australia toward the pro-censorship regimes of China, Saudi Arabia, and Singapore—and they are right.

If it is as difficult to stop the flow of objectionable content as everyone seems to think, Australian ISPs may have no choice but to defend themselves from liability by creating a national web proxy. This proxy would filter all content flowing through Australia, thereby isolating Australian Internet users from the rest of the world. China already employs a national web proxy to block Chinese Internet users from visiting prohibited sites, and it recently forced a number of ISPs to deploy monitoring equipment that tracks individual e-mail accounts. Iran allows Internet access, but blocks web sites dealing in themes considered to be un-Islamic or that otherwise challenge the government. Saudi Arabia has even gone so far as to employ human sensors to intercept user requests and view the requested site for acceptability before permitting the user to have access. Singapore requires its ISPs to deploy banks of proxy servers to block access to sites banned by the government, but this effort seems to have weakened in recent years.

# A Uniform Procedure for Dealing with Content Regulation

In reality, no new type of content is made possible by the Internet that does not already exist in the physical world. The concerns regarding copyrights, child and adult pornography, defamation, gambling, drugs, hate speech, and spam are no different. The problem with content on the Internet is the same as for content in other mediums. The difference, however, is the way in which that content is created and used, the speed at which that content is distributed, the ease of access to that content, and the difficulties associated with controlling that content within an often anonymous and borderless environment. Unfortunately, as more countries attempt to pass laws and regulations directed to each different type of content available over the Internet, an increasingly complex patchwork of laws is being created within and between countries. I first recognized this phenomena in the United States shortly after the first anti-Internet gambling bill was introduced. As with early copyright legislation, this bill did not do a very good job of protecting ISPs from liability for other people's actions that the ISPs did not control. Although a number of ISPs recommended the adoption of DMCA-like protections, that recommendation was only partially followed.

ISPs will have an incredibly difficult or impossible time complying with different processes for every different type of controlled content or activity in every country. Imagine trying to comply with one process for copyright infringement, another for child pornography, and a third for gambling in country A and different processes for those activities in country B. Inconsistent laws and procedures for dealing with different types of controlled content and activities threaten to severely hinder the growth, development, and effectiveness of the Internet and global electronic commerce.

## A Plea for International Uniformity

After the successful adoption of an immunity and notice-and-take-down system in the DMCA and in the draft E-Commerce Directive, I suggested the adoption of a similar model in the broader context of form of regulated content. A worldwide uniform model for controlling content and regulating ISP liability is required to prevent a chaotic regime from developing within each country and among such countries (a patchwork within each patchwork). The World Intellectual Property Organization (WIPO) and the Global Business Dialogue on Electronic Commerce (GBDe) have recognized this need and are beginning the process of considering the issue, but neither effort will be enough. The WIPO's authority to propose a treaty in this regard may be limited to its specific subject matter—intellectual property—and therefore won't necessarily be much help with respect to all of the other types of controlled content. The GBDe is an industry organization and therefore can only suggest policies and principles to governments; it cannot make those governments enact legislation. Hopefully, however, a number of governments will wake up to these efforts and start a competitive trend between the governments around the world.

Any uniform model will have to strike a balance between the need for each government to protect public welfare as it sees fit and the need for business certainty in the global economy. Given the experiences of the EU in attempting to deploy directives within different legal regimes, this model will work only if it only sets forth the process to be followed when controlled content is in question—not the type of content that can be controlled or how originators of such content are to be punished.

Under this proposed system, ISPs that have neither knowledge of nor control over the content traversing their networks would not be liable for illegal content under any circumstances, provided that the ISPs met certain reasonable conditions in the operation of their networks, such as those set forth in the DMCA.

A caching ISP that complies with regular content refreshing requirements should be required to remove cached copies of illegal content only after that content has been removed from the original site and the caching ISP has received a valid, accurate notice of such removal.

Hosting ISPs should be held liable for illegal content if they are aware that it resides on their systems and fail to remove it or block access, or if they receive valid notice from a rights owner or a law enforcement authority and fail to act. Information location tool providers should be treated the same as hosting ISPs.

The distinct treatment of ISPs depending upon the type of service provided and the establishment of sound notice-and-take-down procedures, irrespective of the nature of the content, will go a long way toward responsibly addressing the problem of illegal content and activity on the Internet. A worldwide framework based on the foregoing principles will best serve the important and myriad interests of everyone involved in Internet communications and electronic commerce. These include law enforcement's duty to prevent the availability of illegal content; content owners' interest in preventing the unlawful distribution and exploitation of their goods, services, and property; the uninhibited access to legal content by Internet users; and the business certainty required by ISPs to continue expanding the Internet around the world and offering valuable services.

This uniform model has been my dream since I first realized how difficult it was going to be to export the DMCA model into other legislation within the United States and abroad. Fortunately, the GBDe has recently stated that one of its goals in 2000 is to "create where feasible and appropriate a horizontal approach on the issue of liability for most forms of legally controlled content and activities that could provide a foundation upon which to build a robust electronic commerce environment." The WIPO recently announced, as part of its Digital Agenda, that it would seek to "[d]evelop appropriate principles with the aim of establishing, at the appropriate time at the international level, rules for determining the circumstances of intellectual property liability of Online Service Providers which are compatible and workable within a framework of general liability rules for OSPs." I have a long way to go before my dream will be realized, if ever, but this is a very good start.

# Protecting Consumers and Their Privacy: Tools and Agents

Any time you collect information from anyone on the Internet, you will need to be mindful of the developing laws relating to the protection of consumer privacy and what you can and cannot do with that information. Although the United States has adopted a specific law having to do with the collection of information from children, it has not passed a general law on the subject and does not appear to be willing to bend to the will of the Europeans and follow their Privacy Directive.

## Privacy, Defamation, and Related Concerns

In the United States, the FTC is leading the charge to ensure that consumer privacy is protected on the Internet, but it is primarily doing so through the enforcement of consumer privacy laws. To the extent that you publish a privacy policy (and you are not currently required to do so), the FTC will bring an enforcement action against you only if you fail to live by the terms of your own policy. This is not a privacy issue. This is a consumer protection issue because it has to do with a violation of consumer trust, not privacy. The FTC is also under pressure from the EU, which is in the process of implementing its Data Privacy Directive and its reciprocity provisions. The reciprocity provisions require other countries to treat data in substantially the same manner as the EU or EU residents will be barred from exporting data to such countries and data sent from such countries will not be protected in the EU. As a result, the FTC could be forced to become more aggressive and has already indicated that if it is forced to do anything more, it will focus on what it calls its five principles for its privacy mission:

1. Notice that personal information is being collected and recorded.
2. Choice of how that information is used and/or distributed.
3. Access to the information collected.
4. Security of collected information.
5. Enforcement of online privacy laws.

Throughout much of 1999, there has been an almost constant attempt to negotiate a resolution to the dispute regarding U.S. privacy principles (or lack thereof) and the Data Privacy Directive's requirements. As the lead negotiator for the United States, the Department of Commerce (DOC) has indicated that it is pushing for the establishment of safe harbor conditions for U.S. companies and citizens. The EU has agreed to this in principle, but all of the details have not yet been worked out. A U.S.-based entity would qualify for the safe harbor as long as it complied with the conditions of an independent privacy protection organization that would in turn be responsible for resolving disputes. Details regarding enforcement, notice, damages, and other terms have not been resolved, either. The DOC is supposed to post any new and revised principles and FAQs on its web site (refer to International Trade Administration Electronic Commerce Task Force at www.ita.doc.gov/ecom/menu.htm).

In the meantime, the best example of the type of privacy practices that ISPs will be expected to follow in the EU can be found in the *Appendix to Recommendation No. R (99) f of the Committee of Ministers to Member States for the Protection of Privacy on the Internet*. This *Recommendation* sets forth specific guidelines for the protection of individuals with regard to the collection and processing of personal data and suggests that these guidelines be adopted as codes of conduct for ISPs. The guidelines for ISPs are as follows:

1. Use appropriate procedures and available technologies, preferably those that have been certified, to protect the privacy of the people concerned (even if they are not users of the Internet), especially by ensuring data integrity and confidentiality as well as physical and logical security of the network and of the services provided over the network.

2. Inform users of privacy risks presented by use of the Internet before they subscribe to or start using services. Such risks may concern data integrity, confidentiality, the security of the network, or other risks to privacy such as the hidden collection or recording of data.

3. Inform users about technical means that they may lawfully use to reduce security risks to data and communications (e.g., legally available encryption and digital signatures). Offer such technical means at a cost-oriented price, not a deterrent price.

4. Before accepting subscriptions and connecting users to the Internet, inform them about the possibilities of accessing the Internet anonymously and using its services and paying for them in an anonymous way (for example, using prepaid access cards). Complete anonymity may not be appropriate because of legal constraints. In those cases, if it is permitted by law, offer customers the possibility of using pseudonyms. Inform users of programs that will allow them to search and browse anonymously on the Internet. Design your system in a way that avoids or minimizes the use of personal data.

5. Do not read, modify, or delete messages sent to others.

6. Do not allow any interference with the contents of communications unless this interference is provided for by law and is carried out by a public authority.

7. Collect, process, and store data about users only when necessary for explicit, specified, and legitimate purposes.

8. Do not communicate data unless the communication is provided for by law. In general, data protection laws permit communication to third parties under certain conditions, in particular:

Sensitive data and traffic data for which the person concerned has given his or her explicit consent

Other data for which communication is necessary to fulfill the legitimate purpose or that the person concerned, after having been informed, does not oppose the communication

9. Do not store data for longer than is necessary to achieve the purpose of processing.

10. Do not use data for your own promotional or marketing purposes unless the person concerned, after having been informed, has not objected or, in the case of processing of traffic data or sensitive data, has given his or her explicit consent.

11. You are responsible for proper use of data. On your introductory page, highlight a clear statement about your privacy policy. This statement should be hyperlinked to a detailed explanation of your privacy practice. Before users start using services, when they visit your site, and whenever they ask, tell them who you are; what data you collect, process, and store; and in what way, for what purpose, and for how long you keep such data. If necessary, ask users for consent. At the request of the person concerned, correct inaccurate data immediately; delete such information if it is excessive, out-of-date, or no longer required; and stop the processing carried out if the user objects to it. Notify the third parties to whom you have communicated the data of any modification. Avoid the hidden collection of data.

12. Information provided to the user must be accurate and up-to-date.

13. Think twice about publishing data on you site! Such publication may infringe other people's privacy and may also be prohibited by law.

14. Before you send data to another country, seek advice (e.g., from the competent authorities in your country) on whether the transfer is permissible. You may have to ask the recipient to provide safeguards necessary to ensure protection of the data.

Although some of the preceding guidelines are cumbersome and impractical and would be expensive to implement, you'll find some pretty good advice in a number of the guidelines. This is probably the direction in which the world is headed, so the sooner you get comfortable with these types of requirements, the better off you will be.

## The Communications Assistance for Law Enforcement Act and the Electronic Communication Privacy Act

When the Communications Assistance for Law Enforcement Act (CALEA) was first introduced in the U.S. Congress, it was intended to extend wiretapping capabilities to any form of communication technology. After significant industry and public outcry, Congress subsequently narrowed the scope of the Act to extend wiretapping capabilities to new telephone, cellular, and satellite technologies (referred to by the FCC as "communication services"), but not to computer network services (referred to by the FCC as "information services"). As a compromise, CALEA also was structured so that information services would be exempt only until the FCC determined that informa-

## Side Law: Government Surveillance Activities

Although the EU has pushed for very extensive data privacy and protection laws, it has also ironically sought to force ISPs to provide law enforcement agencies with full-time, real-time access to Internet traffic. In accordance with the Lawful Interception of Communications council resolution, also known as *Enfopol,* ISPs would be required to provide access to all content and user identifier information relating to interception targets and with whom such targets communicate. ISPs would even be required to allow multiple simultaneous interceptions with multiple interfaces provided by the ISPs so the ISPs could then transmit the collected data to law enforcement agencies' premises in a readily available format. Although ISPs have attacked the resolution as highly impractical and vastly expensive, and even though the council's resolution is nonbinding, the resolution itself calls for member states to implement the requirements. Although the Europeans have been very good at doing what they were told by their governments, they are getting much better at protesting the actions of the EU. It will be interesting to see who wins this battle.

The United States, Canada, the United Kingdom, New Zealand, and Australia already operate a cooperative antispy and antiterrorist information-gathering organization called Echelon. The American Civil Liberties Union (ACLU), in a press release announcing a new Echelon web site, stated that Echelon reportedly attempts to capture all satellite, microwave, cellular, and fiber-optic communications worldwide, including communications to and from North America. Computers then use sophisticated filtering technology to sort through conversations, faxes, and e-mails searching for keywords or other flags. Communications that include the flags are then forwarded to the intelligence agency that requested them. Rumor also has it that Echelon requires ISPs in the United States to engage in the same type of behavior contemplated by Enfopol, and that Echelon operatives (wearing scuba gear) have secretly spliced into all of the transatlantic data cables to divert communications traffic.

While I wouldn't be surprised if some limited amount of monitoring of voice traffic from outside each country were being performed, I seriously doubt the transatlantic splicing story and similar stories that I have heard. First of all, that kind of activity could not be performed without the affected communications companies finding out about it. Second, even if the intelligence agencies were so engaged, they couldn't possibly have enough people to review all the information received and gather anything useful. Nevertheless, the Intelligence Authorization Act of 1999 included a provision requiring the intelligence agencies to submit to Congress a report detailing the legal standards under which they conduct electronic surveillance affecting the communications of Americans. The report must be submitted in both classified and unclassified form. For background on the need for a congressional inquiry into the surveillance activities of U.S. government intelligence agencies, see http://www.cdt.org/digi_tele/echelon_signon.html.

tion services had largely supplanted communication services as the primary means of communications within the United States.

Although the FCC has determined that information services have not yet supplanted communication services, that determination may end up being a moot point. When the FCC implements a law, it issues one or more regulatory *rule makings* interpreting the law and specifying how the law is to be implemented. In its second rule making regarding CALEA, the FCC decided that any service that combines a communication service with an information service would be required to comply with CALEA wire-tapping requirements as though it were a communication service. The FCC uses DSL as an example because DSL services include both a communication service component and an information service component. Hence, DSL equipment must be CALEA compliant, unless and until such time that someone successfully challenges the FCC's decision in this regard. This decision has sent equipment manufacturers scrambling to make sure their equipment is compliant, and it presents these manufacturers with a significant dilemma.

For the most part, existing communication equipment, aside from DSL and related technologies, operates in either the circuit-switched environment of communication services or in the packet-switched environment of information services, but not in both. The communication industry, however, has been pushing for the development of equipment that will handle both types of services. Because it is dual-function equipment like DSL, the equipment vendors are concerned that it must comply with CALEA. Because information services do not otherwise have to comply with CALEA, many people are concerned that making dual-function equipment CALEA compliant will open the Internet to abuse, security issues, and privacy violations by law enforcement. A number of equipment vendors requested that the IETF address this issue in the context of developing a standard protocol that would be CALEA compliant within a number of working groups, but the IETF deferred the discussion and decision to a plenary session, which soundly rejected the proposal. Despite the IETF rejection of the proposal, the equipment vendors may still feel compelled to make their equipment CALEA compliant, but now they won't do it in a uniform fashion, so I am not sure anything was actually solved by rejecting the proposal. The IETF may have been better off accepting the proposal to ensure that the CALEA compliance requirements applied only to the portion of the equipment responsible for receiving incoming voice traffic, not to the portion responsible for receiving and subsequently distributing data traffic.

At the same time, certain laws have been passed to protect the specific privacy of communications from interception. The Electronic Communication Privacy Act (ECPA), which is discussed in detail in Chapter 2, requires legal due-process standards to be met before Internet-based communications may be handed over to law enforcement officials, and ECPA prohibits individuals and service providers from "intercepting" communications over the Internet. Because law enforcement officials, your human resources department, and customers may still want you to intercept traffic over your network involving messages to or from employees and/or contractors, you need to make sure you do it right.

First of all, any time you are asked to do anything by law enforcement, contact a lawyer, and make sure law enforcement provides you with the necessary legal documents compelling you to take such action. If you are overly cooperative with law enforcement and end up trampling all over someone else's rights, law enforcement will not be there to cover for you and you will end up with the liability. When it comes to monitoring your own employees, however, you are permitted to intercept and disclose messages and e-mail from and among employees where such actions are necessary to protect your rights or property, as long as you use a device that is used in the ordinary course of business and it is incorporated into your network. You also can intercept e-mail between any two parties where you have the permission of one of the parties to do so. And you can even take action on behalf of a customer provided you have the customer's written authorization to act on its behalf and that the customer has obtained the requisite authorization from the person whose communications will be intercepted. You can also retrieve stored messages from network memory in any way and for any purpose you choose.

In Chapter 7, *Policies and Procedures: What to Ask/Tell Your Lawyer,* I will talk about policies you should implement, but keep in mind that one of those policies involves the use of electronic communication services by your employees and getting their consent to intercept messages and perform other investigations when deemed necessary. Because many employers now include consents of this type in agreements signed by employees and contractors, the employer can pass on the interception right to the ISP.

## Children's Privacy

COPPA provides that web sites cannot collect information from children under the age of 13 without first obtaining parental consent. The FTC has issued rules that take effect on April 21, 2000, that implement the requirements of COPPA. Although the rules may be further clarified, they are not expected to change significantly. The FTC rules apply to commercial web sites directed to, or knowingly collecting information from, children under 13. Such sites are required to obtain parental consent before collecting, using, or disclosing personal information from children. Such sites are also required to provide notices on the site and to parents about their policies. Parental consent must be verifiable.

While the FTC does not commit to any particular verification method, it does suggest the following options:

- A consent form signed by the parent and returned to the operator by postal mail or facsimile
- The use of a credit card by the parent (not by the child)
- A toll-free telephone number that parents could call
- An e-mail accompanied by a valid digital signature

Clever children, of course, could readily forge any of these, so upon request, parents must be given access to the personal information collected from their child and a means of reviewing that information. Sites must also give parents a choice of whether their child's information can be disclosed to third parties and the chance to prevent further use or further collection of personal information from their child.

Industry groups or others who wish to create self-regulatory programs (I am not presently aware of any, but that doesn't mean they don't exist) to govern compliance can qualify under safe harbor provisions. A *safe harbor* is a provision that protects you from liability as long as you comply with the terms. If the FTC approves a safe harbor, ISPs that follow that safe harbor may even be able to tailor their compliance obligations to their particular business model.

Rather than making additional specific recommendations about how to comply with the FTC rules, especially because they might change, I urge you to access the privacy policies of any well-established company that has a business model similar to your own. For example, if you operate a web site that is targeted to children under 13, I would recommend taking a look at the Walt Disney Company web site for some ideas. You can be fairly certain that Disney does not take any chances regarding FTC compliance, so whatever the company has on its site (http://disney.go.com/legal/privacy_policy.html) is probably good enough for you. Do not copy Disney's policies, however, because they are copyrighted, and Disney's lawyers would no doubt take copyright infringement seriously. Use the policies as a guide to the elements that you should include, but rewrite the text in your own words, using your own style and format.

## Publicity

While it isn't likely that a right-of-publicity claim against a customer for whom you provide access, transmission, or web hosting services will get you in trouble, you may nonetheless be subject to a subpoena seeking facts about your service provision, or you may be subject to injunctive orders requiring you to remove offending material. If you post people's pictures on your web site, then you need to be very careful about what you post. Do not rely on someone else's assurance that he or she has obtained the necessary rights to allow you to post the picture in question—make sure you see any such consents or licenses.

## Defamation and Libel

In the United States, in accordance with the CDA (actually Section 230 of the Communications Act of 1934, as amended), "[N]o provider or user of an interactive computer service shall be treated as the publisher or speaker of any information provided by another information content provider." ISPs are immune from any liability as a publisher (which could include defamation and libel) where the ISP only transmitted, published, or resold questionable information from a third-party content provider. AOL has successfully used this provision of the CDA in its defense in a number of defamation and libel suits brought against AOL resulting from acts by its customers and information providers. In particular, AOL was able to use the CDA to protect it from liability when a contributing author (Matt Drudge) allegedly wrote a defamatory column that was published as part of an AOL-produced web site. In that case, called *Blumenthal v. Drudge*, 922 F. Supp. 44 (D.D.C. 1998), the U.S. District Court for the District of Columbia said that ISPs were immune "even where [they] have an active [or] aggressive role in making available content prepared by others."

In other countries, such as the United Kingdom, very different rules apply. Northern Ireland Minister David Trimble sued Amazon UK for libel for selling a book (*The Committee: Political Assassination in Northern Ireland*, by Sean McPhilemy) about Trimble's alleged involvement in sectarian violence. Trimble sued Amazon UK because he can't sue Amazon in the United States, where the damages would be much larger if he could prove the book libelous. The United States also makes it much harder for public figures such as Trimble to pursue such claims. Furthermore, under the U.K.'s Defamation Act, exercising editorial control of posted information may subject an ISP to liability as a publisher or editor, thereby depriving the ISP of any defense. Amazon could get in more trouble if it posted defamatory comments by someone who wrote a review about *The Committee*. Australia, New Zealand, and Singapore have similar laws.

ISP liability for defamation should be one of the content-related issues included in any uniform process for resolving content liability issues. The rationale for such treatment largely parallels the online copyright infringement debate. The perpetrators of defamatory remarks are harder to identify and locate in the online world. As with copyright infringement, ISPs who have access to, and control over, identifiable defamatory content may be in the best position to aid victims of defamation in seeking recourse and remedy. And, as an ISP, you are probably no more interested in becoming involved in disputes over defamation than you are in playing a role in remedying civil copyright infringement claims.

Although ISPs in the United States are unlikely to accept the idea of having to comply with NTD for defamation when they already have an exemption from any liability under the CDA, the CDA does not shelter them from complying with subpoenas, and U.S. courts have been issuing subpoenas requiring ISPs to reveal the names of customers who had anonymously posted allegedly defaming and disparaging messages on message boards. Because IP addresses often cannot be traced back beyond a wholesale ISP or an ISP hosting a service, defamed parties have no choice but to ask the ISPs to identify the posters. Most ISPs, however, refuse such requests because of customer confidentiality concerns. The defamed parties then go to court and force the ISPs to reveal the names, and because most ISPs have provisions in their Acceptable Use Policies that allow them to reveal such information in response to court orders, the ISPs can do so without liability. It is possible that a uniform process could establish a similar, less costly process for revealing names in certain circumstances, so it may still be worth considering in this context.

## Spamming, Spoofing, and Fraud

Unsolicited bulk e-mail poses a serious threat to the integrity, safety, and efficient, reliable operation of the Internet. Instant messaging systems, such as ICQ, are also being used to send unsolicited messages. Vulnerabilities in web browsing software have even been exploited to allow frame spoofing, where a disreputable site inserts its own frames into the window of a web surfer when that surfer visits both sites. Not only does spam hurt the ISP and bother all users, but some big customers are holding their ISPs responsible for controlling spam that is sent to them or that spoofs their address for return mail. Use of the term *spam* for such e-mail allegedly came from a Monty Python skit in which a group of Vikings sang a chorus of "Spam, spam, spam . . ." louder and louder until it drowned out everyone else in the skit. Congress has considered a handful of antispam bills, but has not yet decided on one solution.

State legislatures are introducing and passing legislation to prohibit or restrict spamming and/or to clarify that existing computer hacking and trespass laws apply to spam. The State of Washington's antispam law empowers individuals and ISPs to sue spammers for spoofing, hijacking other e-mail systems, or otherwise "misrepresenting the messages' point of origin." In addition to having an antispam law in California, Intel has won a suit in state court to prevent a former employee from spamming Intel's 30,000 employees. The former employee tried to argue that Intel's e-mail system was akin to a shopping mall and that Intel's attempts to block his spam were violations of his free-speech rights. The court, and a number of experts, felt that the former employee confused his right to express himself with the mechanism by which he did so (i.e., just because he has the right to say what he wants does not mean that he has the right to use any mechanism to do so).

Virginia (where I make my home and which advertises itself as the "Home of the Internet" because of the heavy concentration of Internet-related companies in its northernmost counties, including UUNET, AOL, NSI, and PSInet) has adopted a very strong antispam law as part of its Computer Crimes Act. The Virginia laws make it a criminal and civil offense to spoof when spamming and to knowingly sell or distribute software whose primary purpose is to facilitate the transmission of false e-mail. ISPs are immune from liability if they merely transmit someone else's spam. Virginia-based e-mail service providers are also protected from liability that may arise from any contractual conditions or technical measures that they may implement to prevent the transmission of falsified spam.

The software provision in the Virginia law is important, and I hope something similar to it will be picked up in other legislation. For example, a software product called GeoList Professional had often been used by spammers to target mass mailings to specific states or regions. To make matters worse, GeoList was shipped with a list of domain names for over 4,200 regional ISPs (usually under 30,000 users) that could be used to construct mailing lists. These lists were created by repeatedly sending messages containing made-up names to an ISP's mail server to see if the made-up names matched real mail addresses for that ISP's domain. The processing time and traffic load resulting from such an operation was catastrophic for some ISPs. EarthOnline voluntarily discontinued distribution of GeoList shortly after being informed of the Virginia ban on spam software.

Internationally, if the E-Commerce Directive survives the EU process, it will require member states that permit spam to ensure that such spam be "identifiable clearly and unambiguously as such as soon as it is received by the recipient." Given the foregoing permit language, I take this to mean that some member states either currently ban spam entirely or are thinking of doing so. For those countries that do permit spam, service providers are required to frequently check and comply with an opt-out register for natural persons (not corporations) who do not wish to receive spam.

An *opt-out system* is one in which a person not wishing to receive spam is required to register in order to not be spammed by those that comply with the registry. The Internet Alliance, which recently merged with the Direct Marketing Association (DMA), runs an opt-out registry in the United States. The DMA is an association of direct-marketing companies (a nice way of saying "junk mailers") that maintains do-not-call and do-not-mail lists that its members must follow. The Internet Alliance is trying to do the same thing for the Internet. An *opt-in system* is one in which those wishing to receive spam are required to put their names and e-mail addresses on a list or nothing will be sent to them. The direct-marketing organizations don't think highly of opt-in systems, for obvious reasons, although a couple of these systems have been suggested in legislative solutions. In general, however, most people consider opt-in systems to be impossible to control.

As an ISP, however, you don't need to wait for legislation (although it would be nice) to help you fight spam and prevent liability for the damage caused by spam to your network and/or your customers. The Realtime Blackhole List developed by the Mail Abuse Prevention System (maps.vix.com/rbl/) can be used by ISPs to automatically block a spammer's access to your clients. The Spam Recycling Center, Abuse Net, and other organizations, such as the Coalition Against Unsolicited Commercial E-Mail (CAUCE), and the Forum for Responsible Ethical E-mail (FREE), can be contacted for additional help and advice. Then again, you could always buy a copy of Geoff Huston's *ISP Survival Guide* (published by John Wiley & Sons as part of the Networking Counsel Series) an excellent reference for similar technical concerns.

## Cookies and Other Tempting Tidbits

*Cookies* are mechanisms that allow web sites to identify particular users and to record information about that user and his or her activities on that user's own computer for subsequent retrieval and use by the web site. On their face, cookies sound (and taste) pretty good. Cookies can be used to save a user's password, purchase history, and preferences for when that user visits the same web site again. In this sense, cookies make web surfing easier for users.

Cookies can also be fattening and bad for your health, and accepting too many of them can cause all kinds of problems. Many cookies are received and stored without a user's knowledge or consent, especially if the user has not enabled the function of a browser (if his or her browser is even so equipped) that alerts users of the receipt of a cookie and allows the user to reject it. Even when such functionality is enabled, some web sites send so many cookies that users are forced to disable the function or abandon any hope of using the site in a normal fashion. Furthermore, a cookie usually does not tell you what its programmed function is, so users are forced to blindly accept or reject it at their own peril. For example, in response to a browser query, a web site will usually return a form page that identifies the cookie's name, what it does, and when it expires. The names are usually a meaningless string of alphanumeric characters that tell you nothing. I have never once been provided with an explanation of what a cookie will do, and the expiration date is often set for many years into the future.

The latest problematic use of cookies involves a new tracking tool known as a *web bug* or *clear GIF*. A web bug operates to identify a particular machine that has accessed a web site, the page that was opened at that site, the time of arrival, and other details. A cookie is then used to store that information in that machine's memory. For more information about web bugs, go to www.tiac.net/users/smiths.

The information gathered by a web bug is also sent to a company that provides Internet advertising services, such as DoubleClick Inc., which gathers and analyzes information about computer users at some 1,400 web sites. A company like DoubleClick can use a web bug to determine if the same user has subsequently visited other web sites or pages that are part of the same advertising network. Web bugs present a number of interesting problems. Consumers who have not enabled cookie identification may agree to more than they intended when they agree to accept a cookie associated with a web bug. Acceptance of a single cookie from a company in the advertising network can activate all of the other cookies from within that network without that consumer's knowledge or consent. Although, DoubleClick and a number of Internet advertising companies have agreed to let consumers opt out of such practices, concern about such tracking tools continues to grow, and I would expect to see more industry self-regulation and legislation in this area in the near future.

Although no specific legislation has been introduced or passed to address the cookie problem, the IETF has proposed some standard-oriented solutions in Request for Comment (RFC) 2109 that might help. This RFC and similar standard proposals and discussions can be accessed through www.isoc.com. Regardless of changes in the standards by which cookies operate or the new laws that are adopted regarding cookies, if you operate a web site that uses cookies, do your users a favor and either discontinue their use or make sure you use them correctly. If you do use them, use them only when really necessary, return complete responses when queried by users, and make sure you comply with consumer privacy and protection laws and COPPA. Remember, if you tell people that you will use cookies only in a particular way, the FTC requires that you comply with what you say.

## Microsoft and Intel's Attempts at Embedded Identification

The idea of collecting information with software or hardware without a user's knowledge was not limited to the Internet. In March of 1999, Microsoft acknowledged that a "feature" in its Windows 98 operating system could be used to collect information on authors of electronic documents without their knowledge. Other Microsoft software applications, such as Word and Excel, generate a unique 32-digit identification number, called a Globally Unique Identifier (GUID), that includes a 12-digit number unique to a host computer's Ethernet network adapter (a hardware device that is used to link computers to local area networks and from there to the Internet), containing information about a user's personal computer. Windows 98 accessed this information and transmitted it back to Microsoft when a user registered his or her copy of Windows 98 using the automated "registration wizard" included in Windows.

Microsoft was alleged to have initially claimed that GUIDs were intended for use in tracking broken hyperlinks in Office applications, but they were never actually used for that purpose. When it was discovered that GUIDs were passed back to Microsoft during the registration process, Microsoft was alleged to have stated that GUIDs were collected along with other information about a user's hardware to assist with customer-support issues. Other people have speculated that Microsoft created GUIDs to help identify pirated copies of Microsoft software, because Microsoft could match the application ID against the hardware ID to determined whether a single piece of software had been installed on multiple machines. The truth behind this potential privacy issue may never be known, but interestingly enough, Judge Jackson, in his ruling declaring Microsoft to be a monopoly, indicated that Microsoft had engaged in a number of questionable practices for the alleged purpose of fighting piracy. Microsoft claims to have fixed the problem in its latest release of Windows 98 and has produced a patch for correcting earlier releases.

Intel ran into a similar problem when it announced, in late 1998, that it would ship its Pentium III processors with a security "feature" that creates an identifying number that can then be used to identify particular users. Intel said the number, which would be included in almost any document created on the computer and in all communications from the computer, was intended to be used as an extra layer of security that, when turned on, would enable specific authorization of a specific computer. Privacy critics complained that the ID was basically a permanent cookie that enabled information to be collected and tracked like never before.

Even though people didn't like the idea of the ID number, Intel made matters worse by initially refusing to ship new processors with the security feature turned off by default. After a significant amount of bad press, including calls by privacy groups to boycott Intel products, Intel relented and agreed to ship the chips with the feature turned off by default.

# Hate Speech and Special National Laws

Most countries have laws (e.g., Germany's Constitution) that outlaw hate speech. In the United States, hate speech, speech that incites violence, and other similar forms of speech are not protected by the Constitution and could be repressed by any government authority that wants to do so. So far, the United States has been more concerned with the spread of pornography than it has with the spread of hate speech (probably because some of our most "devout" politicians can also be some of our most hateful), even though web sites devoted to a wide variety of hate groups have proliferated in recent years. For the most part, however, even if a law is passed related to hate speech, it probably won't impact ISPs because that is one area where law enforcement seems intent on focusing on the speaker, not the conduit. This may be true, however, only for mere conduits. Hosters and web site operators may have legal obligations to remove or report hate speech, especially if they know the questionable content is stored on their sites.

ISPs are more likely to be impacted by the efforts of others to have certain content removed. Deutsche Telekom, for example, once cut off access to all of the sites that were hosted by an American ISP in a effort to bar Germans from gaining access to neo-Nazi propaganda that was on one of the ISP-hosted sites. In Zambia, Zamnet Communications, an ISP, was warned by the police that it would be held liable for violating a whole bunch of laws if it did not take down an Internet edition of an opposition-voice daily newspaper that was banned by the president. In New Zealand, computer disks are classified as publications and can be banned and seized accordingly.

---

## Side Law: Other Interesting National Laws

A law in Canada requires all companies operating in Quebec to render its "catalogues, brochures, flyers, commercial directories, and publications," including web sites, in French. A photographer in Quebec was fined for operating his web site in English without an accompanying French translation.

AOL has been sued in the United States for alleged violation of the Americans with Disabilities Act for failure to operate its web sites so that blind users have equal access to the information and services AOL provides. AOL denies that is violating the Act, so this could be an interesting decision, if it gets that far.

Any online service that provides investment advertising (such as the ever present banner ads for online brokerage services) is required to include appropriate disclaimers and warnings on all relevant pages, according to the United Kingdom's Financial Service Authority.

The marketing of alcoholic beverages must comply with the Swedish Act on the Marketing of Alcoholic Beverages and may be banned from the Internet in Sweden if a Swedish court decides that the Internet is a heavy-impact medium.

---

Special national laws also apply to the operations of ISPs in almost every country. I am not familiar with all of these laws, although I suspect that most of them have to do with licensing requirements and restrictions on access by citizens. As mentioned earlier, many countries restrict access to the Internet by ordinary citizens or force the ISPs to perform certain policing activities. ISPs in Thailand, for example, are expected to police their own sites for any sexually explicit material or other content that could violate a law. In the most restrictive countries, the ISPs are actually owned by the government, so you aren't likely to be impacted. If you are, then I am glad you are reading this book because your government could use it to learn something!

In short, before you open up shop in any particular country, including the United States, make sure you learn the law of the land, which may require approaching the local government and asking for copies of all applicable laws and regulations. You can't do that in the United States and certain other countries because no one, including myself, knows what all of the laws are! You may have to hire local legal help to research the issue for you. If nothing else, this book at least provides you with some of the details you need and puts you on track to learn more—but you were smart enough to figure that out already.

# Pornography and Other Touchy Subjects

As noted in Chapter 4, a major portion of the Communications Decency Act (CDA) was found to be unconstitutional. The so-called e-mail provisions, however, did survive with respect to obscene materials. Anyone who makes, creates, solicits, and then initiates the transmission of an obscene comment, request, suggestion, proposal, image, or other communication (which could include e-mail, newsgroup postings, spam, etc.) with the intent to annoy, abuse, threaten, or harass another person can be fined and/or imprisoned for up to two years. If the communication was knowingly made to someone under 18, the requirement to initiate the communication goes away. Furthermore, those who knowingly permit a telephone facility under their control to be used for a prohibited act shall likewise be fined and/or imprisoned. At this time, ISPs would not be considered to be operating telephone facilities, even if providing DSL or voice over the Internet services.

Another portion of the CDA that survived has to do with protecting an ISP from civil liability for any action voluntarily taken in good faith to restrict access to material the ISP considers to be obscene, lewd, lascivious, filthy, excessively violent, harassing, or otherwise objectionable, regardless of whether the material is constitutionally protected. ISPs can also take any action to enable or to make available to anyone the technical means needed to restrict access to such material. Despite its broad scope, the CDA states that these provisions were not intended to limit the application of ECPA or any similar state law—which means that ISPs can't do anything they want.

Given these parameters, with respect to regular adult pornography, the CDA only *permits* you to do certain things. The CDA does not actually *require* you (as an ISP) to do or not do anything, unless you make a business of sending obscene messages.

## Filtering Requirements

Like the CDA before it, the Child Online Protection Act (COPA), otherwise known as the CDA II, is (probably) largely unconstitutional. I say *probably* because portions of it were preliminarily enjoined, and the Third Circuit Court of Appeals seems likely to confirm that injunction. I say *largely* because most of the COPA was attacked and enjoined, except for the portion that requires ISPs to inform a subscriber of the availability of filtering software. Although this portion lacks an explicit enforcement mechanism or sanction for noncompliance, it is recommended that you comply with it because the FCC has the authority to issue criminal sanctions against anyone knowingly and willfully violating the Communications Act of 1934.

ISPs must therefore provide a residential customer (at the time of entering an agreement to provide access services) with a notice instructing the customer that computer software and filtering or blocking systems are commercially available to assist the customer in limiting access to material that is harmful to minors. The notice must identify, or provide the customer with access to information identifying, current providers of such software or systems. You are not obligated to sell such software or systems.

Many consumers, however, are under the impression that ISPs are required to provide free filtering software or systems. Although legislation has been introduced to require ISPs to provide such software or systems for free or at cost, no such legislation has been passed and pending legislation has a very uncertain future. When states have tried to pass similar legislation, it has often been found to be unconstitutional, such as was the case with the Loudoun County, Virginia, library system. In addition, the software and systems that currently exist do not work very well and have resulted in numerous complaints by consumers. For example, software designed to block information considered to be obscene, violent, sexual, or worthless blocked the U.S. Declaration of Independence, the Koran, William Shakespeare's plays, and *The Adventures of Sherlock Holmes.* Worse yet, because most filtering and blocking software and systems don't check images, they can be tricked by clever web site operators who don't use certain keywords.

When you offer filtering or blocking software or systems, you should make sure you promise nothing and disclaim any liability for what that software or system fails to do. In the summer of 1999, a new ISP introduced an Internet access service that promised to review all web sites that its customers tried to enter and to screen out *unwanted* material. The ISP was even backed by a number of high-profile religious leaders who stated that the ISP would weed out poisonous content on the Internet. Shortly after starting up, however, users discovered that the ISP's embedded search engine allowed users to seek out sexually explicit content, which was then framed by the ISP's site. Remember the FTC's golden rule when it comes to the Internet: Don't promise consumers anything you cannot deliver.

If you do want to provide filtering or blocking software or systems to your customers, or at least let them know where they can find it, there are a number of places you can look. America Links Up provides public awareness and education information and has a list of browsers and filters at http://www.netparents.org/parentstips/browsers.html. Portal sites and search engines, like Yahoo!, can also help you find similar information.

# Child Pornography Reporting Requirements

The Protection of Children from Sexual Predators Act (PCSPA) requires providers of "an electronic communication service or a remote computing service to the public, through a facility or means of interstate or foreign commerce" to report incidents of child pornography to the appropriate federal agency. As noted in Chapter 4, however, some forms of child pornography are easier to identify than others, especially if a child is depicted in an artistic fashion or if the model is childlike, but not necessarily a child. A number of pornography web sites try very hard to attract visitors with spammed e-mail messages and news posts about Young Teens and Asian Lolitas. Investigators of such sites often have a difficult time determining if the models depicted are 15 years old or 20.

Although the PCSPA does not require ISPs to monitor for child pornography, it does require ISPs who obtain knowledge of facts or circumstances from which a violation of child pornography laws is apparent to report it to federal authorities, and questionable material should always be reported. Leave it up to the federal authorities to determine whether the questionable material is in fact child pornography. For example, if a customer or an employee reports having received a spammed message that includes sample images for an All-Nude Teen Love Fest, and you think one of the nude models could be under 35 years of age, you probably should report it. I say *35 years* because that appears to be the uniform safety zone across all ethnicities. If you go into any store that sells cigarettes or alcohol, you are sure to see signs warning that the store *cards* (checks the identification of) anyone under the age of 35 who is trying to buy alcohol or cigarettes. Stores have adopted this policy because, in general, anyone who looks older than 35 probably isn't under the age of 18 or 21.

Under current regulations, if you know the perpetrator, you are required to report the violation to the FBI area office in which the perpetrator is located or to the U.S. Customs Service if the perpetrator is outside the United States. When you do not know the perpetrator but believe the message originated in the United States, then notify the FBI in the state in which you are located. If the message originated outside of the United States, then notify the Customs Service. You are required to include whatever information you obtained that led you to conclude that a violation of federal child pornography laws occurred. You can include visual depictions, the identity or screen names of persons transmitting or receiving child pornography, or requests by persons to receive such matter. You are not required to supply any additional information, but you may do so if you desire. I advise you to keep it brief in case you are wrong.

The report to the FBI can be made telephonically to the local number of the FBI, which you can retrieve from www.fbi.gov. The report to the Customs Service can be made telephonically by calling the local number for the U.S. Customs Service or by calling 1-800-BE-ALERT. Proving that you called either agency may not result in a record of your compliance, so I advise following any phone call up with a confirming letter. Or just send a letter or facsimile in the first place.

## Staying out of Jail in Bavaria

The United States is not alone when it comes to banning child pornography or applying extremely strict rules to the Internet. According to some ISPs in the United Kingdom, Scotland Yard threatened to jail the chairpersons of a number of companies if they did not cooperate with the police to track down child pornography. The alleged result of these threats was the Internet Watch Foundation (IWF), which was launched in late 1996 by PIPEX founder Peter Dawe. The police, the U.K. government, and the two major trade associations in the United Kingdom, Internet Service Providers Association (ISPA) and London Internet Exchange (LINX), support IWF. These two trade associations, in particular, adopted and recommended a document called the *R3 Safety-Net*, which advocates the adoption of an ISP content rating and reporting system in the United Kingdom. *R3 Safety-Net* can be found at www.iwf.org.uk/about/ R3Safety.htm.

To me, the most interesting aspect of the *R3 Safety-Net* document is the section on responsibility. This section implores ISPs to take a responsible approach to the provision of services; to implement reasonable, practicable, and proportionate measures to hinder the use of the Internet for illegal purposes; and to provide a response mechanism in cases where illegal material or activity is identified. At the same time, the document also states that ISPs should not have to be responsible for law enforcement and that end users (not the ISPs) should be responsible for the content they place on the Internet.

IWF was initially funded by a private foundation, but is now primarily funded by ISPs. It provides a rating service for Usenet newsgroups that indicates whether a group normally contains illegal material and what sort of illegality is involved. It operates a hot line for accepting complaints about illegal material. Complaints are converted into a standard form and forwarded to ISPs and law enforcement. With respect to web sites, the IWF endorses the Platform for Internet Content Selection (PICS) and the RSACi rating schemes, which were previously discussed.

In the first year of operation, IWF processed 781 reports referring to over 4,300 items. A single report often includes many individual items. It is interesting to note that 85 percent of the reports related to child pornography, with 45 percent referring to Usenet news articles and 39 percent referring to web sites. The vast majority of the child pornography emanated from the United States (63 percent). The success of this program has led to the adoption of similar programs in Holland, Belgium, Norway, Germany, Japan, and Australia. This was quite an accomplishment for the Japanese, given that the Japanese Diet (their legislature) did not pass a ban on paid sex with children until 1999. As for the Germans, on the other hand, I was happy to see that they were following the IWF proposals, and I was relieved to hear that their adoption of the program did not involve throwing all of the ISPs in jail first!

## CompuServe Case Study: Good Law Gone Bad

In 1997, the German government enacted one of the world's first legislative attempts to comprehensively regulate the Internet. While the legislation is generally known as the Multimedia Law, it also establishes rules for the liability of ISPs, requirements for data privacy, and the legal infrastructure for a digital signature system. In Germany, regulating early and regulating often is a way of life. The German *Rechtsstaat*, the constitutional court, has dictated that lawmakers have a responsibility to legislate in all fundamental areas of life. Nevertheless, the Germans did a pretty good job with respect to the issue of ISP liability.

The Multimedia Law established that ISPs are liable for the content they create, but that they are not liable for the content created by others unless the ISP is aware of such content and has the technical means of preventing its use and can reasonably be expected to prevent such use. The reasonableness clause was intended to imply that a balancing test be used in each individual case. ISPs are not responsible for third-party content to which they simply provide access, although they are required to block access to or use of any illegal content pursuant to a court order or administrative process. Finally, ISPs are required to ensure that certain publications, as determined by the Federal Examining Board for Publications Harmful to Children, are not distributed to children within Germany. All in all, the German Multimedia Law was viewed as a well-thought-out and appropriately balanced attempt to deal with illegal content and the responsibility of ISPs.

It therefore came as some surprise to the world when Felix Somm, the former head of CompuServe Germany, was convicted of abetting child pornography by the criminal court of Munich, especially after the prosecution pleaded for his acquittal. In particular, Somm was convicted of having knowingly allowed pornography with children to be circulated via CompuServe.

The German Criminal Code, like the laws of many other countries, prohibits the circulation of pornographic text dealing with the sexual abuse of children. The Multimedia Law modified the definition of *pornographic text* to include *data storage media*. As a result, the circulation and/or storage of child pornography in electronic form had become as illegal as the circulation in paper form.

In response to reports that CompuServe's German customers had access to databases (Usenet groups) containing pictures showing sexual abuse of children, the public prosecutor's office began an investigation of CompuServe in 1995. The public prosecutor claimed that Felix Somm could have prevented CompuServe customers from gaining access to such material by technical means. As it turns out, Somm did try to prevent German customers from gaining access to the material by removing it from the German servers, but the German servers mirrored U.S. servers, so the material was reloaded onto the German servers at night. The resulting May 1998 trial lasted only 16 days because the defense was basically prevented from presenting its evidence, although it was able to get an expert to testify that Somm could not have filtered out the content such that German customers could not gain access. The judge nevertheless sentenced Somm to two years in prison (which was suspended in favor of probation) and fined him DM 100,000.

On November 17, 1999, a German state appeals court (based on appeals from both the defense and the prosecution calling for acquittal) overturned Somm's conviction. The state court agreed that Somm had no technical means of blocking the pornographic sites and that under the Multimedia Law an ISP (CompuServe and therefore Somm) is not liable for such content. Thus, as scary as this case seemed and as quick as people were to blame the Multimedia Law, the real problem was a judge who decided to do what he wanted rather than to follow the law. Thank goodness for appellate courts!

## Insurance

Although ISPs have lobbied hard to avoid accountability for most of what passes through their networks, they will obviously not succeed in that regard all of the time. When it comes to criminal liability, of course, no one but you can or should take the responsibility for what you do or fail to do, but civil liability is different. With all of the different standards for liability for different types of content and activity, and with all of the different conditions for eligibility, it will not be uncommon for even the most careful ISP to make a mistake. For that reason, it may be worth buying insurance to help cover the resulting liability. Don't get me wrong, insurance is not a vaccine that will protect you from getting into trouble—only you can do that. But if you do get in trouble, despite all of your best efforts, wouldn't it be nice not to put your profitability or even your business at risk as a result?

So, what kind of insurance should you get? And where do you go?

Historically, insurance companies offered comprehensive general liability policies that provided broad, standardized coverage for many different types of businesses. Successive waves of hazardous material and intellectual property claims have caused insurers to narrow the coverage of policies by adding many different exclusions and to create niche policies that protect only certain types of industries—such as Internet liability. These policies are directed at the typical kinds of risks that an Internet-related business might see, especially in the context of advertising, such as libel, slander, copyright infringement, trademark infringement, and unfair competition. Traditional policies focused more on personal injury and property damage liability because most businesses operated in a physical context. Modern policies take into account that personal injury and property damage are much less likely to occur in cyberspace. While many of the insurance products are aimed at large companies with significant electronic infrastructures, others can be tailored to smaller businesses. Over time, you should expect to see insurance products become even more tailored to ISPs.

For example, Westport Insurance Corporation, a General Electric company and a subsidiary of Employers Reinsurance Corporation, offers an electronic errors and omission policy that provides coverage for claims brought in the United States and Canada. The coverage includes claims arising from the content of matter, including defamation; disparagement or harm to character, reputation, or feeling; product disparagement; invasion or infringement of or interference with the right of privacy or publicity; plagiarism or misappropriation of information or ideas; piracy; infringement of copyright; infringement of title, slogan, trademark, trade name, trade dress, service mark, or service name; unfair competition; and negligent error or misstatement. In other words, the policy appears to address many of the ISP liability risks described in this book. For more information, see www.westportins.com.

Chubb Insurance offers a policy that protects online companies from lawsuits for copyright and trademark infringement, plagiarism, and liability. This policy is directed toward companies with annual revenues between $10 million and $500 million. Net Secure is a policy offered by a New York broker, J&H Marsh & McLennan, that covers first- and third-party losses due to programming errors; network and web site disruptions; theft of electronic information assets, including intellectual property; content injury, such as web site–related defamation, copyright infringement, and false advertising; and losses associated with breach of privacy and the inadvertent release of personal information. To qualify for this insurance, which is typical of the industry, you must undergo a two-step evaluation that analyzes your need for insurance and your risk to the insurance company. This evaluation might cost as much as $15,000. If you get the insurance, the policy provides coverage of up to $50,000 in the event of a web site disruption or security breach.

Reliance Insurance Company of Illinois offers InsureTrust, which provides coverage for losses resulting from security breaches; inability of authorized individuals to gain access or to conduct e-commerce or transmit e-mail on the Internet; introduction of computer viruses; and theft of data, including credit card information. This policy can cover claims up to $10 million. The policy can also be customized for different types of Internet business, such as merchants or ISPs. Lloyd's of London has added Internet liability as a standard endorsement to its worldwide commercial crime policy, which insures against losses arising from employee dishonesty, check forgery, and third-party computer and funds-transfer fraud.

By now you should have a pretty good understanding of exactly where your greatest strengths and weaknesses lie in relation to ISP liability issues. The type of insurance you require, if any, will largely depend on the type of business you are in and where you think you have the greatest risks. You can manage some of these risks when contracting with other parties, such as customers and vendors, for the provision of goods and services. Chapter 6, *Incorporating ISP Liability Concepts in Contracts,* will discuss many of the issues to consider when drafting and negotiating such contracts.

# CHAPTER 6

# Incorporating ISP Liability Concepts in Contracts

A s the provider of a service, you can find yourself liable for many different things (service interruption, failure to perform a task as agreed with your customer, etc.). These are everyday business risks for any type of service provider in almost any type of industry. An explanation of how to contract to avoid or account for such liabilities would require a book of its own—one that would be more appropriately directed to your legal counsel. Although I highly recommend that you hire a competent attorney to write and negotiate your contracts, I nevertheless provide you with information in this chapter that will help you incorporate concepts and language directed to avoiding or accounting for liabilities that are unique to ISPs into contracts with your vendors, suppliers, and customers. Vendor and supplier contracts include hardware, software, and content agreements. Customer contracts include access and resale agreements, hosting agreements, and so forth. *Porting agreements,* arrangements between backbone operators to exchange traffic between their respective customers, are not necessarily one or the other, so I will deal with those separately. Again, you should use an attorney for such contracts, but you should also understand what the attorneys are attempting to do (or not do, as the case may be). To an attorney, an educated client is the best kind of client.

I have included vendor and supplier contracts in this discussion because many companies overlook the third-party liability issues that are associated with such contracts. For example, if you license software from a supplier and that software damages a customer, the customer is going to look to you to cover the damage. But if your agreement with that supplier does not include an indemnity provision that covers the situation, you may be left holding the bag. In other words, if you do not get protective coverage coming in that is at least equivalent to the protective coverage you gave out, then you will end up in the middle as the only liable party. Of course, you may choose to make a business decision to retain such liability in appropriate cases. I just want to make sure that you realize it when you do so.

# Key Concepts of Contracting

No matter how many contracts I have written over the years, I always see other contracts written by other people with provisions or ideas that I like better than my own. I frequently incorporate those ideas, assuming they are not patented (that is supposed to be a joke), into my contracts. (Notice that I did not say that I *copy* other contracts—which might be a serious case of copyright infringement.) I also see language in other contracts that sends cold shivers down my spine. Hence, my contracts become living documents that evolve as my idea of what they should (and should not) include changes and as the business to which the contracts are directed changes as well. This means that there is no special language that should always be used in every contract of the same type. Twenty different providers of the same equipment or service will each present you with a different contract—each one specially crafted to focus on the primary areas of concern of that particular provider. Do not adopt someone else's form contract without molding it to fit your business. To illustrate this point, in Chapter 7, *Policies and Procedures: What to Ask/Tell Your Lawyer,* I will describe how 16 different ISPs treat spam within the context of each company's Acceptable Use Policy (AUP).

Throughout the remainder of this chapter, rather than provide you with form language to cut and paste into your contracts, I will focus on the concepts you need to develop and/or modify liability-related language to suit your purposes. These concepts will enable you to write your own language—or at least understand language that has been written by other people. Form contract provisions generally teach you very little about why a provision was written in a particular way and how it should be used. For example, my wife and I cofounded a nonprofit charity called CHIBB. Among many other things, children create and donate works of art to CHIBB, which CHIBB then sells or gives away in exchange for donations. The money received from the sale or gift of the art is then donated to select IRS-approved charities that benefit children in need. After operating offline for some time, CHIBB finally decided to start a modest web site at www.chibb.org. While reviewing the web hosting contracts from a number of different potential providers, I discovered one contract from a small company (company H) that was obviously pieced together using provisions from a legal form book and/or taken from other contracts.

While there isn't necessarily anything wrong with building a contract in this fashion, a good contract requires a good deal of thought and understanding about why certain things are included in the contract and why ideas are expressed in certain ways. Company H's contract was not a good contract. It was clearly pieced together from a number of different sources. As a result, the language in the contract lacked coherence, many critical terms were not defined, other terms were used in inconsistent ways, provisions contradicted one another, and there were references to sections that didn't exist. Never use a contract that you do not thoroughly understand. Otherwise, you will not be able to explain it or enforce it when you need to, and there is no point in writing or entering contracts that can't be enforced.

Even if you understand your contract, that contract will not do you much good if it doesn't truly reflect the fundamental principles of your business using language that is understandable to your customers. Going back to my prior example, company H designs and hosts web sites for small, technically unsophisticated businesses. Its web site describes its target customers in this fashion and states that company H was founded to specifically serve this market. Nevertheless, company H's web hosting contract (which was actually called *Contract for Virtual Hosting and Software License*) prominently included a section entitled Competency. The Competency section stated that company H expected its customers to have a certain level of knowledge in the use of Internet languages, protocols, and software. In particular, company H's contract stated that it expected its (technically unsophisticated) customers to have a thorough understanding of HTML, how to use CGI scripts within a Unix environment, tar and gunzip commands, perl, C Shell scripts, POP3 services, and so on. If you were indeed a technically unsophisticated customer of company H, you wouldn't even understand any of the terms used in company H's contract, let alone have the requisite knowledge required by company H. Company H's contract does not reflect a fundamental principle of its business. Moreover, its contract will probably scare away the people the company is trying to attract.

Now I understand what company H was attempting to do. It was concerned that technically unsophisticated customers would come to it for web hosting services, using material that company H did not provide. These customers might require an extensive amount of hand-holding, especially if there were problems with the material that the customers could not fix. Moreover, the material might even disrupt company H's servers. Company H wanted to make sure that it was not contractually obligated to help customers correct technical errors in customer-provided materials. The Competency section was not the right way to go about achieving that result. If company H wanted to make sure it didn't spend all of its profits providing free technical services, then company H needed to include language in its contract to that effect and limit it to customers who provided their own material. This limitation is necessary because it would be very disingenuous on company H's part to apply the same competency requirements to all customers, including those customers for whom company H designed and programmed their web sites. Obviously, if company H created the site because the customer didn't know HTML, or CGI scripts, or anything else about Internet technology, then the customer was going to need a certain amount of technical assistance. Company H would have been better off using different language for different situations or simply including language to provide a limited amount of support to different customers under different circumstances.

This brings me to the single most important concept when contracting with customers—make sure you know your customers and write your contracts accordingly. On the other hand, the single most important concept when contracting with a supplier is to make sure that you actually get what you need and that you give your customers no more than you received from your supplier (in appropriate circumstances).

# Contracts with Vendors and Suppliers

The business process starts with your receipt of materials and services from suppliers and ends with your provisions of goods and/or services to customers, so I will start with vendor and supplier (collectively, *suppliers*) contracts first. What you receive from your suppliers will vary greatly with the nature of your business. If you provide consumer dial-up access services, you will need software from a variety of different providers to enable your customers to access your service, to send and receive mail, to create and operate a personal web site, and so on. You will also probably contract with various content providers so you can offer your customers things like search services, personalized home pages with local weather and stock quotes, and hyperlinks to affiliated services. Unless you are simply reselling/rebranding someone else's services, you will need hardware and much more sophisticated software to operate your modem pools, gateways, servers, and so forth. Because you will have to get many of these items from different providers, you will probably have different contracts for each one. In each case, you need to make sure that you get what you need. This book is about ISP liability, so I will try to refrain from straying into other areas and stick with that.

## Supplier Paper and Contract Structure

Whenever necessary and possible, do not contract on unmodified supplier paper (i.e., a contract). Or perhaps a bit more directly, do not use the supplier's form contract. This does not mean that you should write your own contract every time. Unless you really know the supplier's business, it will be a waste of your time to write an appropriate contract for its provision of something to you. You probably wouldn't let your customers write your contracts, so why would they let you write theirs? Obviously, you needn't spend weeks negotiating a lease agreement for office furniture. Pick and choose your fights judiciously. This does mean that you should try to avoid signing a contract for anything important that was written by the supplier and largely unmodified by you during the negotiation process.

Any supplier with any sense is going to write its version of the contract largely in its own favor in the off chance that you will simply sign the contract. The same principle applies with respect to your customers. Sometimes you will have no choice but to sign suppliers' contracts because you need what they supply, you need it now, and you have no leverage to negotiate different terms. Be careful, however, because I tend to find that people often think they have less leverage than they really do. It is the rare situation where a supplier of sophisticated goods or services is unwilling to negotiate language in contracts. Nevertheless, just because suppliers are willing to negotiate doesn't mean you should negotiate every single term in the contract and make unreasonable and unjustifiable demands.

Make sure the contract has a logical flow. The contracting parties should be defined at the start. The purpose of the contract should be explained, which is often done in the introductory paragraphs, otherwise know as the *recitals.* Any time you use a term that isn't commonly understood or that you intend to have only a specific meaning, define that term. Some people place the definitions at the beginning or in an appendix; others weave them throughout the contract as they are introduced. It doesn't matter as long as you can verify that all of the necessary terms are defined and that they are always used consistently. Next, start with a description of the products or services to be provided, and then list each and every obligation of the parties with respect to such products/services. Do not assume that someone will do something that isn't in the contract, because when the time comes to call into question a verbal agreement, most people will deny it was made and stick to the contract. Furthermore, most contracts include what is called an *integration clause.* This is a provision near the back of the contract that says that the present agreement represents the entire agreement between the parties and supersedes any prior or contemporaneous verbal or written agreements. This means you are stuck with what is stated.

# Important Obligations Related to Liability

Because the obligations of the supplier will vary greatly with the nature of the contract, it is difficult to speak to each different type of liability obligation that might be involved. Nevertheless, common liability-related issues include the following.

### Domain Name Registration and Maintenance

To the extent that a supplier agrees to obtain, register, maintain, enforce, redirect traffic to, or do anything else with respect to a domain name, make sure those obligations are clearly defined and that they adequately protect your interests. The legal and regulatory environments relating to domain names are in a state of flux, so be sure to include language in the contract that gives the parties the flexibility to modify their obligations as reasonable and necessary under the circumstances.

### Branding and Trademarks/Service Marks

If you expect to be able to use a supplier's brand or marks in any way, make sure your right to do so is clearly delineated or you could be subject to subsequent claims of infringement or contract breach. Likewise, if you do not want the supplier to tell people that you are a customer or to talk about your relationship in some way that uses your marks (which includes your brands), you need to make that clear in a separate provision. Do not rely on the terms of a confidentiality clause or separate nondisclosure agreement to protect you in this regard, because the other party may consider only the terms, but not the existence, of your contract to be confidential.

### Amendments, Modifications, and Enhancements

A liability issue could suddenly require you to discontinue use of a supplier's product or service or require that product or service to be modified or changed in some way. Make sure your contract provides you with the flexibility to terminate the contract if necessary under such circumstances and/or provides you with the right to make (or force the supplier to make) the necessary changes. This type of provision is especially important where the supplier is providing content. The contract should also delineate who bears what costs in this regard.

## Legal and Regulatory Compliance

Your supplier may include language relating to its need to discontinue the provision of or otherwise change a product or service in order to comply with any law, regulation, court order, or other governmental proceeding, such as the beloved DMCA described in Chapter 3, *A Special Law for ISPs: The DMCA*. Because you are going to have to have a similar provision in your contracts with customers, it would be unreasonable to deny your supplier a similar right. Nevertheless, activation of such a provision could have a significant and damaging impact on your business, so you do not want to leave this to your supplier's sole discretion. Depending on the nature of the business and issues involved, you may want to reserve the right to confer and agree with your supplier with respect to any particular course of action. In such cases, however, it may also be necessary to draw a distinction between civil and criminal matters. If I were the supplier, and my potential criminal liability were on the line, I would be highly inclined to act first and talk to you later.

## Functionality and Features

The functionality and/or features of a supplied product or service may be relevant to liability issues in certain circumstances. For example, if your supplier of network services contracts to block certain types of traffic and fails to do so, and this traffic gets you in trouble, then the language used in the contract to describe the supplier's obligation will become very important. Although you may have an indemnity from your supplier (as described in greater detail in the next paragraph), that indemnity may be triggered only under certain circumstances, and failure to provide a promised function or feature may not be one. Likewise, if the language used to describe a function/feature is not clear enough, the supplier may be able to get out of its indemnity obligation.

## Indemnification and Defense

To *indemnify* someone means to protect that person against some loss or damage that has already occurred (i.e., to make that individual whole). When a supplier agrees to indemnify you, it is agreeing to cover any loss you incur as a result of some specified event. With respect to the example used in the preceding paragraph, if the supplier failed to block the traffic and the supplier had agreed to indemnify you in that event, then the supplier would be obligated to cover whatever loss you suffered as specified by your contract. To indemnify someone, however, does not mean you agree to defend him or her or you agree to pay the cost of that defense. For this reason, an indemnity provision will often be coupled with a defense provision. The combined provision would typically say that the supplier would defend you in certain circumstances, pay the cost of that defense, and indemnify you if you suffered any resulting loss. It is therefore very important that the types of events that could trigger a defense and/or indemnity obligation be clearly stated in your contracts. It is also important to spell out every obligation of the supplier with respect to your defense and to specify which party has what obligations. You may not want the supplier to represent you in court because the supplier's interests may not be directly aligned with yours. It is not uncommon to have a supplier agree to defend a customer, only to argue in court that the customer, not the supplier, was the cause of the problem. It is therefore a good idea to retain some control over the situation, even if it costs you something. Defense and indemnity issues are particularly important when it comes to *intellectual property issues*, which will be addressed later in this chapter.

## Representations and Warranties

A *representation* is a statement made by either party to a contract regarding some past or existing fact, circumstance, or condition that is pertinent to that agreement and that influences the other party's decision to enter that agreement. For example, if you represent to a software vendor that you have never reverse-engineered someone's software, that software vendor could claim breach of contract if that representation turned out not to be true, because the software vendor might have otherwise declined to enter the agreement. A *warranty* is a statement, generally made by the seller, relating to certain facts or qualities of the offered service or product, and it includes a promise that such facts or qualities are as stated. As with breach of a representation, breach of a warranty can be cause for terminating an agreement, but can also result in an indemnity obligation with respect to any damages caused. Some contracts tie all of these concepts together by including language stating that the supplier warrants the representations, thereby obligating the supplier to indemnify the customer for breach of a representation as well. There are very special legal rules in every state and country regarding how the parties are to word the warranties in their contracts in order for them to be effective against customers, especially in contracts for the sale of goods over a certain amount (say $500). The most common requirement is that any disclaimer of a warranty or representation be stated clearly and conspicuously. This is why you will often see such language in capital letters.

Certain warranties can also be implied (e.g., *merchantability, noninfringement,* or *fitness for a particular purpose*) unless expressly disclaimed, so you will almost always see these mentioned in highlighted text. *Merchantability* means that the product sold shall be of the general kind described by the supplier and shall be reasonably fit for purpose for which it was sold. *Fitness for a particular purpose* is a related concept. Where a product is ordinarily used in one particular way, it is implied to be fit for that particular purpose unless the supplier has expressly stated otherwise. *Noninfringement* of intellectual property rights can also be implied.

## Relationship of Parties

It is very important for liability purposes to make sure the relationship between the parties to the contract is clearly stated. If the contract does not state that you are *not* to act as the agent for the supplier, it is possible that you could be presumed to act in that capacity as a reseller or distributor, or because of some other arrangement. One major purpose of a contract is to make sure that a supplier's liability rests with that supplier and not you; however, that liability could be found to rest with you if it is determined that you were acting as the supplier's agent. Agency relationships are often established by circumstantial evidence, such as how the parties treat and refer to one another in their dealings with other parties. In this regard, the language in any contracts between the parties will be very relevant, especially if those contracts do not disavow the agency relationship. It is better to be independent contractors of one another.

## U.S. Government Restricted Rights

In the event that you or anyone you deal with subsequently provides software to the U.S. government, you need to be aware of a very strange requirement. If you provide any software to the government that does not include a specific restricted-rights legend (refer to the appropriate portions of the Commercial Computer Restricted Rights clause at 48 *CFR* 52.227-19 or the Rights in Technical Data and Computer Software clause at *DFARS* 252.227-7013) and does not specify the contractor/manufacturer of that software, then the government will get the unrestricted right to use, duplicate, and disclose that software. You should expect to see this provision in any contract involving software because no one wants to take the chance of losing copyrights and other rights in this way. If a supplier has provided you with the software, and you provide it to the government, you may end up being liable for the full value of that software (not just your copy) if you fail to comply with this labeling requirement.

## Export

Although encryption export restrictions are becoming less of a problem, it is still very important to make sure that the export laws are being followed. Certain suppliers will require you to comply with certain conditions to make sure that they do not get into trouble for violating the export laws. You would be wise, of course, to pass on similar obligations to your customers.

## Taxes and Charges

Most contracts state that each party is liable for its own taxes, but sometimes one party may agree to pay certain taxes associated with certain transactions. For example, a merchant may agree to pay sales tax that it has collected from you on the sale of a merchant item. I anticipate that contractual tax language in Internet-related contracts is going to get very interesting in the near future. For now, the Internet is largely treated as a tax-free zone, and efforts are under way to keep in that way. If it is determined, however, that electronic commerce is eating into the tax coffers of local, state, and national governments, you can be assured that the situation will change. Furthermore, there is a big push on to extend certain concepts from the regulated telephony market to the Internet, such as the *universal service fund* (USF) in the United

States. The USF was established to compensate certain local telephone service providers for the high cost of providing phone services to everyone in the country. A surcharge, or tax, on the phone services everyone receives funds the USF. A number of local providers are quite anxious to hang onto this supplemental income because in addition to lowering the cost of service to some customers, it goes a long way toward artificially enhancing the profitability of the companies that receive it. New Internet-related services potentially threaten the USF because they offer alternative means of phone service in certain areas and are not subject to USF taxes. Anyway, the key concept to keep in mind when contracting with any other party is to maintain the right to pass on any tax, surcharge, or other government-mandated fee to your customers. Otherwise, you will still be obligated to pay the fee; you will just have to do so at a cost to your business.

# Intellectual Property Issues

In addition to the trademark and copyright issues discussed earlier in this chapter, there are issues related to intellectual property. Intellectual property is very easy to create and is often developed in the course of dealings between two parties, but those parties will often fail to deal with the ownership issues that result from the development of that intellectual property. You may need to go back and read Chapter 2, *Intellectual Property Law and Other Laws Made Simple*, to refresh your knowledge of intellectual property concepts. For example, copyrights are typically created as a result of a web site development agreement, and those copyrights reside with the author in the absence of an agreement to the contrary. If you contract with someone to provide design services for you, you need to make sure you own the copyrights in the materials they create for you. Patentable inventions might also be created as a result of the combination of products or services from a variety of different parties. Since those inventions belong to the inventors and the inventors might be a combination of people from the different parties, it is very important to establish up front, before any inventing can be done, who will own what. The same is true with respect to trade secrets. See Side Law: A Dirty Little Trick—The Residual Clause for something to look out for if you share confidential information with some companies.

It is important to resolve the ownership issues in advance for two reasons. First, at the time two parties are entering a contract, they don't always have a very clear impression of exactly how the relationship is going to evolve over time. They may have great hopes, but that is a different matter. It is much easier to get ownership concessions at this stage than it is once intellectual property has been defined and coveted by one party. Second, if ownership is established up front, you know the consequences of your actions throughout the life of the contract and will not be put in the untenable position of being afraid to do certain things because of uncertain outcomes.

Once you have the ownership issues resolved, you need to figure out your licensed rights. Since a software vendor or copyright owner does not sell you the underlying copyright in the product, you have to get a license. If you then provide this

# Side Law: A Dirty Little Trick—The Residual Clause

Nondisclosure agreements and the confidentiality provisions in contracts require the recipients of certain information to treat that information as the confidential property of the discloser. The recipient can use the information only for a stated purpose and cannot disclose the information to a third party. Tangible information that is disclosed is identified by a confidentiality label or marking. A subsequent written note is typically used to designate the confidential nature of orally disclosed information. This method of protection effectively prevents tangible information from being inappropriately disclosed to third parties. When someone has been proven to have stolen a trade secret or violated a confidentiality agreement, it is usually possible to find some inappropriately disclosed document that was marked as the confidential property of the discloser. The situation can be quite different when the confidential information is only stored away in a recipient's mind. In such cases, the recipient might be able to walk away from the discloser and use what was learned without the discloser's ever being able to prove confidential information was taken. Such occurrences could happen innocently, of course; when the confidential information is similar to many other things that the recipient already knows, it may be very difficult for the recipient to remember what can and cannot be used.

Companies that do a significant amount of consulting work for competing companies in similar areas have a difficult time with confidentiality provisions. IBM and Microsoft, for example, provide consulting for a large number of different companies regarding hardware and software installations and operations. The employees used for one consulting job are often reused for similar consulting jobs at other companies because of the employees' established knowledge base. This practice increases the likelihood, however, that one of these employees will inappropriately use confidential information learned on one job at another job. To avoid liability for violation of confidentiality provisions, IBM, Microsoft, and other similarly situated companies have attempted to use a residual clause to protect themselves.

A *residual clause* is typically incorporated into confidentiality provisions as an exception to the nondisclosure rules. In accordance with a residual clause, the recipient is allowed to subsequently use anything he or she learned, whether confidential or not, if that information was stored in the recipient's mind. The recipient cannot say from where the information was obtained, but its use is otherwise unrestricted. Thus, if you hire IBM to perform consulting work and you have a residual clause in your contract, the IBM employees will be free to take any of your information, even if otherwise subject to protection, and use that information at IBM or at another company without restriction. If you suddenly find out that IBM or a competitor of yours has implemented systems or processes that are similar to yours, you will not be able to pursue a breach of contract or trade secret theft claim against IBM because you agreed that it could take your confidential information. Microsoft has recently backed away from vigorously pursuing residual clauses in contracts, possibly as a result of its problems with the Justice Department. IBM, on the other hand, appears as though it would rather lose business than compromise on this issue. Given IBM's presence in computer-related businesses, it almost always gets its way when it comes to residual clauses. Although it claims the residual clause is needed to protect it from legal exposure, IBM has not been sued that frequently for breach of confidentiality contracts, so one must wonder if fear of legal exposure is the only reason. In other words, be careful!

product to your customers, you need to be able to pass on certain rights. Ideally, you would like to pass on what you received, but the copyright owner may not want you to do that, so you will have to carefully negotiate this. Failure to acquire the appropriate rights can be very costly because you may have to make up the difference between the licensed rights your customers received and the resulting damage they caused because you did not properly police your actions with respect to those customers.

Intellectual property is often subject to different indemnity provisions than other portions of the contract. If you get sued for infringing a third party's intellectual property rights when you use a supplier's product or service, you are going to want to make sure you have some form of intellectual property indemnity coverage from that supplier. Even more important, if your customers get sued for infringing intellectual property rights and that infringement can be traced back to your supplier, you will want to make sure that situation is covered as well. With respect to the latter situation, however, you may not want your supplier defending your customers or even knowing who they are, so you will have to be very careful with the construction of the defense and indemnity clause.

In most cases, vendors will agree to provide you with protection only to the extent that the item they provided was the sole cause of the infringement. This may be an appropriate limitation, in some cases, because the provider of one item cannot be expected to cover you for everything that you or your customers might do with that item, especially things that were within your control, rather than that of the suppliers. It is therefore common to see broadly worded intellectual property indemnity language, but with what are called *carve-out* limitations. A typical carve-out is to exclude any infringement caused by the combination of the supplier's item with anything else not provided by the supplier, where, if it were not for that combination, there would have been no infringement. Not all combinations should be excluded in every case. Sometimes a supplier may know that the item it is providing will contribute to the infringement of a patent, but you do not. Accordingly, it may be appropriate in some circumstances for your supplier to indemnify you when the supplier knows that its product or service directly or indirectly infringes an intellectual property right of a third party or if the supplier is otherwise operating in bad faith.

## Retaining Your Flexibility

You also need to make sure that you have sufficient flexibility in your contracts with your suppliers to modify your business over time. For example, you may currently allow your customers to access software on your servers that enables the customers to perform some function on the Internet. For various reasons, you may decide to move the customers using that software off of your server and have them run that software locally on their own computers. If you properly anticipated your need to do this and built appropriate provisions into your contract to enable yourself to do so, then this will not be a big deal. If you suddenly have to go back to the supplier and urgently request a modification to your contract, you will likely find the outcome to be much more costly and time consuming.

This same principle applies to almost anything you receive from suppliers, so you have to try to anticipate changes in your business over time and build language into the contracts with those suppliers to enable such changes. More often than not, the supplier will be focused on the deal at hand rather than on an unlikely future change, so many suppliers will allow you to incorporate flexible language without any change in their pricing. Negotiating contracts in this fashion requires clever people on your side and patience. If you simply accept the supplier's form contract, you might close the deal faster, but it could also cost you dearly in the future.

## Content Flow

Content supplied to you by third parties is particularly problematic. The DMCA and related legislation stand by the principle that ISPs are responsible for ISP-supplied content. As long as you are in control of this content, most of these laws disregard whether you happened to get this content from someone else first. The only exception that I am aware of involves the Communications Decency Act (CDA), which includes a provision that says that ISPs are not considered publishers for the purpose of defamation and liable law. Using this provision, AOL was able to avoid liability for a defamation allegedly caused by an article supplied to it under contract because AOL did not itself write the article; it only published it.

You need to make sure that your content providers accept all of the liability for any damage caused by their content and your resulting use, storage, copying, distribution, public performance, and so forth, of that content. Accordingly, you need to make sure that they will indemnify you, and possibly defend you if desired, in the event that you get sued by anyone else because of that content. There is an important distinction between having a supplier agree to accept liability for something and having that supplier indemnify you. Do not be satisfied with language that says the supplier is liable for content it provides. The issue of liability for content heavily implicates your relationship with other ISPs with whom you may peer and with your customers, so let's move on to those subjects.

## Peering Contracts between ISPs

The Internet consists of a collection of networks, and these networks need to interconnect in some fashion for the Internet to work. If an ISP attempted to operate in isolation, the clients of that ISP's network would not be able to reach people on any other networks. Because no ISP can claim ubiquitous access, every ISP must rely on every other ISP to offer truly comprehensive connectivity. ISPs typically connect their networks through exchanges where a large number of ISPs locate equipment and interexchange traffic with one another.

A network access point (NAP) is a type of public exchange that was introduced in 1995. A number of different types of ISPs locate equipment at an NAP and publicly connect with other ISPs. Local ISPs typically do not use NAPs unless they are purchasing transit services from another ISP. Local ISPs typically connect their small local networks to a regional ISP that covers a broader geographic area. The regional ISPs then use the NAP to arrange to exchange traffic between their networks for free. An exchange of traffic in this fashion is referred to as a *peering* arrangement. A *peering contract* is therefore an agreement between two ISPs to share traffic between their networks. Regional ISPs also connect to national ISPs at an NAP and purchase transit services from the larger ISPs. There are many other ways in which ISPs can exchange traffic than those discussed here. Geoff Huston's *ISP Survival Guide* is a great reference for learning more about this subject.

Each ISP can have different criteria for establishing a contractual arrangement to exchange traffic with other ISPs, either publicly or privately. A private exchange may in some cases be preferable to a public exchange and vice versa. Either private exchanges are purchased (which is called a *transit service*) or they result from a direct peering arrangement. The capacity of the NAPs is such that any ISP connected to a number of different NAPs can be relatively certain that any customer's traffic will get to any other customer on the Internet. The larger an ISP gets, however, and the greater its bandwidth requirements, the more likely it becomes that the ISP will seek private peering arrangements with other large ISPs. Because the larger ISP already has access to the smaller ISP's customers through other connections, the desire of the smaller ISP for a direct peering relationship causes some tension. The larger ISP gets little value from establishing a private peering relationship with the smaller ISP. Therefore, the larger ISP will often attempt to sell transit services to the smaller ISP instead. If you have the opportunity to enter into a private peering relationship, some suggestions appear in the next section.

## Direct Peering Requirements

A private or direct peering relationship between ISPs must be an equitable and cost-effective alternative to a public exchange for it to make sense for both parties. Although there is no typical list of requirements for the establishment of a direct peering connection in the United States, an example list is as follows:

- Direct peering connections are at DS-3 (45 Mbps) speeds or higher.

- A minimum number of two direct peering connections must be established on a bilateral basis. In general, these connections will be established in pairs, with one party paying for one of the circuit connections and the other party paying for the other circuit connection.

- The direct peering connections are generally geographically dispersed. For example, if there are only two direct connections, one would be on the East Coast and one would be on the West Coast. If there were four direct connections, one would be on the East Coast, one on the West Coast, one in the Midwest, and one in the South.

- Once direct peering connections are established, the parties expect to terminate the peering exchanges with one another at public exchanges, if applicable. The parties are generally not required to interconnect at public exchanges, but doing so can enhance the exchange of traffic with other peers at the public exchanges.

- Peering and transit (customer) relationships between two networks are mutually exclusive. This means that a peering relationship cannot be used to bypass a transit relationship.

Before one ISP will consider peering with another ISP, the first ISP usually establishes a set of infrastructure requirements that the second ISP must meet to qualify for a direct peering relationship. As noted earlier, this prevents the first ISP from entering into a nonbeneficial relationship. With respect to national ISPs, a typical set of infrastructure requirements includes the following:

- Operate a nationally deployed (i.e., across the eastern, midwestern, and western sections of the United States) Internet backbone in the United States operating on dedicated circuits of at least DS-3 (45 Mbps) speed. Each backbone hub must be connected to at least two other backbone hubs.
- Operate a fully staffed, 24-hour-a-day, 7-day-a-week network operations center (NOC).
- Agree to establish trouble ticket and escalation procedures as needed.

When two ISPs interconnect, they trade routing entries: lists of client routes, internal ISP routes, upstream routes, and peer routes. Establishing new routing entries within an ISP's network enables that ISP to appropriately exchange traffic with another ISP. Direct peering contracts therefore typically include provisions establishing the routing entry requirements for the two ISPs, such as the following:

- Carry full routing at edge routers using Border Gateway Protocol, Version 4 (BGP-4) or higher, and aggregated routes.
- Register routes with the Internet Routing Registry (IRR).
- Register the ISP's routing policy with the IRR.
- Filter routes at the network edge, that is, listen only to the routes that a customer has preregistered.
- Provide consistent routing announcement (i.e., the same set of routes announced with the same *autonomous system* path at all peering locations).
- Do not establish a route of last resort (i.e., a default route) directed at the other ISP. A *route of last resort* is defined as a route that covers all possible destinations. Instead, the ISPs will fully exchange explicit routes comprising public Internet service destinations of entities to which either ISP is contractually obligated to handle traffic. An *explicit route* is defined as a route that covers only a strict, limited subset of all possible destinations.
- Announce to the other ISP only one's customer routes, not routes from other peers.
- The other ISP must not receive route announcements of the direct peer network via another provider. This will reduce the number of duplicate routes and reduce continued loading on the public exchange points.

The parties usually try to establish a minimum traffic requirement between the direct peers. Establishing a peering connection with another party, especially at a public exchange, costs money because the connection requires equipment and circuits dedicated to that connection. If insufficient levels of traffic flow through that connection, the costs associated with the connection do not justify such expenses. A typical set of minimum traffic requirements includes the following:

- 20 Mbps per pair of direct DS-3 peering connections, with each individual DS-3 connection carrying a minimum of 5 Mbps. These traffic volumes are typically measured in either direction (whichever is higher) and are weekly aggregated averages. Additional pairs of direct peering DS-3 connections require additional traffic, that is, 20 Mbps. Whether the minimum traffic criterion is met is typically based on traffic exchanged with the prospective direct peer at the public exchange points or through other reasonable means.

- A traffic imbalance must not be disproportionately skewed. An imbalance of traffic (in versus out) at a ratio of up to 1.8:1 in either direction is typically considered to be acceptable. The imbalance of traffic is to be measured in weekly aggregates over all the points where the parties exchange traffic.

Given the large number of requirements for establishing a direct peering relationship, the contracts are usually terminable if it turns out that either peer can no longer meet any of the initial criteria.

# Direct Peering Contractual Terms

Once an ISP qualifies to peer with another ISP, they will establish a contract governing the other terms of the relationship. For the most part, such contracts are like any other type of contract that an ISP might enter with a supplier, vendor, or customer (depending on the circumstances), but such contracts can also include some provisions that are unique to ISPs and the subject of this book.

## Exchange of Traffic

ISPs typically agree to exchange traffic over their respective Internet networks at one or more interconnection points, subject to the terms and conditions of the direct peering requirements previously discussed. When interconnected, the parties will agree not to restrict traffic flowing through the interconnection point(s) to and from the other ISP, based on the content or activities associated with that traffic, unless required to do so by court order or applicable law. This means that you cannot count on a peer to monitor or police traffic flowing to or from its network, and you cannot discount the possibility that your connection might be impacted by its interpretation of the law at any given time. In particular, most ISPs reserve the right to interpret solely for themselves when they are free to restrict traffic. Some ISPs publish the acceptable terms of usage of their networks on their web sites, so you can look there for some advance warning. Acceptable Use Policies (AUPs) will be discussed in greater detail in Chapter 7. The ISPs also typically reserve the right to impose different usage restrictions on their own customers and/or to assist their customers in imposing customer-requested usage restrictions on traffic flowing from the requesting customer.

With respect to monitoring, there is typically no restriction on the ability of either party to monitor or capture data and create statistics associated with data moving through its own network and traffic moving through the interconnection point(s). The ability to monitor in this regard is essential to properly maintaining the connection and the ISP's network operations. There is a significant difference between this type of monitoring, however, and packet payload monitoring, which is not done. Accordingly, the contract will always require the ISP to keep in confidence any data it does monitor or capture and use that information for the sole purpose of operating and managing its Internet network. Since even statistical information about traffic flows through a connection can reveal confidential information about an ISP network, these contracts typically prevent either party from providing any derived statistical data to third parties, although customers can generally be provided with their own statistical data.

### Payments

As noted earlier, there can be a fine balance between direct peering arrangements and transit customers. Direct peering contracts therefore typically include a provision that allows the parties to define the point in time when it no longer makes sense to peer for free. At such time, the peering arrangement will either terminate or be replaced with a transit agreement, which is just another form of customer contract.

## Contracts with Customers

Many of the concepts discussed under *Contracts with Vendors and Suppliers* naturally apply to contracts with your customers—only in the reverse. There are some unique considerations to address as well, and there is an important distinction to be made between contracts with consumers and contracts with businesses. Most businesses are presumed to be sophisticated in the ways of the law and more than capable of protecting themselves when contracting with another party, even if the other party is much larger. Hence, all of the comments regarding contracts between you and suppliers are equally applicable to contracts between you and your business customers. Rather than repeat myself, just keep in mind that you are the supplier now, not the consumer, so switch roles accordingly.

Consumers, on the other hand, are presumed to be incapable of entering a contract without some form of government protection. Given the large number of consumers who end up being the victims of get-rich-quick schemes and many other ploys, this is a prudent presumption. There is also another significant distinction between consumers and businesses: the signed contract. Most companies that deal with consumers do not want to have to get a customer's signature on a contract and try to keep a record of such documents. They also do not want consumers attempting to negotiate the terms because it would significantly increase the cost of sales and would inevitably result in some really bad contracts being signed by overly anxious salespeople. Car contracts are bad enough, but imagine negotiating a contract for the purchase of a new television. For these reasons, consumer businesses rely on form contracts that can be agreed to through various means of acquiescence.

In the Internet realm, the most popular types of consumer contracts involve *shrink-wrap licenses* for physically packaged goods, such as software on disk, and *click-wrap licenses* for intangible goods, such as downloaded software. The very finely printed contract slipped inside the jewel case of a CD, which can be read only once the shrink-wrap on the jewel case has been broken, is a typical example of a shrink-wrap license. The long contract displayed within a scrollable dialog box with accompanying radio buttons that say "I agree" and "I do not accept," which appear when you try to install a copy of a Microsoft program, is a typical example of a click-wrap license. At least in the United States, there is little question that shrink-wrap and click-wrap licenses are legally enforceable under most circumstances, even if the purchaser did not have an opportunity to review the terms and conditions of the contract prior to the purchase. In general, such contracts are enforceable as long as:

- The purchaser has notice that there are additional terms that govern a purchase.
- Those additional terms are presented to the purchaser at a later time.
- The purchaser has an opportunity to assent to or rescind the transaction if the additional terms are not acceptable.

In this context, notice of the terms and the method of assent become pretty important. Most software packages, electronic commerce sites, and other such products and services will include some warning or notice to alert potential consumers of the existence of additional terms and conditions, other than the requirement to pay a certain amount of money for the product or service. The methods used for indicating assent are much less uniform. The most common method is to state that use of the product or service constitutes assent to the terms, but this may not always work, especially where the customer starts using the product before doing anything else, as is the case with many different Internet services. While not very scientific, or legal for that matter, I tend to believe that the more hoops you make people jump through before they can start using the product or service, the better protected you are, from an enforceability perspective. Unfortunately, such practices tend to severely dissuade consumers from wanting to use your product or service, so you have to settle somewhere between adequate protection and undue annoyance.

As for the actual terms of a consumer contract, the end user is again highly determinative of the content. Nevertheless, there are some common terms, in addition to those discussed under *Contracts with Vendors and Suppliers,* that you should consider.

## Disavowing Control of the Internet

It has become fairly standard practice to include language in Internet-related contracts that clarifies that the subject provider does not control the Internet in any way. Although this seems pretty obvious to those of us in the industry, many people still believe the Internet to be controlled largely by whoever provides them with access services. This language is usually integrated into the highlighted warranty disclaimer provisions. Typical language reads to the effect that "neither company M nor any of its affiliates controls any information, products, or services on the Internet in any way, and therefore accepts no responsibility for the content of the information passing through company M's host computers, network hubs, and points of presence."

### Consumer Information

It is probably a good idea, given recent developments in consumer protection laws, to clearly indicate the type of consumer information and data you will collect during the provision of a service or operation of a product, and what you will do with that information. You may also have to provide the consumer with the ability to preview that information and cause you to make changes.

### Parental Control Protections

It is also a very good idea to provide information in your contract regarding parental control protection products, such as screening software, or services, such as filtering services. You should tell consumers where they can find such products or services online or where they can get more information. You may even want to offer those products yourself and reference the appropriate URL in your contract. Be careful about listing URLs in contracts, however, because if that URL changes in any way, the information may no longer be accurate and you may forget to update it. If you do provide such products, especially if you provide them for free, include appropriate language to protect you in the event that they do not work.

### Age

In the same way that beepers and cellular phones have become ubiquitous, no respectable young person can now be found without his or her own web site. Just because some contracts entered over the Internet can be enforced doesn't mean they all can, and a contract entered with minors is one major exception. Generally, if you entered a contract with a minor and didn't take adequate precautions to prevent that minor from entering the contract, then the contract cannot be enforced against the minor, should the minor breach. This is why 16-year-olds cannot buy cars without the cosignature of a parent or guardian. The rules apply to the Internet, so you might want to include language requiring your customer to represent and warrant that he or she is 18 years of age or older. Since it would be impossible (i.e., you wouldn't know the age of the person using the mouse) to get a parent or guardian to consent to a click-wrap agreement, I would consider just abandoning the preadult access market. While you can always cut off their service if they default, you may not have an easy time enforcing liability limitation provisions if they use your services to do something really dangerous.

### Billing Practices

In addition to maintaining the right to pass on government fees and takes, you should make sure you describe how you charge and bill for your products and services, especially if you do so on a monthly basis.

### Limiting Liability

This subject is also quite relevant to the supplier contracts previously discussed, but I deliberately left it out of that discussion. When you are the contractee (on the receiving end), you do not want the supplier's liability limited at all, if you can arrange that. On the other hand, when you are the contractor (on the paying end), you want to make sure you stay profitable in the unlikely event that all hell breaks loose. In addition to the defense, indemnity clauses, warranty disclaimers, and other language you can think to stick in the contract, make sure also to include a limitation on your total liability under all possible circumstances. This way, even if the other provisions are thrown out as unenforceable, you may still be able to keep your damages from getting out of hand. The typical limit is some multiple of the amounts previously paid by the customer, usually over the course of six months to one year. You should also exclude liability for any special, incidental, indirect, punitive, or consequential damages, which include such things as loss of business profits, business interruptions, loss of business information, and loss of conjugal relationships. In the event that Susie's Hog Farm loses access services for a day and doesn't get any new motorcycle orders over its web site, you aren't liable for its lost business.

### Prohibited Conduct, Acceptable Use Policies, and Notice and Take Down

You should tell customers that they are not allowed to do certain things and what you will do to them if they do. There are two ways you can do this: You can include the specific language in your contract or include the language in an Acceptable Use Policy (AUP) or similar document. AUPs are usually referenced in the contract and on web sites, but are separate from the contract so they can be changed from time to time. For example, some ISPs use AUPs and other referenced documents to add terms and conditions so their contracts can be kept to one page, under the theory that most customers will sign short contracts, regardless of what they say. When it comes time to enforce such a contract, this type of reasoning may be difficult to defend. Imagine explaining why you stuck all of the really egregious terms in the referenced documents, rather than where the customer would first look—because you hoped to fool the customer?

I will talk about AUPs in greater detail in Chapter 7, but if you use one, here is what I recommend: State that a customer cannot do anything that would violate the AUP, where the AUP can be located, that you reserve the right to change the AUP from time to time without prior notice, and that you will post notices of such changes when they do occur in a particular location. Then do what you stated. I also recommend making sure that customers receive a copy of the AUP when they first sign their contract or otherwise assent to your terms of service. This way, at least, you stand a pretty good chance of enforcing the terms in the AUP, should the need arise. I think it is the height of irresponsibility to simply reference an AUP, state that customers are obligated to abide by it, and then make it almost impossible for them to find it, even if they try to do so.

If you couldn't already tell, I feel pretty strongly about being up front with people and including terms and conditions in contracts, even if that makes the contract longer. Even as an attorney, I don't usually pay any more attention to a short consumer contract than I do a long one; I often don't read them either, so I don't think the length makes much difference. Since the enforceability of AUPs that are referenced only in your contract or off your web site is still an unsettled area of the law, I would put at least the most important language in your contract.

Examples of prohibited conduct concepts you should consider incorporating into your contract include:

- Any activity that will restrict or inhibit any other user from using and enjoying your service, your network, and/or the Internet. You may wish to indicate that this includes spam, spoofing, mail bombing, address trolling, activities that over-tax your servers or network, self-executing programs that tie up system resources, and many other sundry acts of disruption.

- The transmission of any unlawful, threatening, abusive, libelous, defamatory, racially hateful, obscene, pornographic, profane, or otherwise objectionable information of any kind, including without limitation any transmissions constituting or encouraging conduct that would constitute a criminal offense, give rise to civil liability, or otherwise violate any local, state, national, or international law, including import and export control laws.

- The transmission of any information or software that contains a virus or other similarly harmful component.

- The transmission, distribution, or performance of information, software, or other content that is protected by copyright, or other proprietary right, or derivative works thereof, without first obtaining the permission of the copyright owner or right holder.

Once you have successfully indicated what you will not allow, you need to indicate what you will do if a term or condition is violated. In addition to reserving the right to suspend or terminate a customer's account for any such violation, you will probably want to make sure the customer agrees to indemnify you for any loss or damage you incur as a result of the customer's actions. You may also want to charge the customer something to clean up the mess.

You should at least specify how you intend to respond and the process you will follow in the event that you receive a legal notice as a result of the customer's content or activities. For example, when providing web site hosting services, you may wish to include language that explains what you will do if you receive a notice under the DMCA or from law enforcement, or under some other appropriate circumstance. You should indicate that you may be obligated to block and/or remove the material from the site, which may include suspending the customer's access for some other drastic action. If the customer has a right to file a counternotice, as under the DMCA, you may wish to state that fact, but you are not obligated to do so and may wish to keep the customer in the dark in that regard. Yahoo! apparently receives thousands of notices every month, but very few counternotices. You should make it clear that outside of responding to notices and appropriate responses, you will not otherwise get involved in disputes between customers and third parties. Finally, you should let customers know that under certain circumstances—that is, subject to a subpoena—you may be obligated under the law to disclose their names to another party.

Although I have discussed several different concepts, there is still much to be said about many related topics, such as how to define spam or what to include in an AUP. The definition of these terms is a matter of policy for each ISP, so I have deferred further discussion on those topics to Chapter 7.

# CHAPTER 7

# Policies and Procedures:
# What to Ask/Tell Your Lawyer

N
o matter how well you understand the laws and associated regulations, you will make mistakes implementing these laws and regulations within your company if you do not develop effective procedures for employees to follow. Once you have established such procedures, assuming you do not want to disclose them, you may find it necessary to develop external policies based on these procedures and communicate these policies to the outside world. At least this is how it should work, but most companies do it the other way around; that is, they establish external policies first and develop procedures later. Just to be consistent, I will discuss policies first and procedures second. Since I assume a lawyer will probably be tasked with writing most of these policies and procedures, I will also throw in some advice about how to select and/or communicate with an attorney for such purposes.

## Policies

As with Internet-related contracts, the appropriate policies to adopt on any subject vary with the different types of ISP businesses and the different characteristics of each ISP. Everyone's business is different. A policy or procedure that works for one business may not work for another. Rather than provide you with a one-size-fits-all policy or procedure related to each subject, I will suggest certain policies you should consider adopting and what elements you should consider including in the policy, discuss how different companies adopt different policies to suit their purposes, and delve into the concepts and principles that need to be incorporated into any policy that is adopted.

To start with, there are three different types of policies:

1. *Policies you are required to adopt.* Throughout this book, I have discussed the eligibility requirements of a number of existing laws, such as the Digital Millennium Copyright Act (DMCA), or laws that are likely to be enacted, such as the Internet Gambling Prohibition Act of 1999 (IGPA). You are not technically required to adopt policies in accordance with these laws, but you lose whatever protection they provide you if you do not.

2. *Policies you want to adopt.* You may decide to adopt a policy or two for the purpose of attracting business or to influence another company's own policies. A number of ISPs have recently adopted filtering policies and practices to attract customers who want highly restricted information, such as deeply religious customers. Other ISPs, such as MCI WorldCom, have adopted policies in the past in an attempt to influence the adoption of similar policies by other ISPs, such as spam policies.

3. *Policies that you do not want to adopt and are not required to adopt but that you feel compelled to adopt anyway.* In the United States, at least for now, you are not required to adopt a privacy policy. Unlike policies you are required to adopt, you get no greater protection if you adopt a privacy policy. In fact, you may not want to adopt a privacy policy because you will be obligated to live by whatever policy you do adopt. Nevertheless, if you do not adopt a privacy policy, you may be subject to extreme criticism and could possibly lose business, so you may feel compelled to adopt a privacy policy anyway.

The mere adoption of a policy is not enough; you have to make that policy available to the public and you must implement it. I will discuss implementation within the context of procedures, but basically you can adopt the greatest policies ever known and they will do you no good if they are not implemented properly. What exactly constitutes "available to the public" is a matter of conjecture. What you think is readily available, however, may not be viewed that way by other people, especially if they have to weave their way through a series of web pages to eventually find your policy page or pages. You may not want to use screen space for this, but the best place for a link to your policies is on your home page or index page.

Policies that are required by law must be in writing. It doesn't do much good to adopt a policy and not tell anyone about it or only tell them over the phone. Required policies should also be reasonably visible and accessible to the public, not just to customers. This means that your policies should be at a publicly accessible online location so people can access these policies without first having to provide you with any information or money, as would a customer or a subscriber. Although some ISPs try to be cute by labeling their policies and legal notices as "Legal Junk," "Many Words from Our Attorney," and "The Shark Tank," I recommend the extremely boring "Legal Policies and Notices" label. Cute doesn't go very far in court and that will be the only place your policies will matter. If you feel compelled to do something clever once people get to the policy page, you can decorate, animate, or otherwise spruce up the page(s) in a variety of interesting ways. One ISP played the theme from *Jaws*—I will just assume it had a copyright license to do so—when someone accessed the legal policy section. Aside from the legally required policies, the manner in which you inform the public of your other policies is unregulated at this time.

# Adoption of Policies Required by Law

A number of existing laws—and undoubtedly many more in the future—are going to require ISPs to adopt and implement any of a number of different policies for the ISPs to be eligible for liability protection.

## The DMCA—Again!

As noted in Chapter 3, *A Special Law for ISPs: The DMCA,* the limitations on liability established by the DMCA apply only if you:

- Adopt and reasonably implement, and inform customers of, a policy that provides for the termination of customers who are repeat infringers.
- Accommodate and do not interfere with standard technical measures.

As far as the policy requirement is concerned, this means you must adopt a policy that states you will terminate repeat infringers of copyrights. As discussed in Chapter 3, you are not required to define *repeat infringer* and no specific definition is provided in the law. If ambiguity is your friend, then I recommend you leave the term undefined because it gives you the ability to terminate certain types of customers with great flexibility and complete immunity. If you insist on defining a repeat infringer, I would limit the definition so that it includes only identical entities that were previously the subject of two or more effective DMCA notices to you. I suggest this because you do not want to adopt a publicly stated policy that you cannot consistently enforce. For example, if you state that anyone accused of infringing a copyright multiple times is a repeat infringer, you will be required to terminate any customer meeting that definition, no matter what the circumstances. If you do not state such and you attempt to enforce the policy against a legitimate repeat infringer, you will find yourself subject to a discrimination lawsuit filed by the repeat infringer.

Keep in mind that similar laws have been or are likely to be adopted in other countries and regions, such as Australia and the European Union (EU). If you are operating in different countries, you want to make sure that your policies on different online locations are consistent, that the policies are presented in the official languages of the respective countries (not just English everywhere), and that your translations are correct. If you have ever read funny translations on a Chinese menu, you should have some idea of what can happen to your policies once they are translated to other languages. Although it costs more, I always recommend having them translated to one language, and then having them translated back by a different translator. The secondary translation will never match the original exactly, but it should be close.

## Internet Gambling Prohibition Act of 1999 (IGPA)

As noted in Chapter 4, *Other Internet-Specific Laws,* it is highly likely that anti–Internet gambling legislation will be passed by Congress and signed by the president. Any such laws will be substantially similar to the IGPA, so I would start following this law now rather than later—just to get used to it. As with the DMCA, to be eligible under immunity provisions of the IGPA, an ISP must maintain and implement a written policy that requires the ISP to terminate the account of a subscriber after receipt of an appropriate notice. Unlike the DMCA, the IGPA is concerned with singular alleged violations, not repeat infringers. I would not attempt to delineate the requirements of the IGPA or any other law for that matter. You do not want to get into a debate with anyone about the requirements of the law, which is what will happen if you attempt to describe those requirements in your policy. On the Internet, there are always people who will debate any subject, whether they know anything about that subject or not. I would simply adopt a policy that states:

> We have the right to and may terminate any account of a subscriber as may be required by law, subject to our sole interpretation and discretion.

## Registration of Domain Names

With the adoption of the Anticybersquatting Consumer Protection Act (ACPA), any ISP involved in the registration of domain names will want to adopt a reasonable policy prohibiting the registration of a domain name that is identical to, confusingly similar to, or dilutive of another's mark. As with the other two laws discussed here, the ACPA does not require you to adopt such a policy. Still, you are only immune from liability for refusing to register, removing from registration, transferring, temporarily disabling, or permanently canceling a domain name if you have adopted and implemented such a policy.

## Children's Privacy

The Child Online Privacy Protection Act (COPPA) provides that web sites cannot collect personal information from children under the age of 13 without parental consent. The COPPA's effective date was April 21, 2000. If you collect information from anyone, you need to make sure your web site complies with the FTC Guidelines regarding the COPPA. If you don't collect information from anyone, then you don't need to comply, but I would make sure you collect no information whatsoever before you decide to take that route.

You can access the FTC Guidelines at www.ftc.gov/bcp/menu-children.htm under the heading How to Comply with the Children's Online Privacy Protection Rule. I would check this link or any subsequent link from time to time just to make sure the rules do not change over time. With respect to privacy notice requirements, the FTC Guideline presently provides as follows.

### Placement

> An operator must post a link to a notice of its information practices on the home page of its web site or online service and at each area where it collects personal information from children. An operator of a general audience site with a separate children's area must post a link to its notice on the home page of the children's area.
>
> The link to the privacy notice must be clear and prominent. Operators may want to use a larger font size or a different color type on a contrasting back-

ground to make it so. A link in small print at the bottom of the page—or a link that is indistinguishable from other links on your site—is not considered clear and prominent.

## Content

The notice must be clearly written and understandable; it should not include any unrelated or confusing materials. It must state the following information:

- The name and contact information (address, telephone number and email address) of all operators collecting or maintaining children's personal information through the web site or online service. If more than one operator is collecting information at the site, the site may select and provide contact information for only one operator who will respond to all inquiries from parents about the site's privacy policies. Still, the names of all the operators must be listed in the notice.

- The kinds of personal information collected from children (for example, name, address, email address, hobbies, etc.) and how the information is collected—directly from the child or passively, say, through cookies.

- How the operator uses the personal information. For example, is it for marketing back to the child? Notifying contest winners? Allowing the child to make the information publicly available through a chat room?

- Whether the operator discloses information collected from children to third parties. If so, the operator also must disclose the kinds of businesses in which the third parties are engaged; the general purposes for which the information is used; whether the third parties have agreed to maintain the confidentiality and security of the information; and that the parent has the option to agree to the collection and use of the child's information without consenting to the disclosure of the information to third parties.

- That the operator may not require a child to disclose more information than is reasonably necessary to participate in an activity as a condition of participation.

- That the parent can review the child's personal information, ask to have it deleted, and refuse to allow any further collection or use of the child's information. The notice also must state the procedures for the parent to follow.

In addition to posting the notice on its web site, any ISP is also required to provide a direct notice to parents when seeking their consent. The FTC Guidelines specify the content of such direct notice as follows:

The notice to parents must contain the same information included on the notice on the web site. In addition, an operator must notify a parent that it wishes to collect personal information from the child; that the parent's consent is required for the collection, use, and disclosure of the information; and how the parent can provide consent. The notice to parents must be written clearly and understandably, and must not contain any unrelated or confusing information. An operator may use any one of a number of methods to notify a parent, including sending an email message to the parent or a notice by postal mail.

Many of the guidelines set forth by the FTC, such as the clear and prominent nature of the notice, should be adopted with respect to almost any other policy, whether required or not. The simple, straightforward approach used in the FTC Guidelines is also an excellent example of how to write something for the general public's consumption. Remember, we are not dealing with clever people all of the time.

# Adoption of Policies You Want to Adopt

There probably isn't much of a distinction between policies you want to adopt and those you feel compelled to adopt, but I will attempt to distinguish them anyway. Although you may want to do something once you feel so compelled, that doesn't mean you originally wanted to do that something. This was sort of the case with spam during the earlier days of the commercial Internet. Spam had become an irritant and a number of ISPs were concerned about it, but no ISP had attempted to publicly define spam or state in a policy that they would prohibit it from their network. To help lead the way, MCI WorldCom developed a spam (actually antispam) policy and issued a press release telling the world about it. MCI WorldCom also posted that policy on all its web sites. Shortly thereafter, many other ISPs adopted similar policies. The spam policy was a policy that MCI WorldCom wanted to adopt. The similar policies adopted by other ISPs may have been policies that they wanted to adopt as well but had not gotten around to, or they may have felt compelled to adopt them because of MCI WorldCom. Who knows? Who cares, really? The point is that there can be a distinction between the motivations behind the policies rather than between the policies themselves.

Accordingly, I have included a few subjects in this section that are not presently the subject of many ISPs' policies, at least not those that I have seen. You may know differently. If you *want* to adopt policies in these areas, here are some things to consider.

## *Recognition of Electronic and/or Digital Signatures*

I refer to "electronic and/or digital signatures" in the heading because many people think an electronic signature and a digital signature are one and the same. They are not. In short, an electronic signature is any kind of marking indicating the source of an electronic message. An electronic signature may be your name at the end of an e-mail, or your e-mail address in the header of a message, or a pseudonym you adopted for making posts to message boards. Just because an electronic message includes an electronic signature of some type does not mean that the message was really from the person alleged to have signed the electronic message. It is extremely easy to forge and spoof electronic signatures on virtually any type of electronic message.

A digital signature, on the other hand, is an electronic signature that cannot be forged. Digital signatures are typically created using some form of public key/private key encryption, whereby an electronic signature is encrypted using the private key of the sender. This digital signature is then attached to an electronic document, which may or may not be encrypted as well. Any recipient of the document and digital signature can then use the sender's public key to verify that the electronic signature and/or associated document originated from the sender and was not altered since it was signed.

You may want to consider adopting a policy regarding how you will treat and recognize electronic and digital signatures. In this case, as opposed to the terms previously discussed in relation to the other policies, it may be beneficial to define the different types of signatures in your policy as simply as possible. You may choose to state that, due to the unreliability of electronic signatures, your company will not recognize any form of electronic signature that is not a digital signature and will not acknowledge the content of any electronic document that has not been encrypted and digitally signed. This might include legal notices, such as in accordance with the DMCA, contractual commitments, or any other type of communication. This may sound a bit extreme, but I know of a number of companies that have mistakenly acted upon the content of unencrypted and digitally unsigned electronic documents to their extreme detriment. If you are not going to trust the content of any such documents, you need to let people know that in advance; otherwise, they will expect you to do so.

## Import and Export

Although you are required to comply with the import and export laws of your country and any other country in which you operate (or send employees to), there are no requirements to identify your compliance policies to the public. Nevertheless, it may be a good idea to specify what you will and will not do because of any such import or export laws. For example, the United States has certain export license requirements to export certain types of information and technology. There are occasional debates, to put it mildly, regarding the interpretation of these requirements, such that some customers may assume you will do things differently than you do. In such cases, it may be much simpler to define in advance how you intend to comply with such requirements, thereby eliminating any doubt or at least giving you something to point to when there is a dispute. Once you put it in writing, however, you better make sure you live by it.

Keep in mind that every country has different import and export regulations. What may be okay in one country to import without restriction may be highly regulated in the next. Nazi propaganda is one of the best examples of this when it comes to the Internet. Germany's constitution specifically bars the distribution of Nazi propaganda in Germany, and for good reason. Neighboring countries do not. Since German consumers can access web sites in the United States just as easily as they can those in Germany, the Internet unfortunately makes it much easier for Germans who want access to such material to get it. The German government is not messing around, however, and is actively pursuing legal action against any company they can get their hooks into that is allowing such propaganda to be distributed in Germany. With this type of activity in mind, it may be a good idea to adopt a policy that enables you to take whatever appropriate action you need to take in the event a government decides to attempt to enforce its import or export laws against you.

# Adoption of Policies You Feel Compelled to Adopt

The vast majority of policies fall into this last category. As I have stated numerous times, you do not have to adopt a privacy policy, for example, but you *should*—and your failure to do so may work to your competitive disadvantage. The other policies that I discuss under this heading are similarly situated, especially the Acceptable Use Policy, which I will save for last.

## *Privacy*

In addition to the children's privacy notice previously set forth, you may want to consider adopting other privacy policies as well. There is an extensive discussion of the different privacy principles in Chapter 5, *What Is an ISP to Do (or Not)? Content and Activity Regulations to Live By*, under the heading *Privacy, Defamation, and Related Concerns*, so there isn't much point in repeating all of that information here. Suffice it to say that the FTC wants to make sure that ISPs tell customers when they are collecting personal information, what they will or will not do with it, how customers can access the information that has been collected, and how that information is being protected. The FTC does not want to require ISPs to comply with these principles, so the FTC is only enforcing violations of policies that have been adopted. Since competition requires that you adopt a privacy policy and the FTC enforces the policy against you if you do not do it right, the U.S. program should be fairly effective. The European Union has expressed similar concerns, but so far, the EU has taken a much more aggressive regulatory approach than the FTC and has been trying to force the United States to follow its lead.

As these two bureaucracies iron out the differences between their approaches, it is highly likely that ISPs will be left with a couple of choices. To the extent an ISP is operating in the EU, it will have to adopt the policies required there. The guidelines established by the EU are set forth in Chapter 5, as already noted. Since the United States is likely to succeed in getting the EU to back off its reciprocity requirement, the policies adopted in the EU will not be strictly applicable to the ISP's operations in the United States, or necessarily in other countries. In the United States, the ISP will probably be required to comply with certain safe harbor provisions. It is expected that most ISPs will be considered to have complied with any such provisions if they have been certified to be in compliance with self-regulatory programs, such as the Better Business Bureau's BBB On-line program. It may be very difficult to adopt different policies that are applicable under different circumstances in different countries, so it may make sense to shoot for the least common denominator, which will probably be that of the European Union. No matter what you do, be prepared to do it right.

If you need some help figuring out how to word such a policy, a lawyer can and should help you. You can also access the Personal Privacy Policy issued for the FTC web site at www.ftc.gov/ftc/privacy1.htm. Presumably, if you follow their example, it will be hard for them to complain, unless you don't implement it.

### Personal Information Privacy versus Communication Privacy

In case you haven't figured it out by now, there is a significant difference between personal information privacy and communication privacy. The EU unfortunately blurs the difference between these two forms of privacy in the guidelines discussed in Chapter 5 and in other communications and actions by the EU. Perhaps they don't really understand or care about the difference, but since the difference is important in the United States, I will expand upon it.

*Personal information privacy* relates to the personal information of a customer or user of an ISP's service, such as a person's name, physical or electronic address, spending habits, income level, racial or ethnic background, or shopping habits. *Communication privacy* relates to the privacy of a person's actual electronic communication. In the United States, at least, your personal information is protected only to the extent that you gave it to someone pursuant to an agreement that it would be so protected. If you give your name and address out without condition to anyone who asks, then you cannot reasonably expect that information to be protected anyway. Your private electronic communications are treated differently, especially when it comes to the government. The Electronic Communications Privacy Act (ECPA) protects Internet-based communications from being monitored and/or intercepted. The ECPA requires legal due process standards to be met before such communications can be handed over to law enforcement officials and prohibits individuals and ISPs from monitoring the content of communications over the Internet.

While the EU combines personal information privacy with communication privacy, the FTC does not. Presumably, the FTC does not need to do anything, either, because of the existence of the ECPA, but because the ECPA does not protect every form of electronic communication at all times, it is possible that the FTC will eventually assert similar authority in this area. In particular, the ECPA allows ISPs to intercept employees' e-mail under certain circumstances and to intercept a communication when they have previously received consent to do so from one of the parties to the communication. Federal courts have also determined that the ECPA interception protections do not apply to any information stored by an ISP. ISPs store many different forms of customer communications, such as unretrieved e-mail stored in mail servers. Accordingly, you may want to adopt a policy regarding how you intend to handle the privacy of a customer's private communications and, like everything else, make sure you follow it.

You may also want to adopt internal policies having to do with your treatment of internal employee communications and activities. In different states and countries, under different circumstances, employees and contractors have either some right to privacy or none at all when at work or using company-owned electronic communication equipment. To be safe, you should adopt a common internal policy that applies to all such communications, such as phone calls and e-mail, or to employee activities, such as web surfing.

Some companies are adopting liberal policies in this regard as a means of attracting and retaining employees. The extensive bandwidths available within company networks are typically far superior to what individuals can get at home, so some employees are extremely attracted to such benefits. Other companies strictly exclude any personal use for any reason. I think the latter policy isn't very smart and probably is ineffective anyway. Most employees of most companies use company communication resources for personal purposes at one time or another, whether to respond to an e-mail from a friend, to call home during the afternoon, to check a stock quote, or to just take a diversionary break. There is no question that some people abuse these resources, spending hours playing games, viewing pornography, or web surfing all day for no legitimate purpose. Unless you are prepared to enforce a strict policy against everyone who violates your policy, including the president and CEO, you may live to regret selectively enforcing it against other employees. This would be especially true if any of the employees disciplined for violation of the policy belonged to protected classes of individuals that do not include the nondisciplined employees.

## Acceptable Use Policies

An Acceptable Use Policy (AUP) establishes the terms and conditions under which a customer can access a network and restricts the nature of that customer's use of that network. For example, the original National Science Foundation Network (NSFnet) had an AUP that restricted NSFnet from being used for commercial purposes. Although e-mail existed in this environment, it was the implementation of commercial e-mail services over NSFnet, as proposed by Vint Cerf and originally implemented by MCI Communications Corporation, that changed the noncommercial character of the Internet forever.

ISPs appear to be increasingly relying upon AUPs to establish access and use conditions for their networks and to notify customers and users of the ISPs' public policies on a wide variety of subjects. ISPs have used AUPs to inform customers about the availability of screening software to help filter out material that offends them in some way. For example, rather than adopt specific policies concerning illegal activities relating to guns or illegal activities relating to drugs or obscenity, most ISPs simply dedicate a section of their AUP to the subject of illegal uses.

A typical provision might state that the network can be used for lawful purposes only and that any use or activity that violates any law or regulation anywhere is prohibited. Some AUPs will specifically prohibit any violation of copyright, trademark, trade secret, or other intellectual property laws, and prohibit any user material that is obscene, constitutes an illegal threat, is defamatory, or violates import or export control laws. Most ISPs also reference system and network security prohibitions, such as hacking attempts, denial-of-service attacks, and network or use interference. Almost all AUPs include some reference to spam and related behaviors. If the AUP does not include the entire spam policy, it will at least reference the policy and provide an additional reference for the location of such a policy. Given that spam policies are sometimes separate, I will address them as such.

## Spamming, Spoofing, and Other Irritating Behaviors

Everyone identifies spam differently. Some ISPs define spam as any unsolicited mail message and any excessive cross-posting or multiple posting within a newsgroup or

## Side Law: To Be or Not to Be an AUP

Most ISPs make some references to the terms and conditions for use of their network in their service contracts. These terms and conditions are frequently stated in something called an AUP. Contrary to the title, however, some ISPs throw in all sorts of additional terms that don't have anything to do with use of the service or network, such as warranty provisions and other terms that really belong in the contract. While this is a convenient way to squirrel away certain terms and conditions to which some customers might be inclined to object, it can also be a big problem if it turns out that the AUP is not considered to be enforceable because the customer never agreed to its terms.

What I am talking about is this: An ISP might specifically state in its service contract that access to and use of its network and services are subject to the terms and conditions of the AUP. The ISP then includes a copy of the AUP with the contract before the customer signs it. The ISP also includes language requiring customers to acknowledge that they have read the AUP, that they understand the AUP, that the terms of the AUP can be modified from time to time upon posting of a new AUP at a specific online location, and that they will be bound by the present or future terms of the AUP. Another ISP might include all of this language, but not provide the customer with a copy of the AUP at the time the contract is signed. Instead, the ISP simply references where the AUP can be found online. Contract laws in different states and countries may establish that AUPs that were not physically provided to customers are not effective. If you need to rely on the terms and conditions, warranty provisions, and any other language buried in an AUP, you are better off sticking it in front of the customer up front and dealing with any resulting complaints, rather than trying to hide it and losing your ability to enforce any part of it later.

message board. As with other policies I have discussed, all-or-nothing policies tend to have enforcement problems because they are not consistently enforced. I therefore recommend adopting a specific policy that targets the primary evildoers and that can actually be enforced when needed. An effective spam policy prohibits users from participating in any of the following activities through use of an ISP's service or network (where *you* refers to the ISP offering the service):

- Posting 10 or more messages similar in content to a newsgroup, forum, e-mail mailing list, or similar group or list.

- Posting to any newsgroup, forum, e-mail mailing list, or other similar group or listing articles that are off topic according to the charter or other owner-published FAQ or description of the group or list.

- Sending unsolicited e-mail to more than 25 e-mail users, if such unsolicited e-mail could reasonably be expected to provoke complaints.

- Falsifying user information provided to you or users of your service in connection with the use of one of your services.

- Engaging in any of the foregoing activities by using the service of another ISP; by channeling such activities through an account with you, through a remailer, or otherwise through your service; by using your service as a mail drop for response; or by otherwise using the services of another ISP for the purpose of facilitating the foregoing activities such that the use of the other ISP's service could reasonably be expected to adversely affect your service.

The latter two provisions have to do with spoofing and mail and news bombing, but are so related to spamming that they should be included in any spam policy. Your spam policy should also specifically provide you with the authority to terminate users for any violation of the policy, to use any technical measure to combat a prohibited activity, and to collect any information about the spammer and turn that information over to the legal authorities, without limiting your ability to deal with spam in any way. Finally, your policy should direct users to where they can report spam or network abuse and how they should go about doing so to enable you to act upon their report.

In the summer of 1999, the AUPs of 14 other ISPs were examined to see how they treated spam and mail/news bombing and how they presented their AUP to customers. The URLs for some of these AUPs give you some idea of how easy they were to find. Since this examination represented only a momentary point in time, there is no guarantee that any of the practices stated here were actually accurate at the time or are accurate now. I present the information only for the purpose of getting some idea of how other ISPs could theoretically have dealt with spam and other annoying behaviors in the past. Given the foregoing disclaimer, a synopsis of the various AUPs is as follows:

1. *AOL.* AOL integrated its AUP into its service agreement, which each user must accept when subscribing to the AOL service. The AUP referenced the unsolicited bulk e-mail policy, which stated that AOL did not authorize the use of its network to accept, transmit, or distribute unsolicited bulk e-mail sent from the Internet to AOL members. AOL prohibited the sending of e-mail through the AOL network in violation of its terms-of-service agreement. AOL did not otherwise define the terms *spam* or *unsolicited*. AOL also prohibited the collection or harvesting of personal information, including Internet addresses, of AOL's users, thereby proscribing any mass spamming or news bombing predicated upon such collection.

   www.aol.com/copyright.html

2. *AT&T.* The AUP defined *spamming* as the posting of a single message, or messages similar in content, to more than five online forums or newsgroups. The posting of more than one message to a newsgroup in violation of that newsgroup's or forum's rules was considered to be a violation of the AUP. Any unsolicited e-mail that could be expected to provoke complaints was prohibited as *spam,* as was any e-mail with a charity request, chain mail, or related items. AT&T reserved the right to determine, at its sole discretion, whether any use of the AT&T network was a violation of the AUP.

   www.ipservices.att.com/policy.html

3. *Bigfoot.* The AUP prohibited users from reselling or commercially exploiting the names, addresses, or other data obtained by use of the Bigfoot service. The AUP

proscribed the use of Bigfoot e-mail accounts as return addresses for commercial e-mail solicitations, advertising, offensive or illegal communications, or communications that harass, intimidate, or otherwise violate the rights of others. It did not specifically mention spam.

www.bigfoot.com/RUN?FN=legal_mail$locale=en&Cook=&SEQ=& . . . :4014& ver=3.0

4. *CompuServe.* CompuServe incorporated an AUP that addressed spamming through its member agreement, which was integrated into the CompuServe terms-of-use agreement. This was consistent with AOL's practice, and since they are commonly owned, this was hardly a surprise. Nevertheless, the CompuServe policy was not identical to AOL's policy. CompuServe proscribed the uploading, posting, or other publication of advertising, promotion, or solicitation of commercial goods or services. The member agreement prohibited spamming or any similar conduct but did not define *spamming*. Newsgroups and off-topic posting were not specifically addressed. An alternate AUP addressed newsgroups, chain letters, and excessive posts, although none of those terms were defined, either.

http://support.csi.com/cshelp%5Fdocs/sr052.htm

www.compuserve.com/gateway/terms.asp

http://support.csi.com/cshelp%5Fdocs/sr2007.htm

5. *Earthlink.* The AUP was quite detailed and was integrated into the member access agreement. It prohibited the use of personal e-mail accounts for high-volume or commercial mailing or receiving. *Mail bombing* (sending more than 10 similar mail messages to the same e-mail address) and *news bombing* (sending more than 10MB of data to a newsgroup) were prohibited, as was spamming. *Spamming* was defined as the transmission of the same or a substantially similar unsolicited message to 50 or more recipients or 15 or more newsgroups in a single day. The AUP stated that sending unsolicited e-mail where the recipient objected to the content or receipt of the message in general was prohibited. *Unsolicited* was defined as posted in violation of a Usenet or newsgroup charter or sent to a recipient who has not requested or invited the message. Cross-posting advertisements of 10 or more unrelated newsgroups was likewise proscribed. *Off-topic postings* to newsgroups were prohibited but undefined.

www.earthlink.com/about/policies/aupolicy.html

www.earthlink.com/about/policies/accessagrment.html

6. *Erols.* The AUP prohibited *spamming*, which was defined as posting or cross-posting, regardless of content, the same message to 20 or more newsgroups. Erols also proscribed the mailing of chain letters and *disruptive activities*, which were defined as activities that disrupted the normal flow of online dialogue, or otherwise acting in a manner that negatively affected other subscribers, users, individuals, or entities.

www.erols.com/erols/index/agreement.htm

7. *Excite.* Excite regulated the use of its mail, PAL, chat room, and bulletin board services at four different locations in the terms-of-service agreement. Basically, the terms proscribed the use of the Excite product for chain letters, junk mail,

spamming, solicitations (commercial or noncommercial), or distributing lists to any person who had not given specific permission to be included in such a process. Excite further prohibited the use of its service to advertise or offer to sell any goods or services, or to conduct or forward any surveys, contests, or chain letters. None of these terms were defined.

http://reg.excite.com/mps/terms

8. *GTE.* GTE employed the use of an Internet access agreement that proscribed the distribution of *junk mail*, which was broadly defined to include any unsolicited mail of a business or commercial nature. GTE prohibited an inappropriate or irrelevant posting (that includes some of my writings) to a newsgroup. GTE proscribed blanket postings to all or large numbers of newsgroups simultaneously with disregard to the newsgroup's subject. GTE prohibited *spamming,* which was defined as the transmission of unsolicited e-mail to multiple recipients. GTE's explicit and lengthy spamming policy was incorporated into the Internet access agreement. *Usenet spamming* was defined therein as the posting of a single message to 20 or more Usenet groups. *E-mail spamming* was also described as a violation of several portions of the Internet access agreement.

www.gte.net/hotlinks/policies/acceptable.html

www.gte.net/hotlinks/policies/spamming.html

9. *Hotmail.* Hotmail prohibited the use of its service for sending chain letters, junk mail, spam, or any duplicative or unsolicited messages (commercial or otherwise). Hotmail did not specifically define any of the terms. The terms of service also included a liquidated damages clause, whereby each user agreed to pay Hotmail at least $5 for each piece of spam or unsolicited bulk e-mail transmitted from or otherwise connected with the user's Hotmail account.

http://lwllg.hotmail.com/cgi-bin/dasp/tos.asp?_lang=

10. *Juno.* Juno employed a service agreement prohibiting the transmission of or receipt of responses to chain letters or pyramid schemes of any kind or the dissemination of any e-mail message in broad-based mailing. *Broad-based mailing* was defined as a single message sent through the service directly to more than 50 e-mail addresses simultaneously. Juno prohibited the mailing of offensive material of any kind, but did not define *offensive.* The AUP prohibited the use of the service for transmission of commercial solicitations or for the receipt of responses to commercial solicitations. Juno proscribed the sending of unsolicited advertisements for goods or services of any kind. Off-topic postings to any newsgroup were proscribed as was *newsgroup spamming,* which was defined as the posting of a single article or substantially similar article to more an 15 newsgroups. The Juno spam policy further indicated that Juno's software was designed to prevent spamming.

http://home.juno.com/Juno/Policies/home_policies_agreement.html

http://home.juno.com/Juno/Policies/home_policies_guidelines.html

http://home.juno.com/Juno/Policies/home_policies_spam.html

11. *Mindspring.* The AUP was fully incorporated into the terms-of-service agreement. The AUP prohibited sending unsolicited e-mail or collecting responses

from unsolicited commercial e-mail. The mailing of large volumes of unsolicited e-mail was proscribed. Mindspring defined *Usenet spam* as the posting of substantially similar articles individually to multiple newsgroups. The AUP considered multiple postings to 10 or more groups within a two-week sliding window excessive. Spam was not otherwise defined. The cross-posting of a single article to more than five for sale, test, job, or binary groups was forbidden.

www.mindspring.net/aboutms/policy.html

www.mindspring.net/prod-svc/users.html

12. *Prodigy.* Prodigy did not provide an AUP to nonusers on any accessible (nonproprietary) portion of its web site. The Prodigy terms-of-use agreement did not specifically address either spamming or off-topic posting. It is possible that Prodigy employs an AUP governing spamming and off-topic posting, but access to such information was evidently limited.

http://prodigy.com/pcom/company_information/copyright.html

13. *Raging Bull.* The company employed a terms-of-service agreement prohibiting users from advertising or selling products or services to others. No other user limits were imposed. Perhaps this helps to explain the name of the service.

www.ragingbull.com/member/termsofservice.html

14. *Yahoo!* The terms-of-service agreement for Yahoo! prohibited the use of the service for the transmission of junk mail, spam, chain letters, or unsolicited mass distribution of e-mail. The agreement prohibited the mailing of objectionable material of any kind. None of these terms were defined. Yahoo! employed similar language of proscription governing message boards. Users must agree not to post or transmit any unsolicited advertising, promotional materials, junk mail, spam, chain letters, pyramid schemes, or any other form of solicitation.

http://edit.yahoo.com/config/form?.form=agree&new=1&.accept=928961 . . . /
mail%3f.intl=lg=u

http://messages.yahoo.com/disclaimer.html

At least one conclusion that can be drawn from the preceding list is that there is certainly no single way to regulate spamming and other such acts.

### Obscene Communications Intended to Annoy

The last thing to consider adding to your spam policy is some reference to the obscene communication provision of the Communications Decency Act (CDA). The Supreme Court has upheld this provision, so it is okay to repress any obscene communication, such as an e-mail or bulletin board posting, that was made with the intent to annoy. How you go about figuring out the sender's intent is up to you.

# Procedures

Any time you adopt a policy of any type, you should have a corresponding procedure for implementing that policy within your company. You should also identify those laws that have some applicability to you and require you to take some action, such as the Digital Millennium Copyright Act and the Internet Gambling Prohibition Act of 1999. A good start is to go back and make sure you are following the steps that are set out in various places throughout this book. For example, the Protection of Children from Sexual Predators Act of 1998 (PCSPA) requires ISPs to report incidents of child pornography to the appropriate federal agency. You need to make sure you have a procedure in place for identifying when you need to make such a report, who should make it, what agency it should be made to, how it should be made (e-mail, phone call, letter, etc.), and what kind of records you keep once the report has been made. You don't want to have to go through the process of figuring out what to do each and every time you are required to make a report. You also need to consider the ramifications of complying with any law of this sort. You may not want to keep child pornography in an open file in your office to evidence the need for the report, so it would be a good idea to think of a process in advance for safeguarding such informa-tion. I suggest storing the materials in a sealed envelope that is locked up in a file cab-inet that does not reside in someone's office. The specific requirements for complying with the PCSPA are otherwise discussed in Chapter 5.

You also need to think about internal procedures. You need to make sure you have agreements in place with your employees and contracts regarding ownership of intel-lectual property rights, the treatment of confidential information of your own and of third parties you deal with, their use of electronic communication systems, and so on. You need to make sure someone or some group is responsible for getting such agree-ments signed by existing or new employees and contractors and that those agree-ments are then stored some place you can find them. There is nothing worse than suddenly deciding that you need to take action against someone who has stolen your business plans and gone to a competitor, only to find that you have no agreement with that person and have failed to properly safeguard the trade secrets associated with those plans. Properly written and implemented procedures will help to prevent this from occurring—and it happens more often than you might think.

Procedures also help you automate processes that otherwise require some amount of thought and human intervention. This is not to say that you shouldn't think, but it is to say that you shouldn't let some of your employees think when they don't need to or when their doing so could cause problems. You don't really need employees responding to a DMCA notice by trying to figure out whether the alleged material infringes a copyright or whether the poster had a fair-use right to post it. If the notice is effective, take the material down. Thinking about it involves time, costs you money, and ultimately leaves you holding the liability bag if the wrong decision is made or you don't act quickly enough. The same can be said for almost every other law or regulation that has been discussed that requires some action by you. Now that you have read the entire book, if you didn't already do so, you might want to go back and outline your procedures right from the text of this book. My providing you with pro-cedures in this chapter will not really do you any good because I have no idea how your company is organized, who does what, what authority is required for what decisions, how you operate your service, and so on. These are just some of the things that need to be considered when crafting appropriate and effective procedures. Also, be sure you assign someone the responsibility for making sure the policies and procedures are current and are being followed by your employees.

## What to Ask/Tell Your Lawyer

When I first entered the legal profession, the personal computer industry was really just taking off. At that time, any lawyer who had used a computer appeared to refer to himself or herself as a computer lawyer. I find that a similar fate has befallen many fellow practitioners with regard to the Internet. Perhaps they have represented an Internet company, maybe they have used the Internet, they may have even had some relative degree of involvement with some aspect of the Internet's development, but behold: They are now *Internet lawyers*.

Perhaps I am being a bit harsh, but my point is that marketing should not fool you. Any attorneys who define themselves in that way are trying to market their services to you and figure the mere mention of the Internet will help to attract your business. Check them out. Ask them what they have done. If they say that they cannot tell you what they did because it will reveal client confidences, ask them simply to describe the nature of the matter in general terms, leaving out any identifiers. If they can't do this, you don't want them representing you. It may turn out that these attorneys have never done whatever it is that you need them to do. You may need to educate them to bring them up to speed on the subject matter. This is okay and appropriate in many circumstances. I know quite a bit, but there is quite a bit that I don't know. The key is to get people who are open and honest about what they don't know (yes, there are a number of us out there) and who have the mental capacity to pick up what they need to learn quickly. The best thing you can have is a lawyer who asks questions (not too many, however, because it can get really annoying) and doesn't just make assumptions about what you want and how you want to do something. You may have to work harder with someone who needs some training, but the net result will be better.

As with almost any professional service, word-of-mouth recommendations are the best. If you can get a recommendation, you could also surf the Internet for attorneys in your area, or check the Yellow Pages, or call the state bar or the county bar association and ask them if they have a referral service. The first meeting or initial consultation should always be for free, but they may not tell you much. Bigger law firms are generally not interested in small clients with little money. Come to think of it, small firms aren't too thrilled with such clients, either, but some are more willing than others to take a chance. Keep in mind that many law firms have serious problems collecting from nonpaying clients; however, sometimes you just have to do work for people, whether you want to or not, because you represent them and it is generally against legal ethics to withdraw from a representation just because you are afraid you won't get paid. It is therefore not uncommon to be asked to provide a retainer (pay some amount in advance) before they will begin to provide services. You can generally trust attorneys not to take this money, but I still wouldn't give them too much. The most common cause for attorney discipline involves the misuse of client funds.

When you have finally selected an attorney (and before you e-mail me and ask, I am not presently available because I work in-house for a company—although you never know), you need to supply very clear, very specific directions regarding what you want. You also need to get the attorney to estimate the cost in advance in writing and to agree to a cap that cannot be exceeded without your written authorization. Vague legal projects have a way of becoming really expensive projects. The best way to control your legal expenses is to control yourself. Do not expect your attorney to do it for you because he or she expects you to be mature enough to specify what you want and how you want it. Your attorney may assume that you have worked with other attorneys before and know what to expect. If the attorney does a lot of wasted work, you may be able to get him or her to write off some but not all of the time, and if you don't want to end up in a dispute over your bill, learn how to manage your legal affairs. Remember that attorneys often act pompous, but it is an act. You really can tell us what to do—and you should.

With respect to the various matters discussed in this book, you will probably need an attorney to help you draft some procedures and some policies. You may need an attorney to do some research on changes in the laws and regulations and how those changes affect you. You may need an attorney to represent you in contract negotiations in the event something goes right (you tend to negotiate only bigger contracts) or in litigation in the event something goes wrong. Everything I have talked about in this book can help you immensely with respect to figuring out when you need an attorney, what you need the attorney to do, how much work is required, and what to expect. Good luck!

# CHAPTER 8

# Technical and Legal Glossary

**ARPA** *Advanced Research and Projects Agency.* A U.S. federal research funding agency credited with initially deploying the network now known as the Internet. The agency was referred to as DARPA (Defense Advanced Research and Projects Agency) at the time.

**Authentication** The verification of the source, uniqueness, and integrity of a message. Authentication describes a procedure whereby recipients of data can assure themselves that the data was not tampered with—tampering with the data would have rendered the original message unreadable. Cryptographic keys, also known as *public keys* and *private keys,* are use to encode and verify the integrity of the message and its source.

**Backbone network** The part of a communication network that carries the heaviest traffic and that interconnects a variety of other, lower-speed networks at various points called *nodes.*

**Bandwidth** The amount of electronic data that can be transferred through an electronic connection in a given period of time. Modems connected by analog telephone lines to the Internet, for example, generally have a maximum possible bandwidth of 56.6 Kbps (kilobits per second). Such a modem would be referred to as a 56K modem, even though it may not operate at is maximum speed due to other technical constraints.

**Banner** An advertisement that is displayed in a visually prominent location on a web site and that includes an embedded hyperlink to a web site associated with the advertiser. Banners can be static boxes, frames to other Internet locations, or software-animated. Banner advertisements on popular sites are changed every 10 to 20 seconds.

**Browser**   A type of software used for locating, requesting, and displaying web pages on a computer. Brands of browsers include Netscape Navigator and Microsoft Internet Explorer.

**Browsing**   The act of using a browser to request, search for, and locate various Internet locations or other forms of automated information system storage to acquire information with or without a particular purpose in mind.

**Cache**   A cache is a form of high-speed memory for storing information that is possibly soon to be required by another system connected to the memory. A microprocessor uses a cache for storing operating instructions. A personal computer uses a cache for storing frequently accessed files or recently accessed web sites or images that may soon be needed again. A web server may operate as a cache that enables users of certain web sites to quickly locate frequently requested data without overusing network bandwidth.

**Caching**   Caching involves the automatic storage of information in a cache. Caching is a fairly essential part of surfing the Internet. As a user leaves one Internet page for another, the information relating to the first page is not deleted from the designated memory of the user's computer. Instead, that information is temporarily stored on the computer's hard disk so that it is easily accessible if the user decides to return to that page shortly thereafter. A cache server operates in a similar fashion at the network level rather than in a particular user's computer.

**CFR**   *Code of Federal Regulations.* The complete listing of published regulations of the federal government of the United States.

**Click-wrap licenses**   A form contract that can be accessed, reviewed, and agreed to on a computer. The contract is agreed to by locating a computer cursor within an appropriate box and hitting the Enter/Return key or by clicking a button on the mouse that controls the cursor.

**Cookies**   Small test files that are automatically downloaded from a web site and stored on the computer of someone browsing that site. Cookies are used to store information about a particular user. That information can then be accessed whenever that computer returns to that site. Cookies allow web sites to store passwords, track preferences, personalize their appearance by identifying visitors, enable quick checkout procedures, and so forth.

**Country code top-level domain (ccTLD)**   The Internet network is segmented into a hierarchy of domains, or groupings, and ccTLDs correspond to the top-level domains assigned to each country. For example, the United States is assigned .us, the United Kingdom .uk, and Germany .de.

**Deep link**   A **hyperlink** to a particular page of information below the level of the home page for a particular web site. The home page for MCI WorldCom's mail web site is located at the following URL: www.wcom.com/main.phtml. A URL that deep-links to the stock information page within that web site would be www.wcom.com/about_the_company/investor_relations/stock_information/. If you entered this letter URL, you would go directly to the stock information page and bypass the home page.

**Descriptive**   In the trademark context, a name that serves to describe a feature or function of a service or product. With respect to MCI WorldCom's On-Net service offerings, the term *On-Net* is descriptive of an on-the-network service (i.e., it describes the company's ability to transport a customer's traffic entirely over the MCI WorldCom network from point of origination to point of termination).

**DFARS** *Defense Federal Acquisition Regulations Supplement.* A set of U.S. federal regulations that apply in purchasing contracts entered into on behalf of the Department of Defense. The Federal Acquisition Regulations (FAR) apply to purchase contracts entered into by other federal agencies. The federal government relies on these regulations to control all aspects of contracting for sales to the government and even to fill in terms that may have been left out of contracts. This means you must be aware of the detailed provisions in the DFARS and FAR whenever you negotiate a purchase contract with the government.

**Digital signature** A digital signature is an electronic signature that cannot be forged. Digital signatures are typically created using some form of public key/ private key encryption, whereby an electronic signature is encrypted using the private key of the sender. This digital signature is then attached to an electronic document, which may or may not be encrypted as well. Any recipient of the document and digital signature can then use the sender's public key to verify that the electronic signature and/or associated document in fact originated from the sender and was not altered after it was signed.

**Domain names** A designation for a particular location on the Internet. A domain name corresponds to the files, if any, stored on a host computer at that location in association with that particular domain.

**Dynamic IP addressing** Every time an Internet user accesses the Internet through a dial-in connection (i.e., via a modem), the user's computer is dynamically assigned a different IP address to use during the course of the dial-in session. This is in contrast to dedicated access users, who often have the same IP address assigned to their computers at all times. Dynamic IP addresses are usually assigned from a block, or pool, of IP addresses assigned to a particular ISP.

**Electronic commerce (e-commerce)** Business interactions and transactions carried out over the Internet. Business-to-business (B2B) e-commerce involves interactions between one company and its trading partners, such as suppliers and large customers. B2B e-commerce applications include online marketplaces, auctions, claims processing, order management, and Internet-based procurement. Business-to-consumer (B2C) e-commerce involves the processing of economic transactions through electronic communication. B2C e-commerce is one of the most common forms of e-commerce occurring on the Internet (e.g., credit card purchase at web sites). Although B2C e-commerce is growing, the vast majority of all e-commerce is B2B e-commerce.

**Electronic signature** Any kind of marking that indicates the source of an electronic message. An electronic signature may be your name at the end of an e-mail, your e-mail address in the header of a message, or a pseudonym you adopted for making posts to message boards. Just because an electronic message includes an electronic signature of some type does not mean that the message was from the person alleged to have signed the electronic message. It is extremely easy to forge and spoof electronic signatures on virtually any type of electronic message.

**E-mail**  A computer program and/or service that allows computer users to send electronic messages to other computer users. An e-mail message is a message sent using an e-mail service. Most browsers include e-mail software that enables a user to use the Internet as the transport mechanism and enables any other Internet user with e-mail software to receive the message and read it. The formatting of the message can change if the e-mail is sent and received by different brands or versions of e-mail software. Most access ISPs provide e-mail services and store your e-mail messages on an e-mail server (or just *mail server*) until you download those messages from the ISP's network.

**Encryption**  The use of a mathematical algorithm to scramble bits of data into other forms that cannot be read or easily decoded by people who do not have the cryptographic key needed to decrypt the data. The algorithm uses an alphanumeric key of a certain bit length to encode the data. The longer the key in bits, the stronger the encryption (i.e., the harder it is to decrypt an encrypted message without the key).

**Famous mark**  In the trademark context, this refers to a mark that has become so well known in a particular country that it is extended an extra level of trademark protection. For example, even though a certain brand name is not registered as a trademark in a class of goods or services, that brand name may be so well known that it will be protected from being used in that class of goods or services despite the lack of registration. Countries have varying definitions of what constitutes a famous mark. In South Africa, a trademark is considered famous if it is well known to persons interested in the goods or services to which the trademark relates. In 1996, McDonald's Corporation successfully protected the golden arches logo and the McDonald's, Big Mac, and McMuffin brand names from being used by others in South Africa because they were considered famous, even though McDonald's Corporation has not been using them there because of an international embargo against the former apartheid government.

**FAQ**  *Frequently Asked Questions.* Compiled lists of commonly asked questions, along with the answers, on various topics of interest to Internet users. FAQs generally can be found in various formats, such as HTML web pages and traditional printed material.

**Frame**  In the Internet context, a frame describes the appearance and layout style of a web site within a portion or window of a user's computer screen. It particularly refers to the simultaneous loading of two or more web pages at the same time within the same computer screen. Internet users who access frame-enabled web sites may actually access multiple web sites at the same time, with one web site displayed in one window, a second web site in an adjacent window, and so on. Frames can be any size or shape that is available to display windows on a computer screen (i.e., a frame could be used to create a thin boarder around a first window, thereby making the frame appear to be part of the first window rather than a separate window).

**Generic**  In the trademark context, a generic name is one used by a majority of the relevant public to name a class of goods or services. No one can trademark the name *Electronic Commerce* for an Internet-based commercial business, for example, because that is a generic name for such businesses. Generic names are often confused with **descriptive** names because a name can be both generic and descriptive.

**Generic top-level domain (gTLD)**   The Internet network is segmented into a hierarchy of domains, or groupings. The term *gTLD* has been used to describe a class of top-level domains assigned to different subject areas. The top-level domains currently available are *com* (commercial organizations), *edu* (education organizations in the United States), *gov* (government agencies within the United States), *mil* (U.S. military organizations), *net* (networking organizations), and *org* (nonprofit organizations). When responsibility for the registration of the com, org, and net top-level domains was turned over to NSI, no attempt was thereafter made to restrict the use of these top-level domains, so the aforementioned subject areas are no longer accurate for those top-level domains (i.e., they have become generic). Various proposals have been made to ICANN and its predecessors to introduce a number of additional gTLDs, such as *firm* and *store,* to expand the number of possible alphanumeric combinations.

**Host**   Any intelligent device (i.e., under programmed control) connected to a network. In the context of the Internet, a host is any IP-enabled device, including computers, lightbulbs, and chewing gum (okay, maybe not chewing gum), with two-way access to the Internet.

**Hosting**   Refers to the operation of or the service of operating a **host.** If you are hosting a web site, you are operating a computer server connected to the World Wide Web. Companies that provide hosting services often host many different web sites on each computer server.

**HTML**   *Hyper Text Markup Language.* A simple hypertext document-formatting language used to format content so it appears in particular ways on web pages on the World Wide Web. HTML has been released in a number of different versions. Most popular web browsers can read the earlier versions of HTML code.

**HTTP**   *Hyper Text Transfer Protocol.* An Internet (TCP-based application-layer) protocol used for communicating between web servers and web browsers.

**Hyperlink, hypertext link**   These two terms are used interchangeably, but they really describe different things. A *hyperlink* is any object (word, phrase, image, etc.) displayed by a computer program that can be used to create a connection between the Internet-enabled computer running that program and some other Internet host. By clicking on a hyperlink, a user of one web site can be quickly connected to another web site. Hypertext is created using **HTML** and similar programs and refers to nonsequential writing made up of text blocks that can be linked by readers in different ways. In other words, if the words *Dr. Suess* were in hypertext, you could click on the words with your cursor and be transported to text about Dr. Suess. That text would either be in the same document or in some other document. A *hypertext link* is sometimes used to refer to hypertext that is associated with a hyperlink and therefore connects you to a different web site.

**Internet**   Commonly used as a reference to the loosely administered collection of interconnected networks around the globe that communicate via the Internet Protocol to exchange packets of data and that share a common addressing structure for the exchange of such packets. These networks are joined together by a vast array of high-speed backbone data links supporting the TCP/IP protocol, which stands for Transmission Control Protocol/Internet Protocol. **TCP/IP** is a family of networking protocols providing communication across interconnected networks, between computers with diverse hardware architectures, and between various computer operating systems. Basically, any computer can use TCP/IP. **TCP** operates by taking data to be sent from one computer to another and breaking it into manageable pieces of data, called **packets.** The amount of data in each packet is quite small, so even a small message requires many packets. TCP marks each of these packets with sequence numbers so they can be reassembled in the correct order and checked for errors using a checksum. TCP also uses port IDs to specify which applications running on the host are sending or receiving the data. The port ID, checksum, and sequence number are inserted into the TCP packet in a section called the *header.* The header is located at the beginning of the packet and includes other control information. The actual data in a packet is called the *payload* of the packet. **IP** operates as the messenger protocol of TCP/IP and is basically responsible for addressing, sending, and receiving the packets created by TCP. Through use of the TCP/IP protocol, different hosts are connected only through the sending and receiving of packets, as opposed to traditional communication systems (such as the public telephone network), which required a fixed connection between the communicating devices during the entire communication session.

**Internet address**   A unique identifier for a specific **host.** Also called an **IP address.** IP addresses are in dotted-decimal form (e.g., 126.345.34.229), with each of the four address fields assigned as many as 255 values.

**Intranet**   A private network that uses the Internet Protocol for communication purposes, but which is either not connected to the Internet or is limited in some way so only certain users can have access outside of the private network.

**IP**   *Internet Protocol.* See **Internet.**

**IP address.**   See **Internet address.**

**ISP**   *Internet service provider.* The term *ISP* originally referred to a vendor who provided access for customers to the Internet and the World Wide Web, as well as **e-mail** services and other services. The term has been significantly expanded over time and presently encompasses a wide array of different types of service providers. An ISP may provide Internet access services on a retail basis to residential and/or business customers. An ISP may operate only a **backbone network** and provide access services to that backbone network on a wholesale basis to other ISPs. Some ISPs provide **hosting** services. Some ISPs provide server **caching.** Other ISPs do not provide any of these services and only operate **portals.** An ISP may provide only a **search engine** or some other **e-commerce** tool.

**LAN**   *Local area network.* A network that has a limited geographic range and that is typically constructed using privately operated wiring and communications facilities. The network set up within a particular building or campus of buildings is typically a LAN. Remotely located facilities might be connected to a *wide area network* (WAN).

**MAE**   *Merit* or *metropolitan access exchange.* A huge interconnection point for ISPs where traffic from customers on one ISP network can be routed to customers on other ISP networks. Physically, a MAE is a building with tons of computers, switches, and other equipment, with millions of wires connecting all of them together, typically owned by various ISPs. MAEs are often run by other ISPs that collect fees for transmission, switching, and interconnection services, as well as equipment colocation and maintenance fees.

**Metadata content labels**   See **Metatag.**

**Metatag**   Metatags are elements of **HTML** code embedded in a web page that are normally hidden from the view of people looking at that web page. Search engines read these hidden words to determine how closely a web page matches the search request of a search engine user who is looking for specific content. Thus, your search request for a car loan could return a web site for an automotive repair shop hoping to lure you into fixing your present car rather than into buying a new one.

**Mirror cache**   A computer server that is used as an alternative access site for data available on another computer server at a different online location. The mirror server includes an identical copy of the data on the original server and is updated when the original server's data is changed, or at programmed times if the original server's data changes frequently. If the mirror server is not updated immediately, it is generally not referred to as a mirror cache, which is not really an accurate term in the first place, considering the definition of **cache.**

**Modem**   A device used to convert serial digital data (0s and 1s) from a transmitting terminal (your computer) to a signal suitable for transmission over a telephone channel (beep deep boop), or to reconvert the transmitted signal to serial digital data for acceptance by a receiving terminal.

**MPEG**   *Moving Pictures Experts Group.* A joint committee of the International Standards Organization and the International Electrotechnical Commission. MPEG is more commonly known as a series of hardware and software standards designed to reduce the storage requirements of digital video (i.e., video recorded digitally or converted into a digital signal).

**MP3**   A digital file format for compressing and recording music for distribution over the Internet. MP3 is an acronym for MPEG 1, Audio Layer 3. A 4-megabyte MP3-formatted file can represent about three minutes of high-quality music.

**NSF**   *National Science Foundation.* A U.S. government agency that funds U.S. scientific research programs. This agency funded the operation of the academic and research NSFNET (a successor of ARPANET and a predecessor to the current commodity Internet) from 1986 until 1995.

**Packet**   See **Internet.**

**Patent claim.**   The part of a patent that defines the technology that is the exclusive property of the patentee for the duration of the patent. A patent claim sets the technical bounds that legally exclude others from making, using, and selling a patent owner's product.

**Portal**   A web site that aggregates and organizes information about the content of other web sites so users can readily find desired information.

**Proxy server**   Software that runs on a computer and that serves to relay packets between a trusted client (a host inside a network) and an untrusted host (a host outside the network). Proxy servers are used to provide World Wide Web access, or *selective access,* to selected people inside the network. A proxy server can also serve as a **cache** server.

**QoS**   *Quality of service.* In the Internet context, QoS refers generally to the differentiation between the bandwidth dedicated to, and therefore the amount of network delay associated with, certain types of data. Live videoconferencing data requires a high QoS because the transmitted data is very sensitive to network delays. E-mail is largely unaffected by such delays because it is often stored first before being downloaded and has time to accommodate delays.

**Real Audio**   Real Audio, now called RealPlayer, was a type of software that enabled Internet users with multimedia computers to browse, select, and play back audio or audio-based multimedia content on demand, in real time.

**Real Media**   A broadening of the **Real Audio** idea.

**ROM**   *Read-only memory.* A static form of memory used to record information that can be read by computers and/or associated software but cannot be changed (i.e., written).

**Root name server**   The base or top-level server on the **Internet** used to store the tables associating **domain names** with **IP addresses.**

**Router**   In the Internet context, a device or software on a computer that determines the next network point to which a **packet** should be forwarded on its way to its final destination. The router is connect to at least two networks and decides which way to send each packet based on its current understanding of the state of the network to which it is connected. Routers are often included in network switches.

**Search engine**   A mechanism for finding documents on the Internet. Examples are Yahoo! and Alta Vista.

**Server**   A computer dedicated to storing information for use by other computers. In the Internet context, a web server stores the various files that make up web pages, as well as the protocols needed for communication with other computers via the Internet.

**Shrink-wrap licenses**   A form contract that can be accessed and reviewed either through the shrink-wrap on a package, such as a box containing software disks, and that can be agreed to only through certain specified actions, such as installing the software or not returning the software to the place of purchase within a specified period of time.

**Stream** and **streaming**   In the Internet context, the ability to look at or listen to data corresponding to a larger message as that data is received over the Internet by your computer, as opposed to waiting until your computer has received the entire message. This is an effective way to hear music or watch video over the Internet.

**TCP**   *Transmission Control Protocol.* See **Internet.**

**TCP/IP**   *Transmission Control Protocol/Internet Protocol.* See **Internet.**

**URL**   *Universal Resource Locator.* An address, such as www.wcom.com, for a file or files located on the Internet, usually via the World Wide Web.

**User interface**   The means by which users interact with other objects. The user interface of a telephone is the handset and buttons. The user interface of a computer is the collection of images displayed on your computer and the associated software that enables you to interact with those images.

**Watermarks**   A technique for embedding within a digital recording identifying data that cannot be readily detected and removed by users. Watermarks of nonaudio data embedded within each track of a music CD can be used to distinguish legal CDs from pirated CDs and to control the playback and copying of legal CDs. For example, a Secure Digital Music Initiative (SDMI)–compliant music player may prevent you from making more than four copies of a particular track on a CD and from playing those copied tracks on another SDMI music player.

**Web site**   A location in the World Wide Web that holds documents or files (e.g., HTML or XML files) that are interpretable or downloadable by a web browser. All web sites have a given URL and reside on a server.

**World Wide Web (WWW)**   The entire collection of files written in **HTML** and similar languages and available on the Internet at any given time. Internet users enter **URL**s into their **browsers** to request these files from web **servers** and then display them as web pages. The web is only a portion of the Internet—it is not the Internet.